# Praise for *Unborn Bodies*

Conceived with care and delivered with wisdom, *Unborn Bodies: Resurrection and Reproductive Agency* does more than fill a gap in feminist theology. It articulates an enlivening alternative to the caricatures of miscarriage and abortion. Its delightful prose carries its courageous and all-too-timely message to a wide Christian public.

—Catherine Keller, George T. Cobb Professor of Constructive
Theology, Drew Theological School, and
author of *Facing Apocalypse: Climate,
Democracy, and Other Last Chances*

Neither miscarriage nor the exercise of moral agency to end a pregnancy precludes eschatological longing for reunion with persons that never came to be in this world. Kamitsuka reclaims the neglected Pauline metaphor of bodily resurrection as new life sprouting from a seed of the old, providing a nontoxic eschatology that can speak to reproductive loss. This book engages submerged knowledges and experiences to shift the entire framework of the discussions it enters, and the result is compelling and healing.

—Sandra Sullivan-Dunbar, Loyola University, Chicago

Every now and then a book appears that reshapes the entire discipline of theology. Kamitsuka gifts readers with just such a work. Kamitsuka challenges readers to reconsider what it means to be a self in the afterlife, no matter at what point mortal existence ended. She resists convenient categories while maintaining a steady grasp on Christian tradition and justice. At once prophetic, provocative, and pastoral, Kamitsuka blends together an incisive knowledge of Christianity's two-thousand-year history with feminist analysis and scientific facts to challenge readers to reconceptualize their understanding of what happens in the liminal spaces of pregnancy loss, abortion, and the afterlife.

—Danielle Tumminio Hansen, Candler School of
Theology, Emory University

In poetic prose, Margaret Kamitsuka develops an eschatology that ventures where the traditional imaginary of resurrected life refuses to go. Taking her interpretive cues not from Aristotelian soul-body talk but instead from the materialist sensibilities of evolutionary biology, she offers the prospect of a heavenly life in which the unborn flourish bodily as undiminished participants in eternal joy. Creative and caring, Kamitsuka's theology offers hope and consolation to those who have suffered reproductive loss and affirmation for reproductive decision-making.

—John E. Thiel, Fairfield University

# unborn
# bodies

# unborn bodies

## Resurrection and Reproductive Agency

Margaret D. Kamitsuka

Fortress Press
Minneapolis

UNBORN BODIES
Resurrection and Reproductive Agency

Scripture quotations are taken from the New Revised Standard Version Bible, copyright © 1989 by the Division of Christian Education of the National Council of the Churches of Christ in the USA and used by permission. All rights reserved.

Library of Congress Control Number: 2023932827 (print)

Cover image: Conflorescence, Etching and thread on Japanese paper, Eleanor Havsteen-Franklin
Cover design: Kristin Miller

Print ISBN: 978-1-5064-9262-9
eBook ISBN: 978-1-5064-9264-3

*Now the green blade riseth, from the buried grain,*
*Wheat that in the dark earth many days has lain;*
*Love lives again, that with the dead has been:*
*Love is come again, like wheat that springeth green.*

                    J. M. C. Crum (1872–1958)

# CONTENTS

# ACKNOWLEDGMENTS

My first words of thanks go to my family—husband David and sons Mark and Paul. They cheerfully and patiently supported me in all things great and small, which made possible the labor of beginning, sustaining, and completing this book project. A special word of thanks goes to my longtime dear friend Evantheia Schibsted, writer and media maven, for all her encouragement along the way.

Ideas for and sections of this book were presented at various conferences (Zoom and in-person), where I benefited enormously from feedback, suggestions, and mutual collegial support. The Third International Conference on Philosophy and Meaning in Life (July 2020); Princeton Project in Philosophy of Religion Inaugural Conference (Oct. 2020); Society of Christian Ethics Annual Conference (Jan. 2021); Disability Studies Unit and Women and Religion Unit at the American Academy of Religion Annual Conference, San Antonio (Nov. 2021); Society for the Study of Theology, Warwick University, UK (March 2022); Societas ethica, Zurich, Switzerland (Aug. 2022). I give particular thanks for the insights from Hille Haker, Danielle Tumminio Hansen, Karen O'Donnell, and Dean Zimmerman.

Earlier versions of parts of this book appeared in the following journals: "The Resurrection and Unborn Beings: The Seeds of a Materialist Emergence Proposal," *Theology Today* 78, no. 2 (2021): 170–81. "Disabled Bodies on Earth and in Heaven: Eschatology and the Ethics of Selective Abortion," *Journal of Religious Ethics* 49, no. 2 (July 2021): 358–80.

This book gratefully acknowledges the women who entrusted to me their private stories of reproductive endings and experiences of stigma in the church. They await serious theological reflection that includes their voices.

I am indebted to my editor, Carey Newman, who emboldened me to see how far from the theological shallows my prose could take me.

# INTRODUCTION

DEATH CIRCLES AROUND life. Fear of death casts the living into liminal shadows. From ancient days, religion offered rituals that lit the way to the nearest exit. These rituals, the métier of shamans, priests, and preachers, prepared adherents for their inevitable journey into the mysterious realms beyond this vale of tears. Incense and hyssop branch, ephod and crozier designated their high holy work, the attempt to make supreme sense of humanity's ultimate limit experience.

The scut work of living and dying, however, falls to the women. Their labor is the societal glue. They nourish fragile newborns and watch over reckless children. The women wash and shroud the bodies of their dead. Their pregnancies and birthings bring them infirmities, bring them to the brink of death. They do what they can to survive.

Women survive by gathering around the hearth and at the well, sharing secrets. How to ensure conception, keep the wanted pregnancy, end the mistimed one. They make humble ritual gestures: a votive cake for the goddess of fertility, an amulet tucked beneath the birthing stool, a bitter potion to bring on the "flowers."[1] Women and marriageable girls whisper together, glancing over their shoulders, wary of scarlet letters, inquisitions, burning stakes. Their survival is a cloth woven of secret knowledge and mother wit, disguised as old wives' tales and chin-wagging.

The world religions—all patriarchal—ignore this domestic female gossip. They think father knows best, but they stutter when they pontificate about the mysterious fertile female body. They avoid commenting on an ended pregnancy, unless they can find a way to call it sinful. Alpha male religions prefer safer theological ground: teaching adherents how to live during their brief stay on earth and how to reach the serene realms of the hereafter. By the Greco-Roman period, the motif of the journey through the underworld was a papyrus meme. Women's daily grind fell below the radar of this sacred interest. Elysium enticed the male gaze.

The new Christian religion took the motif and ran with it. The story of discarded grave clothes and a risen Jesus circulated. Doctrines coalesced. Creed and catechism taught "the resurrection of the body and the life everlasting." The church relegated the women's part in the passion narrative to a theological footnote. Scripture, however, did not write them out of the story. The myrrh-bearing Marys trudged to the tomb to find the body of their Lord. They were given kerygma instead. And they believed.

Women believe and continue to fill the pews every Sunday. They fold their secrets into the pleated cloth of a tradition that disregards the gifts they bear. Keeping a low profile, they wash the vestments of patriarchal religious hubris. They still whisper together in darkened naves and the corners of church halls. A clueless church presumes their dutifulness and misreads their capacity to wrestle with angels and absorb the wound. Women demand their blessings and resurrections.

## Undomesticating Resurrection

Bodily resurrection baffles. Religious and nonreligion-affiliated people hold to a belief in some kind of heaven,[2] though bodily resurrection is viewed as a quaint, embarrassing idea. If the afterlife comes up in genteel dinner table conversation, "one may admit to believing in life after death, at least if one's beliefs are appropriately spiritual, involving leaving one's body behind, heading toward the light, and so on."[3] Serious discussions of the afterlife are relegated to highbrow shows on PBS.[4] Popularized notions of the afterlife fill the big screen in blockbuster films such as *Heaven Can Wait* and *Ghost*. These domesticated images of life after death entertain.

The resurrection of the body, however, in its undomesticated form is feral. Personal postmortem existence snarls at demythologized renditions of the risen Christ. Theologians, pastors, and believers make a wide berth around this wild and unpredictable species of doctrine. They prefer resurrection curled up by the fireside, tame as a tabby.

A doctrine of resurrection that speaks to the realities of bleeding women's bodies has yet to be thought. How the promise of the dead rising from their graves applies to death in the womb has yet to be thought. Believers who can get pregnant, who have lost a pregnancy, stand waiting with their jars of myrrh. They wait for a wild word about unborn bodies and the afterlife.

The afterlife is not just esoteric theological marginalia but a concern at the core of some of the most intimate and fragile moments of family life. Death in a wanted pregnancy is heartrending and spirit-gutting. Grieving parents cry out for answers, turn to their faith communities for solace, and wonder if their lost one has found final rest in heaven. The viewpoint that labels it "irrational to engage in mourning for the sake of an insentient cluster of cells" makes a determination that rational capacities are the basis for legitimate grief.[5] Such a viewpoint misrecognizes the phenomenology of grief and implies that unseen deaths in the womb are somehow irrelevant for ethical and theological reflection. Far from irrelevant, these deaths demand theological attention.

Believers who pass through experiences of reproductive loss have difficulty catching the church's eye. They have trouble locating (nonpoliticized) liturgical or pastoral resources for commemorating an ended pregnancy. Ordinary Christians are left to google "heaven" for religious answers to their earnest questions about eternal life after a miscarriage or abortion. The afterlife continues to influence Christian understandings of how one should live now in light of God's eschatological promise for a time when "sorrow and sighing shall flee away" (Isa 35:10).

The dearth of serious theological reflection on, sacramental spaces for, and pastoral resources about reproductive endings has left a gap. Into that gap have stepped diverse conservative Christian groups focused on protecting the rights of what they consider preborn children. Their literature assures parents who have suffered a miscarriage that their unborn child went immediately to heaven. Women who have had an abortion are forewarned: you "have no hope of joining your child in heaven" unless you repent and ask forgiveness for that "grievous" sin.[6] Believers, vulnerable in their grief or guilt, latch on to peddled rococo social media images of miscarried or aborted cherubs cavorting in heaven.

For the modern scientific mind, bodily resurrection raises eyebrows.[7] The resurrection of unborn bodies seems beyond the pale. Philosophy scoffs. The notion of resurrected unborn beings would mean a heaven populated by "shapes that can neither think nor speak, and resemble tadpoles."[8] Secular feminism is mildly repulsed by the fetishizing of angel-babies in heaven.[9] Theology is inclined to find questions about resurrected babies "faintly ridiculous."[10]

Fetuses appearing in heaven as infants with angel wings is ridiculous. However, asking about whether or how infants—and the unborn—will be resurrected is speculative but not ridiculous. Infants are included in biblical prophecy about who shall inhabit God's "holy mountain" (Isa 65:25).[11] Bereaved parents interpret the prophet Jeremiah's words as a promise of heavenly peace after miscarriage, stillbirth, or infant death:

> *There is hope for your future,*
>   *says the Lord:*
> *your children shall come back to their own country.*
> *(31:17)*

Philosophy and theology ridicule such imagery as antiquated. Ridiculous is as ridiculous does.

A relevant doctrine of the resurrection will resist being cowed by the cultured despisers of religion or the mainline church's attempt not to ruffle their feathers. Too much is at stake to marginalize the question of the unborn and the afterlife. A theology that wishes to bring eschatological relevance to the upheaval of reproductive loss cannot play it safe but will have to confront the obstacles to rethinking resurrection, untamed.

## Nontoxic Eschatology

Standing in the way of theologizing about the unborn and the afterlife is the church's ambivalence about the eternal destiny of beings that die in utero. Visceral misogyny as well as theological confusion on prenatal life impede rethinking eschatology. The church's banal platitudes about hope for heaven and its reticence to ritualize reproductive endings are toxic for women's experience.

The Christian tradition and Christianized society perpetuate an irrational and harmful association of women's bodies with evil, temptation, and ritual impurity. The church is uninterested in women's wombs—other than the Virgin Mary's inviolate one. Paeons flow about Mary's immaculate uterus and painless birth. For every other woman, conception, gestation, and birth take place in leaking, lusting, bleeding, and expanding female bodies. The male ecclesiastical gaze both desires and abjects the female body. Even secular society experiences a visceral recoil from the seemingly uncontrollable fluids and fleshiness of fertile and gravid bodies.

The church's confusion about the eternal destiny of those who die in the womb derives from its confusion about the status of uterine life. Whenever the topic arose about life developing in the womb, the early church shuffled its feet. Contrary to present-day prolife certitude, the ancient church hemmed and hawed on the question of when an ensouled person begins.[12] The magisterial imaginary did not tenderly embrace beings knit together in their mothers' wombs. Even born unbaptized babies were relegated to spend eternity in a dim anteroom of hell. The toxicity of centuries of the Vatican's defense of infants in limbo cannot be measured.[13] The Protestant Reformation suppressed talk of limbo but avoided pronouncing on the afterlife of fetuses, leaving their followers as much in doctrinal darkness as Catholics.

Ignoring fetuses in heaven began early in church history. Very few early church fathers gave a minute's thought to fetal resurrection. Augustine alone agonized, speculating that "there is a resurrection for them" but only if their bodies have finished forming. All the other amorphous uterine beings would, he thought, "perish, like seeds that did not germinate."[14] Heated medieval debates about the timing of ensoulment in the womb "made the resurrection of *abortivi* a hard case in eschatology."[15] Taking a life by abortion received decisive condemnation;[16] promising salvation for miscarried or aborted uterine beings—a rare occurrence.

Reticence to reflect on reproductive endings and eschatology is the church's legacy. Perpetuating that reticence cedes the theological stage to popularized messaging that distorts Christian doctrine and inflicts spiritual injury on women. Pontificating about the preborn pervades prolife literature. The reassurance that their baby is safe in heaven is dangled in front of parents after a reproductive loss. The stick of damnation is brandished to women who abort.[17] This carrot-and-stick approach is toxic. There are good pastoral, theological, and philosophical reasons to rule out any eschatological family separation policy where parents are accorded salvation and their unbaptized lost child is relegated to limbo. Or, conversely, aborted babies ascend to heaven while their mothers burn in hell.

Prolife rhetoric churns out stereotypes about women that are spiritually harmful. Women who experience reproductive endings are corralled into two groups: those who have abortions and those who suffer a miscarriage. Murderous mother versus grieving mother—these cardboard characterizations are used to pit women against each other. The tactic is reminiscent of the Eve/Mary binary, a pernicious product of patriarchal thought in search of supremacy.[18] The bad mother/good mother trope infuses even nonpoliticized pastoral and practical theologies and ministries. Compassionate support is extended to the victim of miscarriage; disapproval is telegraphed, even if unwittingly, to women who have terminated a pregnancy.

Feminist and other progressive theologies push back against such caricatures. These theologies, speaking from the margins, lobby to change the script on the meaning of sexuality, gender, bodies, and their place in a fragile ecosystem. They warn against preaching otherworldly hope that leaves unacknowledged the traumatic "despair and hopelessness" experienced by those struggling with infertility or mourning miscarriage.[19] Feminist theologians craft new eco-friendly and justice-oriented eschatological imaginaries.[20] However, the eschatological question of the unborn and the afterlife remains unanswered, and this silence harms. A nontoxic eschatology that includes unborn bodies eludes feminist thought.

## Running toward the Resurrection

Eschatological toxicity lurks around every theological corner, but theology cannot avoid addressing the resurrection without consequences. Theological silence on the afterlife creates a vacuum that will be filled by those who leverage that idea as an opiate or cudgel for vulnerable believers—including and especially those who suffer spiritually after a reproductive ending. Instead of running away from resurrection's dangers, theology should run toward them.

Embryos and fetuses die—often. These dead beings exude ritual danger. Excluding them from theological reflection about bodily resurrection perpetuates old lacunae and theological confusions about their status. For most of church history, a developing being in the womb was meaningless, until ensouled, and barred from beatitude, unless cleansed by baptism's waters. This legacy tarnishes the church. A relevant and nontoxic theology will move beyond hand-wringing about the eternal destiny of "the weakest members of the human family."[21]

A "literal" or "'plain' sense" biblical approach to bodily resurrection may not be popular in secular academe.[22] However, skirting fetal salvation because some call it a fetish that erodes women's reproductive rights would be to fetishize secularism. Feminist believers want to have their rights and heaven too. Theology should explore how to deliver both.

Seeking shelter in demythologized meanings of Jesus's resurrection exhibits a failure of theological nerve. No one said that belief in the resurrection was going to be easy. The apostle Paul assumed the contrary when he chided the cultured Corinthian believers to "hold firmly to the message" of bodily resurrection (1 Cor 15:2). Things are even harder today. The resurrection of the body teeters on a precipice for modern minds. However, those already in the abyss of bereavement do not have the intellectual luxury of flicking away the idea of life after death, like so much lint on one's coat. This constituency's questions deserve theological attention.

Clarifying the possibility and nature of an unborn body in heaven depends on understanding its beginnings in a very earthly woman's body. There is never only one type of pregnancy-capable person or one essential experience of pregnancy. Pregnancy eludes, overjoys, hounds, befalls, catastrophizes. Women bear children they find they cannot raise and grow to love an infant born disabled. They pray for a miscarriage that never happens and regret ending a mistimed pregnancy. Women even bring themselves to death's door to get their baby born. Sometimes people choose their own well-being and decide to end a pregnancy. In so doing, believers fear they have endangered their eternal life.

Women's sometimes conflicted conscience about reproductive endings is proof to conservative sectors of the church that women need constant pastoral oversight. As flawed daughters of Eve, they never quite understand the divine directives about good and evil. Women, however, have read Genesis chapter 3. Their lot is to survive under conditions of patriarchy and painful birth. They understand that difficult reproductive decision-making is the God-given load they carry in a fallen world. Those who believe in an afterlife bear this burden, like women walking with jars of myrrh.

# 1

## LEVERAGING HEAVEN
## WHEN A PREGNANCY ENDS

A PREGNANCY BEGINS in a limited number of biological ways in the female body, but the emotional experiences of reproductive endings are as different as each individual woman who carried the pregnancy. The death in utero of a wanted child can be devastating. The miscarriage of an unwanted pregnancy can bring a mixed reaction of relief and guilt. An abortion may be a private trauma for one person and an open door to well-being for another. However it is experienced, an ended pregnancy is a transition in the woman's life that also marks the premature death of a developing uterine being.

Pregnancies occur in religiously taboo areas of the female body. Religions, not wanting to dwell on these uterine transitions from life to death, perpetuate ancient "cultural taboos regarding bodily fluids, blood and corpses."[1] Women, however, cannot avoid the reality of reproductive endings.[2] Sisters, nieces, aunts, colleagues, and foremothers through the ages have been through this trial and have stood before this open door. The diversity of their experiences of an ended pregnancy demands recognition. Theology should not turn away but should recognize the woman who is the subject of these experiences.

The problem with recognizing the person who experiences an ended pregnancy is that she is a construct. This subject's outlines are molded by religious authorities with a vested interest in controlling women's bodies, the meaning of pregnancy, rituals of death, and requirements for entrance into whatever lies beyond the grave. The identity of the woman whose pregnancy has ended is scripted by discourses (as the postmodern philosophers say) that "contour the materiality of bodies" and frame the very categories by which she understands herself.[3] There can be a comfort in conforming to an expected identity. However, women who adhere to these scripts pay a price because of how their very self-understanding is policed by those who exercise influence over them.[4]

In religion's shaping of pregnant women's identity, heaven is a sharp tool. If she has an abortion, she is contoured as a sinner who murdered her unborn baby. She is obligated to pass through the fires of repentance and to wear forever the scarlet A of abortive woman. Popular and pastoral writings on miscarriage carve out a space for the woman as traumatized victim—on the condition that she distance herself from the evil woman who aborts. Those who turn to clergy for post-miscarriage rituals may be cast in the role of inconvenient mourners for whom there is a paucity of sacramental resources. The person who terminates a pregnancy is celebrated by secular feminists for exercising her right to bodily autonomy. This identity of rights-bearing person is also a script, and anyone who deviates from it, in order to express hope for their "baby" in heaven, is escorted off the reproductive rights stage.

The assortment of scripts is dizzying, and the scripts can be harmful. These identity constructions imply that the woman who miscarries is fundamentally different from the one who has an abortion. This implication, even if only suggestive, pits two stereotypes against each other: people who grieve miscarriages and people who procure abortions. This imposition of stereotypes masks the complexity of real reproductive lives and damages solidarity within the sisterhood.[5]

A second harm occurs when the trope of heaven is leveraged to control the narrative of ended pregnancies. Conservative Christian rhetoric imposes on a believer who has miscarried the idea that she should imagine what she miscarried as a baby who awaits her in heaven. This imagery locks her into a calculus where salvation is contingent on her assenting to a particular understanding of beings in the womb. Secular feminism ridicules the notion of fetuses going to heaven. This viewpoint imposes a self-silencing on the person who is feminist and Christian. Her feminism means that when she miscarries, she must keep her hope for heaven to herself, as if it is something shameful. Heaven in the hands of prolife or prochoice ideologies polices the experience of reproductive endings that pregnant people are allowed to have.

The afterlife is an open question. It punctuates the inchoate and poignant prayers after a reproductive ending. Or heaven is pushed to the side by women who do not think eternal life applies to what they lost. The drumbeat message from ecofeminist theologies repudiates an otherworldly eschatology. Hope of heaven is off the table in feminist sectors where it is considered to be a toxic concept. This theological move forecloses too much too soon. The work of discerning a new theological script about reproductive endings depends on first exposing how heaven is leveraged to control the meaning of death in the womb. A nontoxic eschatology waits to be written.

## Constructing the Female Subject of Reproductive Endings

Murderous mother. Traumatized victim. Inconvenient mourner. Rights-bearing pregnant person. When a pregnancy ends, women are channeled toward these four different identities, depending on the community with which they primarily associate. Societal communities are porous. Any woman—secular or religious, conservative Christian or progressive believer—might be impacted by a number of discourses and practices associated with the meaning of death in pregnancy. Drawing back the curtain on these communities' meaning-making tactics reveals how the afterlife factors into the construction and policing of the female subject of reproductive endings.

### Murderous Mother
The image of babies can be powerful. In commercials, babies sell any number of products. Babies doing adorable things fill the social media

posts of new parents. Emaciated babies in distant, war-torn lands accompany donation pleas from charitable relief organizations. It is no wonder that images of babies in heaven are mobilized by conservative Christian groups to promote the message to believers that they should never abort their vulnerable preborn child.[6]

The tone used in popular preaching about murderous mothers ranges from pastoral to severe. Prolife blogs and websites, depicting infants in an idyllic heavenly landscape, assert that women who abort are forever linked to their baby by a "motherly bond that even abortion cannot dissolve."[7] An abortion memorial shrine website features an appealing image of two babies with Photoshopped angel wings posed on clouds.[8] Another social media page depicts aborted fetuses in the guise of infants and toddlers frolicking in a heavenly meadow.[9] Their cherubic faces and smiles are meant to induce an urge to maternal protectiveness in any woman who might stumble upon these websites.

Fervent antiabortion Christians do not mince words. Abortion is the "killing . . . of vulnerable unborn children—*by their mothers.*"[10] Extreme prolife rhetoric indicts anyone involved in this "unjustified homicide," from the doctor to the woman herself.[11] Some antiabortion legislative activism focuses on getting abortion on the books as a federal crime, as in El Salvador, Nicaragua, Senegal, and Madagascar.[12] Beyond the threat of earthly punishments are threats of eternal damnation. Aborted babies go to heaven. Murderous mothers who abort must repent. Those who do not turn penitently to Jesus "will NOT see their children in Heaven."[13] Hell awaits murderous mothers.

Damnation as a preaching strategy is not new and was known to be effective in boosting conversions in the First Great Awakening.[14] American society is a long way from the eighteenth century, however. Believers today may not take kindly to the threat that heaven's gates will be closed to them if they do not embrace a particular conservative Christian understanding of life in the womb. Even without the threat of damnation, the church can still wave the stick of stigma. Believing women rarely reveal to their pastors or congregations that they had an abortion. Women self-shun by remaining silent about a past abortion. Labeling women as murderers of their unborn children comes at a cost for their spiritual well-being and injects a poison of secret shame into the fellowship of believers. This stigma falls on anyone who ends a pregnancy, even those who do not believe in heaven or hell.

A more severe variation on the theme of murderous mothers invokes the notion of fetal martyrdom. This morally rigorous Roman Catholic and Eastern Orthodox approach promotes the notion of aborted fetuses as martyrs of the faith who ascend immediately to heaven at death.[15] Aborted fetuses give implicit witness to Christian faith in their death because abortion, in rejecting unborn life, rejects the "Author" of life, God. Abortion is "absolute hatred of Christ."[16] Mothers who abort their children subject them to a martyr's "baptism of blood."[17] Aborted fetuses are seen as "companions of the Holy Innocents of Bethlehem," referring to the biblical story of Jewish male children slaughtered shortly after Jesus's birth (Matt 2:16, 18).[18] The biblical Rachel wept for her lost children (Matt 2:18).[19] Mothers who have abortions do not weep. These mothers are the cruelest of dry-eyed, murderous anti-Rachels.

## Traumatized Victim

"I struggled mentally for years, feeling like I didn't deserve to be alive." "I experienced guilt, shame, anger (actually rage), difficulty having healthy relationships and a divorce." "I cried a lot. I had nightmares of hearing a baby cry in the distance. I wanted a way out of the emotional pain and perpetual inner darkness."[20] The experience of abortion traumatizes: so say many women who post testimonials like these on postabortion recovery websites. Their tearful repentance is warmly welcomed in moderate prolife circles, where the language of abortion-as-murder is avoided in favor of compassion and healing. This "pro-woman/pro-life" approach purports to advocate for "*both* the woman and her unborn child."[21] The offer of compassionate Christian understanding, however, comes with strings. This prolife

approach frames women with unwanted pregnancies as morally inde-
cisive. They are depicted as vulnerable to manipulation by selfish
partners, overbearing parents, and abortion providers who are just
in it for the money. Women who have had an abortion, even those
who seem to be coping, are pronounced as deluded victims, unaware
that they are suffering from emotional, psychological, and spiritual
trauma.[22]

Prolife groups offer these women a particular script. Spiritual healing awaits them, contingent on accepting their own traumatization as
a result of their complicity in the death of their unborn child. They are
offered an identity—victimized sinner. These women are directed to
postabortion counseling, step-by-step healing programs, and spiritual
retreats with bereavement rituals. Attendees at these retreats can ask
forgiveness from God and their baby in heaven.[23] One retreat partici-
pant remarked that she was now reassured that her aborted "children
are alive in heaven with Christ."[24] Repenting publicly before witnesses
and participating in group healing processes counteract the trauma of
keeping the abortion "a carefully guarded secret."[25]

Prolife groups also facilitate public repentance on a grand scale.
One can attend a national "day of remembrance for aborted children"[26]
or go on a postabortion pilgrimage tour to notable Marian shrines.[27]
Instead of being told they are murderers excluded from heaven, participants are assured that God will have mercy on anyone struggling with
the "emotional carnage" of having had an abortion.[28] This approach
recognizes abortion as sin but lessens the stigma by invoking the mother's own trauma and victimization.

Science disputes the notion of postabortion trauma.[29] With little to no evidence of abortion precipitating a psychiatric trauma syndrome, these postabortion spiritual therapies and rituals constitute a
constructed identity that manipulates women's emotions after abortion. However, women in the pews may be responding positively to
this soft-sell prolife tone. They comply with the identity of traumatized
victim, preferring it over cold-blooded murderer.

Heaven as a component in postabortion victimization messaging is exemplified in a novel way, literally. The hugely popular genre of Christian romance fiction has a growing subgenre of stories focusing on abortion.[30] The novel *Tilly* by Frank Peretti uses a quasi-fantasy genre that invokes the trope of aborted children in heaven. *Tilly* tells a story of a woman who suddenly has to grapple with a past abortion.[31] The narrative creates the perfect medium for constructing the protagonist, and therefore all readers who associate with her, as an abortion trauma victim.

In the novel, the protagonist Kathy Ross, an ostensibly happily married, white suburban mom of three, has an experience that causes her to confront her past abortion. In an extended dream sequence, Kathy encounters a group of children of various ages who mysteriously appear in her backyard. Kathy is drawn to one young girl named Tilly. Kathy and Tilly spend a seemingly timeless and fantastical afternoon together, talking, walking, and picnicking in an idyllic meadow beside a creek filled with jewels. They eventually work out their relationship: Tilly is Kathy's aborted daughter, now age nine, who is cared for by Jesus, along with other aborted children in heaven.[32] Tilly, however, is not fully happy in heaven and desires to know and be loved by her mom. Just as Kathy emerges from her dream, the two reconcile. "I forgive you, Mommy. I love you. Don't cry . . . Jesus forgave you a long time ago," Tilly assures her. She implies that they will meet again in heaven, and then Tilly fades away in a fog.[33]

The story gives a gentle antiabortion message. Kathy and her husband are depicted as caring Christians and loving parents to their other children. Kathy's abortion trauma is mild, a periodic but persistent inchoate sadness. The trauma is alleviated by the healing encounter of mother and child, even if only in a dream, and by the hope that dream inspires of an eternal reunion in heaven.

## Inconvenient Mourner

Imagine that a woman has delivered her twenty-week-old child stillborn in a hospital. Her wailing fills the hallways of the birthing center, and the nurses run to close her door. She is visited by a Catholic chaplain, who finds her still holding the tiny bundle that the nurses have tenderly washed and swaddled. She turns to the priest, "Father, can you baptize him? We had chosen Gregory for a name." Awkward silence. The very presence of an unbaptized dead fetus and its grieving mother puts hospital chaplains in an uncomfortable position.[34] They would prefer not to cross the sacramental line. The woman's grief-filled request for her fetus to be baptized is inconvenient.

The sacrament of baptism is so closely linked to salvation in Catholicism that ordinary believers equate the two. Practically, baptism is optimal for facilitating a funeral mass and burial in consecrated ground.[35] The US Conference of Catholic Bishops' ethics manual for Catholic hospitals urges baptism for a miscarried fetus, if it is born alive.[36] Not all priests follow this directive to the letter, and some may agree to conduct the same funeral mass for an unbaptized stillborn infant as for a baptized born infant. One Catholic chaplain reasoned that "when a pregnant woman receives communion, her child also receives it" in the womb, and "the child will certainly be in heaven."[37] Thus, a Catholic burial is appropriate. (He probably knows his bishop would not be pleased with this sacramental interpretation.) Concern for the spiritual well-being of the parents is top of mind for one Episcopal priest who said that she would conduct a stillborn infant baptism to comfort the family, even knowing that doing so is "heretical."[38]

Imagine that a married couple arrives at their pastor's office. It's been a month since she miscarried early in her pregnancy. Still distraught, they want to have a service for their baby. Even though they have no body to bury, the ritual will give them closure. They ask, "Can we see a sample service that we can personalize for our situation?" Pause. The pastor blinks. He blinks again. His mouth is open but no sound is coming out. Pastoral confusion about where to go for resources in this situation makes these parents inconvenient mourners.

Ministers note that "baptism is the only sacrament that is expressly anticipated for infants."[39] Denominational liturgies for fetal death are difficult to find. Caring and attentive ministers who have some pastoral training regarding reproductive loss will be able to work interactively with bereaved parents in a cooperative process to construct their own unique service.[40] These pastors will be able to listen and let the grieving parents "reach their own conclusions" about death, salvation, heaven, and other such religious questions.[41] Ministers may find themselves faced with their own questions, admitting that they have "no clear answers" on complex theological issues such as whether fetuses go to heaven.[42]

Some denominations have worked to develop services to use after miscarriage or stillbirth.[43] However, one size does not fit all when it comes to commemorating the many types of reproductive endings. For miscarriages that happen at home, many families just do what grieving families from time immemorial have done: bury whatever remains they can save in a grave in the backyard or some other meaningful spot. The request for a church funeral service after miscarriage can be complicated and upsetting, especially when those requesting it are viewed as inconvenient mourners.

Imagine a young woman, newly appointed as an associate minister, unexpectedly falls pregnant. After prayerful consideration, she acts quickly and has an abortion. No one knew; it was so early in her pregnancy. She experienced some severe cramping, but the process was uneventful and done in the privacy of her own home. Still, she wants closure. She shares what happened with the senior minister and asks if he will help her create a ritual to mark this important transition in her life. He immediately agrees and they get to work. After choosing the hymns and scriptures, he says, "Here is where we'll do the confession of sin and affirmation of forgiveness." She looks up. Her eyes narrow. "What sin?" People who wish to commemorate an abortion, *sans* regret, may find that they are viewed as inconvenient mourners.

Postabortion memorial church services, which are welcoming and accepting of all reproductive decisions, may not be that common.[44]

Even recent worship manual rituals for miscarriage and stillbirth avoid crafting words to address abortion, categorizing it as a "sociopolitical . . . crisis event" that they apparently want to avoid.[45] A progressive congregation may wish to offer a service that affirms the person's abortion decision, respects a range of emotions, and welcomes trans and gender-nonconforming persons. The minister and service planners will have to hunt for such a ritual.[46]

If the pastor and congregation are prolife, the postabortion rituals will likely be crafted so that "every lost fetus that is memorialized *becomes* a child" in the mind and heart of the woman who had the abortion.[47] A welcome may be extended to the woman who "repents an abortion."[48] She may be handed a prayer, giving her the proper words to say to "cleanse" her of her sin.[49] Planners of memorial services or reproductive endings might issue an invitation to anyone in the congregation who has "suffered the loss of children in utero through a miscarriage or a regretted abortion."[50] The qualifier for abortion is not insignificant. An attendee who does not express regret would be an inconvenient mourner.

## Rights-Bearing Persons

Women today have rights. Even the most conservative Christian women are thankful for their intrepid foremothers who fought for women's rights. Activist women of past centuries marched, leafletted, and even went to prison to secure women's rights to vote, divorce, retain custody of their children, attain higher education, and have a fair wage. Childbearing was unavoidable for married women. Until the advent of reliable birth control and the legal right even for married women to use it, spontaneous miscarriage was often experienced as a relief and a "blessing" by families overburdened with many dependents, unstable incomes, chronic health issues, and other stresses.[51] In the 1960s the fight for reproductive rights began in earnest.[52] With reproductive rights came a script of how the modern, liberated, rights-bearing woman should think and act.

American women are better off with the modern women's rights script than with the two miserable options they faced in past centuries: "the odium of being called old maids," or married into the "torture of bearing children every year . . . at the expense of her own life and health."[53] However, changes in societal attitudes occur slowly. By the waning decades of the twentieth century, women had rights, but conservative social mores still held sway in polite society. America had barely emerged from the era of the tabooed use of the term *pregnant* on television.[54] Even with the advent of legalized abortion in 1973, there remained in place a widespread societal "miscarriage taboo."[55]

In feminist circles, speaking of one's miscarriage as a lost baby is taboo. Some feminist approaches solve the baby-talk problem by asserting personhood only at birth.[56] Or the personhood question is written off as unsolvable because it is mired in controversies and unanswerable ontological questions.[57] Concerns about eroding the rights of pregnant persons are top of mind.

The feminist prochoice position protests the use of fetal ultrasounds to construct developing life in the uterus as a baby with "person-like qualities" and hence person-like rights.[58] Any "blurring of boundaries between the concepts of 'foetus' and 'infant'" is seen as creating an expectation of the woman's ethical obligation to her unborn baby.[59] If baby talk about one's fetus is taboo, adding a layer of religious imagery is even more so. Depicting a fetus that dies as a cherub in heaven strikes many secular feminists as a kind of "fetish"[60] and borderline "creepy."[61] Today's rights-bearing person who has an abortion is encouraged to "shout" it, but if they have a miscarriage, they should only grieve *sotto voce*.[62]

Some prochoice scholars who have suffered a pregnancy loss did not get this feminist memo on miscarriage. One philosopher's autoethnographic account of her miscarriage unmasks the widely known secret that feminists mourn their miscarriages. She admits to "having trouble squaring my losses with my pro-choice politics" and to finding "the notion that I had lost 'babies' oddly comforting." She sees nothing wrong with women calling the being they miscarried a child, as long as they do not imply that the "prenatal being is a 'person' in the moral sense."[63] There is an odd public/private ideological dichotomy at work when feminists urge pregnancy-capable persons to celebrate openly their reproductive rights but to keep a low and private profile when mourning a reproductive loss. Women, including secular feminist philosophers, might acceptably grieve a lost pregnancy but should avoid talk of lost babies, especially as angels in heaven.

There is a common thread running through the various ways the female subject of reproductive loss is framed: leveraging the trope of heaven (positively or negatively) to entice her to conform to a particular identity. Even if one can deconstruct the tactics of how the female subject is constructed and policed, one will still be faced with a binary—also constructed—between abortion and spontaneous miscarriage.

## The Stereotype of Miscarriage versus Abortion

Women suffer, individually and as a group, when they are pitted against each other. Nowhere is this adversarial situation more acute than in the experience of reproductive endings. A widespread "cultural assumption of the enormous difference between miscarriage and abortion" has succeeded in making pregnancy loss a wedge issue.[64] The wedge is a construct. In reality, miscarriage and abortion are two sides of the same coin of people managing their fertility and making parenting decisions in different contexts and at different times in their reproductive lives.

### Two Sides of the Same Coin

Discussions of reproductive endings too often construct wedges. Sympathy is extended to those who innocently and tragically suffer a spontaneous miscarriage; opprobrium is voiced toward those who procure an abortion and do not repent of it. Another wedge forms because of an imposed normative view of women's maternal nature. Prolife positions characterize women as maternally devasted by miscarriage, in order to draw a contrast with women who have an abortion. The latter are presented as either cold-hearted or traumatized psychologically (whether they admit it or not) for having gone against their essential maternal nature. A third wedge forecasts two opposing eschatological futures. The woman who miscarries is given the hope of a joyful reunion in heaven, whereas the unrepentant woman who aborts faces dubious salvation. These wedges, based on damaging caricatures, breed disinformation about women's actual reproductive experiences.

Women are ill-served by religious attitudes and practices that pit women who abort against those who have miscarriages. Believers should not be forced into self-identifying with a moralistic stereotype, a psychological box, or a particular view of salvation. Looking beyond simplistic binaries reveals unmet needs for more fluid reproductive identities that match all types of pregnancy endings.

The binary between miscarriage and abortion runs deep. The church has a history of comforting women who feel guilty about their miscarriage by telling them how different they are from women who contemplate or commit evil acts like abortion and infanticide. Sixteenth-century Protestant reformer Martin Luther gave these instructions regarding pastoral care for women who miscarry:

> *We ought not to frighten or sadden such mothers with unkind words. It is not their fault. It is not their carelessness or neglect that caused the birth of their child to go wrong. One must distinguish between them and a woman who resents being pregnant, deliberately neglects her baby, and even goes so far as to strangle or destroy it.*[65]

This good-mother/bad-mother message has been deeply internalized by many faith leaders and ordinary believers. This message may contribute to why women who have miscarriages feel guilty and fend off that guilt by disassociating their experience from that of women who abort.[66]

Women with a wanted pregnancy, who subsequently undergo a termination due to fetal anomaly (TFA), react strongly to having their procedure described as an abortion.[67] Moreover, those who understand that their TFA was, technically, a selective abortion will not speak about it openly as such, fearful of condemnation from prolife family and friends. The "self-silencing" in light of antiabortion sentiment is detrimental and, in one woman's words, "has severely compromised my ability to seek support for my loss in a public way."[68]

Women recoil strongly against any language that associates the medical treatment for their miscarriage with abortion. They "hated" when their medical providers called their miscarriage a "spontaneous abortion."[69] The use of abortion-related medical terms for miscarriage contributes to their feelings of culpability.[70] Individualized medical care that respects each patient's preferred terminology is usually best; however, the need to monitor language about miscarriage reveals a deeper cultural problem. Stigmatizing abortion spills over onto other reproductive events.

Seeing abortion and miscarriage as two sides of the same coin does not discount the visceral desire of women who suffer the loss of a wanted baby to distance themselves from any notion of an unwanted pregnancy. There are real differences in intentionality and context between the loss of a desperately wanted child and the intentional termination of a mistimed and unwelcome pregnancy. Nevertheless, to think of miscarriage and abortion only in terms of this binary promotes an inaccurate picture of reproductive endings. Just because a woman who miscarries rejects any abortion-related terminology does not mean that she wishes to reject other women who have abortions.

## Reproductive Endings beyond the Binary

The experience of pregnancy—the emotions around it and the sheer physicality of it—can be unpredictable. Pregnancy is like an expanse of ice upon which women are thrown, sometimes finding traction, sometimes in a free slide. Pregnancy-capable people know that they could find themselves suddenly in either scenario. The lines between different types of ended pregnancies can be very blurry, as these vignettes demonstrate.

Vignette 1. In terms of the medical procedure, treatment for a miscarriage and an abortion may be indistinguishable. Imagine a woman who is happily pregnant. Suddenly, she begins to miscarry spontaneously at home, but after a few days the bleeding increases drastically. She requires dilation and curettage (D&C) that will empty her uterus to prevent sepsis or hemorrhage. She is distressed that she lost the baby but relieved that the miscarrying is over. She had been alone, frightened, and in pain at home, passing wads of bloody tissue sitting on the toilet. Several days later she recounts her harrowing experience to her two longtime friends. One friend reveals that she had had a medical abortion at home a year ago; the other shares about her past clinic abortion. They could relate to what each other's bodies went through.[71]

Vignette 2. The emotional aftereffects of miscarrying an unwanted pregnancy and the aftereffects of abortion may have similarities; in both instances, the women may feel relief. Imagine a teenager busy with her life activities who is not planning on having a child before college, marriage, and beginning her career. She has an unusually heavy, late menstrual cycle where she passes some large clots. When she checks her calendar and her sexual activity that month, she realizes that she may very well have been pregnant, despite the use of birth control. She is enormously relieved that the possible pregnancy failed on its own and that she did not have to face an abortion. Her friend was not so lucky. Her friend did not realize she was pregnant until she was well into her first trimester. When her own gynecologist refused to do the procedure, she ended up going to Planned Parenthood. Even with her mom there for support, it was an experience she never wants to repeat, but she is enormously relieved that she found safe abortion care where she was not refused treatment.[72]

Vignette 3. There can also be similarities between miscarriage and abortion having to do with the stigma women feel.[73] Imagine a woman finds herself unexpectantly pregnant with her third child at age forty. Her husband is over the moon that it's finally a boy. She is starting to get excited too, but she sometimes complains to her women's Bible study group that her ob/gyn recommended no alcohol and stopping her marathon training (half-jokingly, she admits she still sneaks a glass of wine and a short jog occasionally). Then, unexpectantly, she miscarries. She is conflicted—feeling sad, feeling it was probably for the best, but also worried about being blamed by her Christian friends. She is uncertain about whom to confide in regarding these mixed feelings. Finally, she calls an old friend who had once spoken openly of her abortion and was subtly snubbed by some of the people at church. Somehow, she had the feeling that her old friend would understand.

These vignettes are fictional but based on medical facts and social scientific studies about the many facets of miscarriage and abortion experiences. These vignettes do not recount a woman who had an abortion suffering subsequently from infertility or repeated miscarriages, because that would not be a fact-based story but a prolife myth.[74] That said, because of the prevalence of early miscarriage, it is highly likely that a sexually active woman who gets an abortion has already had one or more miscarriages. Miscarriage is common. In one sense, losing a pregnancy is more natural than completing it for a woman who has experienced repeated miscarriages or for a woman in her late thirties or forties using her own (not previously frozen) ova.[75]

When prolife groups spread the myth that abortion causes later reproductive problems, they inadvertently cast aspersions on any woman experiencing fertility problems, implying that a past secret abortion might be a contributing factor to her repeated miscarriages. Prolife writers try to segregate the two reproductive experiences, implying that the woman who has an abortion has never been a woman mourning the miscarriage of her wanted pregnancy. As one prolife writer asserts, "The woman who aborts is a different woman from the one who chooses not to."[76] On the contrary. Statistically speaking, she may be the same woman.

These vignettes do not show women deeply traumatized by abortion. The claim of postabortion trauma syndrome is based on faulty science, but trauma is associated with miscarriage. The miscarriage or stillbirth of a wanted child correlates with a risk of developing mental health problems.[77] Thus, some distinctions between miscarriage and abortion are valid, but these distinctions do not justify propagating misleading moralistic binaries. In terms of family planning, fertility management, contraceptive use, and sexuality, there is more of a continuum between miscarriage and abortion than many would care to admit. Trying to pit so-called innocent maternal women who miscarry against so-called guilty antimaternal women who have abortions turns out to be a political tactic rather than a window into real people's reproductive lives. If anything, the dividing line between miscarriage and abortion for believing women, even prolife ones, can be very narrow and fluid.

Consider the story of Shannon Dingle. A mother of six, including several special needs children, Dingle is well known in Christian prolife circles for writing and speaking on disability and the sanctity of life. She discovered she was pregnant a mere one week after a freak tragic accident took the life of her husband. Grieving and battling her own medical complications, she began making plans to have an abortion. Then she miscarried. Dingle reveals the details of this painful period of her life in order to combat distorting prolife caricatures about reproductive decision-making. Such caricatures "make for good propaganda but terrible policy. People, real people, become pregnant" and may need not to be pregnant. As Dingle writes, "I knew I couldn't have this baby."[78]

The moral of Dingle's story is not that some pregnancies happen in such tragic contexts and to such otherwise exemplary mothers that they meet some casuistic criteria for a morally permissible abortion. Rather, her story supplies more evidence about the misleading and constructed dichotomy between miscarriage and abortion. Dingle grieved the loss and also was relieved. She does not try to explain or justify that paradox. Dingle says she is "not pro-life anymore, not in the political sense";[79] however, her deconversion is not the point. Rather, her account illustrates how the abortion/miscarriage binary harms by ignoring the complexities of reproductive lives and undercutting women's ability to navigate those complexities.

## Feminist Theologies and Reproductive Endings

Women's reproductive experiences have long been a taboo subject in the church. Feminist theologies have for decades warned that what is rendered invisible is disempowered. Feminist scholarship is slowly breaking the silence and making visible the person who experiences an ended pregnancy.

The growing focus on reproductive experiences is, in part, due to the turn to the body in current feminist and other progressive Christian scholarship.[80] Discussions of corporeality are breaking down the taboos on theologizing about sexuality, the life cycles of female bodies, and the realities of pregnancy, birthing, and childrearing. Opportunities now exist for women of faith to come out of the closet about their reproductive lives and have their voices heard. Surely this is good. Yet here is where a tension arises.

Some believing individuals who have suffered from an ended pregnancy wonder what might await beyond this vale of tears. Heaven remains a motif in Christian faith and practice. In many feminist theological circles, however, heaven is taboo. Liberation theology and ecofeminism have long seen appeals to eternal life as an opiate for poor and marginalized communities. Heaven threatens the fight for justice in the here and now. The sweet by and by will not serve the needs of a fragile planet and, thus, "an otherworldly afterlife, and eternal life need to be abandoned."[81]

Feminist theologians (and the communities of women they serve) are pulled between two apparently incommensurable sets of values: support for embodied experience, including spiritual needs surrounding an ended pregnancy; and justice on behalf of an endangered earth and the dispossessed. In terms of lived reality, given that believers who gestate also are affected by ecological disasters and social injustice, the two sets of values can intersect. However, these two sets of concerns represent a theological rift, and not an inconsequential one.

The believer whose pregnancy has ended finds herself caught in the middle of this theological fissure. On the one hand, if traditional views of salvation and resurrection promote damaging concepts for the earth, it would be ethically questionable for her to give serious credence to the notion of heaven, even if it comforts her after an ended pregnancy. On the other hand, if solidarity with a woman's experience of reproductive loss means respecting her hope for life after death, then it would be ethically and pastorally questionable to use ecojustice to silence her talk of heaven. The believer is left adrift between these dueling theological discourses with their apparently competing ethical values. The competition need not be divisive. It is possible to bring into balance the two sets of concerns: attention to one's individual bodily identity after reproductive loss, and willingness to imagine a future wider than one's own story.

## Rebuilding One's Bodily Self

A reproductive ending is a corporeal undoing. Whether welcomed or mourned, it is still a significant bodily event. The pregnant embodied self that was, now has unraveled. One needs to find a new way to live in one's own skin, alone. Believers who suffer reproductive loss want to know that God is not absent when a pregnancy ends. In a miscarriage or self-managed abortion, the pregnant person's body takes on the literally gut-wrenching task of expelling that which it had at one point nurtured. The process can extend over hours or even days—a long time to feel bereft of God's Spirit.

Rebuilding one's bodily identity after a reproductive ending is hard. Women face impediments from church and society in their "attempts to construct meaning when confronted with the pain of death before birth."[82] Overcoming or mitigating those impediments requires at least two things: community and anger.

Many women miscarry spontaneously or have a medical abortion completely alone. Shame or secrecy impels some to seek privacy—in a dorm bathroom stall, at home while one's children are at school, in an impersonal hotel room. Some would prefer a supportive community. This preference is voiced in testimonies about the tender ministrations of nurses, doulas, friends, and family members who were there not to preach but to keep vigil, not to chide but to care. After the undoing of reproductive loss—whether it is experienced as great or small—one needs a "way back to wholeness" and that path is "found as community, self and body are cobbled back together over time."[83] One can survive a reproductive ending alone, but it takes a village for the body to thrive again.

Women need to express their anger. First-wave theological feminism counseled that anger is the catalyst for breaking free from patriarchy. Anger challenges the overt and "subtle conditioning that reinforces our reluctance to develop a sense of our own power."[84] The first generation of scholars in religion who put anger on the feminist agenda also put female bodies back into theology—not as a locus for temptation and sin but as a site of oppression and resistance.[85] They gave Christian women back their bodies. They gave women permission to celebrate their sexuality and develop new rituals for female-bodied life events.[86] They called them to anger.

Feminist theology channels women's anger regarding the church's "profound silence"[87] and lack of "any serious, sustained theological reflections" on issues of infertility and reproductive loss.[88] Women mourning an ended pregnancy are doubly wounded when their spiritual need "rarely seems to be met with a theology—and especially an eschatology—that can support or make sense" of their loss.[89] Anger overflows when a child-free professional woman is made the target of biting criticisms and suspicions from those in her church who think that she "misused her youth, getting pregnant and aborting," and that she wasted her "fertile years on education and a profession."[90]

Anger can be channeled in generative directions. Righteous fury about silencing and shaming can empower a community to band together. Indignation can motivate believers to protest a church that condemns the taking of life in abortion while doing little in its "theological, pastoral, and liturgical responses to women who experience the loss of a pregnancy."[91] Anger is a tool feminism puts in the hands of the mourning woman so she can rebuild her identity after reproductive loss.

### Imagining a Wider Future

"Where there is no vision, the people perish."[92] People who experience a reproductive ending need not only community and anger but also an imagined future. Whether one's state of mind is inconsolable grief or breathless relief, one's life has changed. One needs to find one's bearings again, and that requires a wider horizon line.

Some imagined futures are grassroots, improvised spiritualities. Believers may find that the devastation of an ended pregnancy "cemented their hope and expectation of a heavenly afterlife." Little, insignificant things take on new meaning. Catching sight of a child's balloon drifting into the sky triggers a reassuring spiritual sense of one's miscarried baby somewhere in heaven.[93] The first steps toward an imagined future may entail a homemade ritual—a poem read while planting a tree in one's backyard where the miscarriage remains are buried.[94] Rituals for child loss can become customary over time. Poor Catholic women in a shanty town in Brazil bury their dead infants "with their eyes left open, ready to see God, and with the coffin lid left unfastened so as to quickly enter into heaven."[95] Theology calls these *eschatological imaginaries*, which capture "life at its most tender and tenuous moments."[96]

Grassroot rituals arise during a time of emotional vulnerability and spiritual exposure. Misguided comforters and bad actors materialize at these moments to offer a "facile palliative for those who mourn."[97] Tone-deaf preachers promise an otherworldly peace that encourages people who are suffering now to "postpone hope and expectations to the next world."[98] Dishing out hope to those mourning reproductive loss leaves "no room for despair and hopelessness."[99] This hope is toxic. Instead of affirming the pain of an ended pregnancy, hope in a benign eschatological future is "weaponized to minimize and belittle suffering and trauma."[100] This otherworldly pablum is inadequate for the spiritual hunger of reproductive grieving.

Some ecofeminists, liberation theologians, and womanist theologians offer compelling reasons for doing away with an eschatological imagery altogether. Even before ecotheology deconstructed the notion of an otherworldly realm after death, theological teachings about heaven were never women friendly. The church begrudgingly included women among the saints in heaven "but only through accepting their subordination on earth and transcending their sexuality and sexual bodies in the resurrected life."[101] Feminists are correct to categorize the male theological "preoccupation with death and other worlds" as a "symptom of the deep misogyny of western culture," with its "fear, dread, and fascination with the maternal body."[102]

To combat the androcentric individualism of the afterlife, ecofeminists advocate for nonpersonal postmortem continuity. They reconfigure the meaning of Christian resurrection not as individual survival in "heaven or another world" but as a way to affirm the "physical basis for life" on earth, humanity's home and God's body.[103] Salvation is viewed not metaphysically, as blessedness in another dimension of existence, but ethically, as a commitment to living justly and sustainably on this planet. Life and death are aligned so that "everything that lives and dies goes back into . . . the matrix of life."[104]

Womanists recount the exploitation of African Americans from the slave era to the present and call for "eschatological hopes for change within history."[105] They critique the "other-worldly eschatology" foisted on enslaved or downtrodden people of color[106] and preach a "prophetic eschatology" focused on combating societal injustices.[107] These prophetic visions challenge believers to think outside of the box of traditional anthropocentric, individualistic, and classically theistic views of resurrection and the afterlife.

Many women, including those who suffer reproductive loss, are deeply committed to movements for environmental, economic, and racial justice in the "here and now of history."[108] They are drawn to eschatological imaginaries of justice, healing, and ecological flourishing in this world. These women find peace in the spiritual vision of rising "from the womb of the earth" and returning at death to that dark womb in a natural circle of life.[109] There is a power to these justice-oriented and eco-friendly Christian commitments to the flourishing of life on earth.

Christians whose pregnancy has ended may not need or want to believe in heaven. Many suspect that in its traditional form, it is a construct of white, male, body-phobic religious authorities attempting to pacify the oppressed, squelch movements for environmental justice, and downplay the importance of corporeal well-being related to sexuality, sexual expression, and reproductive agency.[110] Believers suffering from reproductive broken dreams are not interested in a heaven that resembles an eternally happy family reunion in a great rumpus room in the sky. Neither are they interested in an eternal life framed as an ever-spinning eco-mandala. Many pregnant persons long for an imagined future after reproductive loss that will fill their achingly empty arms.

It is not a question of either/or: either a natural circle of life or being transported to heaven at death; either attentiveness to injustice on earth or hope for one's tears to be wiped away in the New Jerusalem. Rather, remaining within the tension between these two ways of thinking propels feminist theology toward more expansive and dynamic images of the afterlife.

• • •

"One is not born a woman, but rather becomes a woman."[111] This concept from Simone de Beauvoir opened the door to analyses of the culturally constructed nature of sex and gender. It has taken longer to convince people that the meaning of pregnancy is also culturally variable and not a univocal, natural process for a woman.[112] The female subject of pregnancy and of reproductive endings is constructed. She is not, however, a mere puppet. This subject, who is also an agent, is capable of grasping how various cultural spheres (advertising, social media, sermons, the medical profession, etc.) work overtly or inadvertently to impose upon her an identity, a piety, a politics, and a maternal sensibility. The more aware she is about the scripts for how "one becomes a woman," the more she can assert her agency, resist certain forms of moralistic policing, and explore new meanings for her reproductive life cycles.

The woman who has had an abortion may learn to resist rather than internalize the identity of murderess. She may begin to look suspiciously upon claims that she has been traumatized by her abortion. After a miscarriage, she may grow impatient with the blank stares of clueless ministers who deem her to be an inconvenient mourner. If she is a feminist, she may challenge the secular prochoice talking point that lamenting the miscarriage of her "baby" will endanger her sisters' reproductive rights. She may understand the harm that is inflicted by the divide-and-conquer strategy of pitting women who miscarry against women who abort.

A recurring thread running through many Christian discourses of reproductive loss is a hope of heaven. That hope can turn toxic in many ways. Feminist theology is on the cusp of developing a nontoxic response to reproductive endings that maintains the creative tension between the here and now and the afterlife. More critical thinking is needed. Not to reflect Christianly on whether there will be fetuses in the afterlife is to cede the stage to conservative Christian groups who would use that trope to leverage prolife compliance.

People who wish to remain connected to the church deserve to know the basis for and contours of a Christian hope of heaven. They deserve to know if assenting to the resurrection of the body—including unborn bodies—requires them to sacrifice their reproductive rights. They deserve an explanation for how eschatology can sustain an embodied sense of self, which is sometimes fractured by the experience of reproductive loss.

# 2

# CLOSING HEAVEN
# TO THE UNBORN

PARENTS THROUGHOUT CHRISTIAN history experienced reproductive loss. Women had miscarriages and abortions. Small bodies were buried, their graves as shallow as the church's recognition of their passing. It borders on astounding that a religion that revolves around the promise of life eternal would say so little about whether infants or unborn beings might attain heaven.

When theology did entertain the idea of infant salvation, it was wrapped in a theological fog. An afterlife for the unborn hardly occurred to the church fathers. A fetus in heaven was a surd; it could barely be thought. This theological conundrum continued as the church struggled for settled meaning regarding issues of personhood in the womb, whether infants should be baptized, whether unbaptized infants are saved, and whether attaining heaven is possible for those who die before they have the ability to profess faith in Christ. The idea of unborn bodies in the afterlife, vivid in the minds of mourning parents, languished in the theological mind.

The history of theological and sacramental fumblings over unborn bodies is a story of repeated cul-de-sacs. The church circled back around, again and again, to the same resurrection riddle, wrapped in a magisterial mystery, inside an eschatological enigma. Having started with the same set of premises, the conclusion was always the same. The gates of heaven are closed to the unborn. Focused on issues of ensoulment and baptism, the church missed the real subject of the story: the reality of a body, wrapped in a womb, inside a woman's body.

The degree to which Christian history ventured to answer the question of the unborn manifests in two parallel historical stories. One track is the dominant narrative of the church. This story recycled—sometimes couched as a traducian issue, sometimes in hylomorphic language, sometimes under the banner of *sola gratia*. But the story always ended with the same conundrum. The salvation of an unborn being could not be thought.

The other story is one the church did not even know was being told. Across history, the always, everywhere events of reproductive beginnings and endings unfold. Babies conceived in love, in violence, as a duty, by accident; babies dead on arrival, born too soon, never born at all. Hidden within this history of birthed and birthing bodies is another understanding of salvation and resurrection. This story emerged, as Foucault said, as subjugated knowledges.[1] Random, submerged yet insistent counterstories of women's reproductive bodies hum throughout history. One finds their fragments by reading between the lines of historical texts, across the surfaces of artifacts, and even in patterns of scattered bones in a graveyard. It is a story worth hearing and is still being told.

A tale of two stories. The official church bequeathed to centuries of grieving families abysmal teachings along with tone-deaf and callous sacramental responses to reproductive loss. Unable to conceptualize resurrected fetuses, theology declared the matter closed. For women who have carried life only to lose it, the dead do not remain complacent in their graves, and the matter is not closed to them. Theirs is a ghost story.

The specter of resurrection faith hovers over the fragile contents of wombs. Pregnant women shiver when this ghostly mist lifts the hairs on the back of their neck. They utter a prayer, touch the amulet hidden in their bodice, throw a pinch of salt. They take this visitation as a promise uttered. Let there be life, even in death. Holding on to that promise, they demand their resurrections—not for themselves alone but for the lives never born.

## The Ambiguity of Unborn Beings in the Early Church

One need not be an expert in the Greco-Roman era to discern that the early church's attitude toward the unborn was ambiguous. One can find a rare instance of an ancient writer, such as Clement of Alexandria, who spoke of aborted fetuses as tenderly given over to the care of angels.[2] When they discussed deceased infants at all, early church theologians spun a narrative that a fetus was not a person to whom any talk of heaven should apply.

### Abjecting Women's Bodies

The early church fathers had a visceral abhorrence to the workings of women's uteruses and gestational processes. Early third-century theologian Tertullian wrote graphically of "the filth of the generative seeds within the womb, of the bodily fluid and the blood; the loathsome, curdled lump of flesh which has to be fed for nine months off this same muck."[3] Much of the ancient world thought of the womb as a place of "'unclean' . . . blood and debris"[4] and a place of "decay, excrement, foul smell, and disease."[5] The remnants of a miscarriage, or *abortivi*, were singled out as indicating something "polluted and filthy."[6] These early notions of filth associated with wombs and birthing had a continuing impact in subsequent centuries. Women absorbed these religiously inflected sentiments and grew to hate and abject their own bodily processes. One fourteenth-century French woman explained her difficulties, after having given birth, in accepting Christ's incarnation in Mary's womb because pregnancy culminated with "the disgusting afterbirth that women expel."[7] To associate Christ with a placenta was abhorrent.

Medieval treatises and iconography of the Virgin Mary strove to emphasize the purity of Mary's womb,[8] in part to contrast it with widespread notions of ordinary women's tainted bodies. Other than Christ and Mary (or possibly John the Baptist and Elizabeth), fetuses and their corporeal housing were objects of disgust and abjection in

Christian writings. This visceral revulsion was the cultural backdrop for theology's failed attempts to imagine fetuses in heaven.

## Personhood in the Womb

The question of when and how a uterine being became an ensouled person with moral and spiritual status confounded the early church. Tertullian rejected the (creationist) notion of an infused immaterial soul at some point in development. Instead, he took a traducian position. The fetus received a corporeal soul at the moment its father's semen congealed the mother's uterine blood.[9] The embryo's body and soul both had to develop in order to achieve a formed state of personhood later in the womb.[10]

Tertullian was a strong apologist for bodily resurrection, defined as an event whereby souls are given back "the self-same bodies in which they died."[11] Tertullian would have faced a quandary about how to conceptualize the bodily resurrection of an embryo, with its seminally received material soul joined with the bloody uterine tissue that still "for the most part shares its own state with the mother."[12]

Tertullian was married and may well have witnessed the progression of pregnancy. No record mentions that they had any children, but he was interested in and knowledgeable about the obstetrical and gynecological science of his day.[13] Tertullian allowed the science of gestation to inform his theology. Bodies took time to form in the womb, so it made sense to him to think of souls and personhood developing over time. He apparently would not, or could not, speculate on how those still-developing fetal bodies and souls might be resurrected if they died before birth.[14]

Augustine of Hippo, a theological giant in the Western church, was drawn to both traducian and creationist views of ensoulment. He eventually espoused the creationist notion that God creates a soul and infuses it into the developing body in the womb.[15] Augustine was rare in voicing concern about uterine life, but he did not have clarity on its status in the womb or in the afterlife. In his early fifth-century treatise

*Enchiridion,* Augustine confessed that a "question may be most carefully discussed by the most learned men, and still I do not know that
any man can answer it, namely: When does a human being begin to
live in the womb?"[16] Espousing creationism did not solve the quandary
of the timing of ensoulment.

The issue of fetal resurrection was not a marginal concern for
Augustine. He grappled with the question for years as he struggled
with the tenuousness, in his mind, of a developing fetus's personhood.
Augustine could imagine that "there is a resurrection for them" but
only if they "are fully formed"; otherwise they will simply "perish, like
seeds that did not germinate."[17] They will simply return to dust.[18] The
"vacillating Augustine of the *Enchiridion*" appears differently in the
massive tome *City of God.*[19]

In *City of God* Augustine entertained two possible options for
fetuses who have received a soul but whose bodies were not fully developed. They would exist in the afterlife as "souls without bodies though
they once had them . . . only in their mother's womb." Or, he speculated, God would miraculously and speedily enable their resurrected
bodies to mature to a more appropriate size and age. Augustine seemed
to prefer the latter option, in theory. He speculated that fetuses will not
"rise in that diminutive body in which they died, but shall receive by
the marvellous and rapid operation of God that body which time by a
slower process would have given them."[20] Where and how, after death,
this growth process might happen, he did not offer further elaboration.
These comments appear to be musings rather than the kind of firm
theological stance Augustine took on so many other issues of import
for the church.

Augustine did not envision heaven as a place of bodily growth
but imagined the resurrected bodies of the saints as having achieved
static perfection. "Non-stasis" in heaven was conceptually unthinkable.[21] It is doubtful that he could have endorsed, beyond some musings, the final resurrection as anything other than a fetal soul being
joined with a body that had matured at least to infancy. Augustine

was theologically honest enough to concede that he had no biblical or philosophical basis for identifying when a fetus could be said to be a person whose body would be resurrected at all.

As someone who lived in a long-term relationship with a woman with whom he had at least one son, Augustine had direct, existential experience of pregnancy. Even if he can be castigated for his sexist and patriarchal views of women, he understood parental grief, having lost his beloved son when he was a teenager. There may be a paternal concern in Augustine's musing about the eternal destiny of unbaptized fetuses. Nevertheless, it was an "agonized and agnostic counter-example" to the church's near-silence on the matter.[22]

Augustine took bodily resurrection seriously, having worked through his own early Manichean denigration of the body. He would not have settled for an insipid eschatology of fetal souls in heaven. However, the solution for their resurrected bodies eluded even his expansive theological mind.

### Infant Baptism and Burial

Infant baptism ignited a controversy in the early church. The notion of infants needing cleansing from original sin was most famously promulgated by Augustine, but this doctrine was already being discussed and debated in the Western church.[23] A significant contingent of leaders in the early Christian communities believed that infants were born tainted by the sin inherited from Adam.[24] The practice of infant baptism eventually took hold in the Western and Eastern churches.[25] To be saved, one needed the cleansing waters of this sacrament. By the fourteenth century, the papal bull *Benedictus Deus* linked salvation with baptism for born infants, effectively codifying the sacrament's necessity.[26] No doubt, countless families still hoped that their miscarried fetus or dead unbaptized infant went to heaven, but that idea was now sacramentally embargoed. In official church teachings and practice, heaven was closed to those unfortunate souls.

The church's attempt to impose by fiat the unthinkableness of unbaptized infants in heaven affected burial practices. Burial in consecrated ground was reserved only for the baptized. Families (willingly or not) conformed to and resisted this imposition from on high. Parents with economic means engraved the term *neophyte* (meaning, baptized) on the tombstone of their deceased child, indicating to the community its saved status.[27] Parents tried in whatever way they could to access sacramental spaces after reproductive loss. Archaeologists have found clusters of fetal remains close to the walls of churches or near defunct outdoor baptisteries, as if the sanctity of these places might leach out and be efficacious to save those who died unbaptized.[28] Some parents brought their dead neonate to church, invoking the saints for a miraculous resurrection with just enough time to complete a baptism and ensure salvation.[29] These are heart-wrenching accounts. Parents acted within sacramental strictures, while still attempting to bend the rules and get their child a place in heaven.

There is also evidence of families resisting the church's burial rules. When authorities denied a Christian burial for an unbaptized infant, the families created their own private mourning rituals.[30] Domestic burials of fetal and infant remains under the floorboards or sealed in walls or foundations of homes indicate humble ritual attempts to recognize an infant whose death the church ignored.[31]

Only a baptized infant could receive ecclesiastical recognition, which impelled the church to take increasingly extraordinary measures. The church allowed midwives to conduct emergency baptisms for sickly infants.[32] Roman Catholic leaders in the Middle Ages began authorizing or even requiring a crude form of a postmortem caesarean section on a mother who died in childbirth so that the fetus might be baptized before it died.[33] However, being able successfully to extract and baptize a still-living fetus from a dead or dying woman was highly unlikely.[34]

If the church sanctioned extreme obstetrical procedures in order to produce a live, baptizable infant, it forbade life-saving procedures for the mother. A fetal-destructive operation (embryotomy) kills the fetus in a surgical attempt to save the mother's life during an obstructed birth. Emergency embryotomy, a procedure known since Greco-Roman times, is mentioned in medieval obstetrical manuals.[35] The procedure was forbidden for Christians.[36] In terms of fetal salvation, however, nothing was gained by banning embryotomy, since before the advent of modern obstetrical surgery, the fetus in an obstructed birth would have died unbaptized along with its mother.

The torturous logic underlying emergency baptism did not raise the status of fetuses. If anything, such practices opened the door to medieval superstitions about fetal bodies. Myths circulated that the birthing mother's exposure to her dead unbaptized fetus "might pollute her soul" or desecrate "the sanctity of a Christian cemetery" where she would be buried.[37] If not successfully baptized, a fetus's corpse would have been seen as dangerous refuse to be thrown into "privies and midden heaps."[38] The fetus, for whom salvation was unthinkable, morphed into a subhuman category.

Roman Catholic policy on infant baptism and burial practices flip-flopped through the modern era. Even late into the twentieth century, Catholic women who lost a pregnancy experienced emotional suffering due to the Catholic notion of limbo and the lack of access to a church burial after miscarriage.[39] Limbo has officially been dropped, and fetal burials are now promoted by Catholic dioceses.[40] Postmortem c-sections are out, but delivery room invasive baptism measures are still in.[41] The practice of baptism after miscarriage is encouraged in the ethics manuals for Catholic hospitals.[42] These twistings and turnings of sacramental logic in the Catholic Church demonstrate the ongoing instability of the idea of the unborn beings achieving a place in heaven.

The concept of limbo has lost its hold for modern Catholics. They apparently do not want to return to the bad old days of postmortem c-sections, vials of holy water in the delivery room, and mass unmarked graves of fetuses and unbaptized neonates dotting the landscape in Catholic countries.[43] However, today, the church increasingly is poking it head into doctors' offices and operating rooms, to the consternation of physicians and pregnant women.[44]

### Infant Damnation

The church's stance regarding infant baptism and fetal burial dampened the confidence of many believers about their deceased child attaining heaven. Any remaining flickers of hope for heaven were doused by the shift in church teachings from musings and doubts about the salvation of unbaptized infants to assertions of their damnation.

The notion of infants in the underworld arose in the early centuries of the Christianity. The idea of babies in the devil's domain pained even the promoter-in-chief of the doctrine of original sin, Augustine. He tried to soften the teaching, arguing that these little ones would only suffer "the mildest punishment."[45] Other early church writers were not so soft-hearted. The second-century pseudepigraphal Apocalypse of Peter describes an afterlife for aborted fetuses, but it is in hell where they torment their mothers who sit up to their necks in a pit of blood.[46] A North African bishop in the sixth century similarly asserted that unborn beings "who begin to live in the wombs of mothers and die there . . . will be punished with everlasting punishment of eternal fire."[47] The narrative of fetal damnation continued in subsequent centuries. Even Pope Sixtus V, who notoriously called for the death penalty for any procured abortion, nevertheless affirmed in his 1588 papal bull *Effraenatam* that aborted fetuses do not go to heaven.[48]

Unbaptized infants were caught up in a complicated geography of the underworld, which had its origins in the early church's Greco-Roman context. An underworld with levels and topography was well established by the time of the advent of Christianity.[49] This imaginative idea took hold in theology and art.[50] A region of hell reserved for less sinful denizens cohered with accounts of Christ's harrowing of hell between his death and resurrection. The early church taught that "the Lord descended into the regions beneath the earth, preaching his advent," thereby freeing the worthy ancient biblical patriarchs and matriarchs, whose souls had been languishing there.[51]

These notions about the underworld were consolidated in the high Middle Ages and the Reformation period. Albertus Magnus developed an intricate geography of hell, explaining that the souls of unbaptized infants and ensouled fetuses would reside in the *limbus puerorum* (infants' limbo) in the dim, though not fiery, upper regions of hell. They would be deprived of the vision of God, but they would not suffer.[52] Thomas Aquinas concluded that Christ did not rescue the infants in hell because they did "not possess reason, [and therefore] they were unable to make the choice" to hope for a savior.[53] Dante immortalized this medieval theology of a tenebrous life of "grief without torment" in his *Divine Comedy*.[54] Albrecht Dürer's and Lucas Cranach's paintings of Christ freeing the captives in limbo show infants standing alongside Adam and Eve, giving visual solidity to the notion of unbaptized infants in hell.[55] Supported by treatises, art, and poetry, the infants' limbo was supremely imaginable; the unborn in heaven, however, never materialized in the church's mind.

## Thinking with Aquinas about Fetal Salvation

Even if Thomas Aquinas had rejected the medieval notion of the infants' limbo, the question still remains whether his theological anthropology could accommodate the idea of the unborn in heaven. Much depends on how one interprets his claim that a fetus, until "animated" with its rational soul, was not yet a human person.[56] At the core of a Thomistic view of personhood are two technical terms: *hominization* and *hylomorphism*. They determine the degree to which the idea of uterine beings as resurrected persons is thinkable.

Hominization means God's infusing of the soul in a developing human organism, thus animating it as a person. Hylomorphism is the model of personhood Aquinas adapted from Aristotle, which specifies the way in which the soul, once it is endowed by God, is joined with bodily matter. The human soul (medievals mostly called it a rational soul) is not a preexistent spiritual substance that God injects into the body's shell. The soul actually configures or forms bodily matter into a human individual. The pithy formula for hylomorphism is "the soul is the form of the body."[57] The soul gives matter its "own brand of existence."[58]

Aquinas was clear that hominization happened in the womb—but not at conception. A rational soul cannot inform a human organism developing in utero "unless the body is properly disposed" with the organs that can receive it.[59] Aquinas's Aristotelian understanding of gestational development caused him to think in ways that appear to most people today as quaint or even "*completely bogus*,"[60] because he thought there was a succession of different types of souls informing a developing organism in the womb. A "vegetative" and then an "animal" soul precede the divinely infused rational soul.[61] Mostly following Aristotle's embryology, Aquinas thought this hominization would happen around forty days after conception for male embryos and after ninety days for females.[62] Prior to hominization, resurrection would be unthinkable. Only persons can be resurrected.

Present-day prolife theologians looking for a Thomistic basis for personhood from conception argue that Aquinas's strange embryology (and his related, less stringent views on abortion) can be jettisoned.[63] His embryology can be updated with modern science, while preserving his essential theology. The science of human development demonstrates that the embryo is "a single, complex, actively developing human organism" and thus can be claimed as having a body prepared to receive its rational soul at conception.[64] Indeed, "the early embryo" is such "a stunningly complex entity" that one cannot doubt it is the bearer of a rational soul, even if the powers of rationality are only potential.[65] These modern Thomists conclude that the embryo's "DNA genes *are* organs" that meet the criteria for ensoulment readiness.[66] If Aquinas lived today, he would have to agree that even a pre-embryo could "come to participate supernaturally and eternally in the life of God."[67] With a new embryology, Thomism can support personhood from conception, which in turn would make uterine beings in heaven thinkable.

Traditional Aquinas interpreters argue that these attempts to update Aquinas for prolife purposes misunderstand what undergirds his commitment to delayed hominization. Aquinas, if he were alive today, would no doubt be fascinated by the wonders of DNA and the complex biochemistry of embryology. However, Aquinas would not need a modern biology lesson to understand that an embryo is a complex developing organism, even at its vegetative stage. He would not need persuading about biochemically complex uterine life. Aquinas would stipulate complexity from the beginning. However, he would insist that one needs the right sort of complexity to receive one's rational soul. The developing uterine organism needs the "requisite organs" perfected enough to begin sensing or having the real (not just theoretical) potential to do so, which is the basis for cognition. It is not enough to have the genetic "coding" in place for organs expected to develop at some future point.[68]

Aquinas could not have anticipated genes. He was, however, aware of traducian ensoulment-from-conception arguments in his day. (Traducians thought the soul was a material substance carried to the embryo in the father's semen.) Aquinas categorically rejected this theory—not on biological grounds but on ontological ones:

> *It cannot be said that the soul, in its complete essence, is in*
> *the semen from the beginning and that its operations do*
> *not appear because of the lack of organs. For since the soul*
> *is united to the body as its form, it is united only to a body*
> *of which it is appropriately the actuality. But the soul is the*
> *actuality of a body with organs.*[69]

Aquinas rejected the biologically based argument about ensoulment at conception not just because it was traducian but because it was based on a mistaken definition of potentiality. One cannot posit a potential future development without some basis in actuality. Aquinas insisted that fetal matter must have acquired a potential for material organs appropriate for hominization. DNA would not have cut it for Aquinas if he lived today. In fact, he would probably be more interested in how neurobiology supports his view of delayed hominization. It is even possible that the science of fetal brain development might actually convince him that ensoulment must happen significantly later in fetal development than what Aristotle taught.[70]

For theological not just embryological reasons, hominization has to happen later in gestational development. This hominization position seals the eschatological fate of beings who die before receiving a soul. Aquinas reiterated accepted church teachings that at death, the soul survives until the final judgment, when it will be reunited with "matter that is qualitatively the same" as the body it configured on earth.[71] The hylomorphic model cannot conceptualize a resurrected unensouled uterine body. Decomposition, cannibalism, and other degradations of a fully formed person's body are not impediments to resurrection. However, an undeveloped uterine body would be an impediment for resurrection. Without a minimally developed body with which the soul could be reunited again as its form, resurrection is rendered incomprehensible. At best, Aquinas offers limbo for unbaptized infants. For unensouled beings, not only are the gates of heaven closed but also those of limbo.

## The Reformers' Agnosticism on Infant Salvation

The classic Protestant tradition was either inconclusive about or not disposed to see unborn life as bound for heaven. The impediments to thinking about fetal salvation arose at Protestantism's beginnings. Martin Luther and John Calvin, both fathers, were aware of pregnancy loss and infant death. However, they did not develop a robust theology of unbaptized infant salvation. Instead, they settled on a "cautious, agnostic view" of infant salvation. Only in later centuries did this agnosticism morph into "an ever-growing universality of conviction" that unbaptized infants are "included in the election of grace."[72] By the late nineteenth-century, Baptist preacher Charles Spurgeon declared that "there would be more infants in heaven than adults."[73] This comment indicates not continuity with a Protestant past but a theological sea change regarding infant salvation. The reformers, no shrinking theological violets, could not or would not formulate a definitive stance on the unborn and the afterlife.

## Luther's Missed Opportunities

Martin Luther was theologically unsystematic in his writings, which affected his ability to untangle issues of infant baptism, infant salvation, and the resurrection. In some writings, Luther insisted on the necessity of infant baptism, and he permitted midwives to conduct an emergency baptism, implying its importance for salvation.[74] That Luther saw infant baptism as a catechetical moment is revealed in his instruction that the rite be administered in the vernacular so that the participating adults would understand their spiritual obligations.[75] This instruction deemphasized baptism as a sacramental transaction ensuring salvation.

Luther even entertained the notion that infants might have the capacity for faith (*Kindertaufe*). Luther's example of infant faith was John the Baptist leaping in his mother's womb in the presence of Mary, newly pregnant with Jesus.[76] While Luther might have used this biblical story as an opportunity to assert fetal personhood and the possibility of salvation, he did not.[77] Luther should have been theologically disposed to the idea of fetuses and unbaptized infants in heaven, based on his principle of *sola gratia*—salvation by grace alone.[78] He might have made a strong *sola gratia* point in relation to fetal salvation, but he did not.

Personal and pastoral reasons caused Luther famously to address pregnancy, birthing, childrearing, and infant loss. Notwithstanding some hyperbolic statements by Luther (perhaps in an exasperated fatherly moment) that "infants were possessed by the devil,"[79] Luther was known for his affection for his children. He even published a letter addressing miscarriage. His "Consolation for Women Whose Pregnancies Have Not Gone Well" (1542) was penned several years after his wife Katharina von Bora, then in her forties, nearly died from a miscarriage.[80] This letter calls on those grieving a pregnancy loss to think of their ardent desire for their unborn child's salvation as "effective prayer" accepted by God. Nevertheless, regarding the question of whether or how the "*abortivum* . . . or 'one untimely born'" would be resurrected on the final day, Luther did not speculate.[81] Another missed opportunity.[82]

Luther held a traducian view of ensoulment from conception.[83] This view, however, did not impel him to offer an opinion on how an ensouled but corporeally undeveloped miscarried fetus would rise on the final day. He retreated into a kind of vague apophatic platitude that God has planned for us "more than all we can ask or imagine" regarding life after infant death.[84] Though Luther seemed reticent to pronounce on the eternal fate of a fetus or unbaptized infant, he did not shy away from extemporizing about what the final day will be like.[85] The final resurrection was thinkable; fetuses in heaven were not. If any historical theologian might be poised boldly to preach bodily resurrection for those who die unbaptized before birth, it would have been Luther.

## Calvin's Systematic Silence on the Unborn in Heaven

John Calvin worked to bring Protestant beliefs into more systematic coherence, including the topic of infant salvation. Infants are born with original sin and should be baptized, but baptism is not a requirement of salvation.[86] Calvin developed the covenant-based notion that unbaptized infants were elect, if born to believing parents—a notion that cohered with his views that it was not the baptismal act that effected salvation.[87] He simplified the baptism ceremony, doing away with exorcisms and the anointing of oil. He insisted on including a sermon, which made the hearing of God's word take priority over rituals.[88] The widespread practice of emergency infant baptism was suppressed in Calvin's Geneva.[89]

Calvin spoke about infant death. He accepted that scripture recounts how God sometimes allows the death and possible damnation of "infants as yet in their mothers' womb."[90] Infant death was not just an abstract idea to Calvin. He was married, and his wife Idelette de Bure suffered several miscarriages or stillbirths. They also lost a son shortly after birth.[91] Calvin wrote poignantly in a letter to a friend, "God had given me a son. But God had taken away my little boy."[92] Presumably their infant son was baptized soon after his birth,[93] but even if not, the infant would have been presumed to be elect, given that he was born to believing parents. Calvin and Idelette may have comforted themselves with assurances of God's superabundant grace.[94]

The soul was a central concept for Calvin. A creationist, he taught that infants are infused with a soul at conception.[95] He even thought that there is a natural knowledge of God, "of which each of us is master from his mother's womb."[96] Calvin affirmed the traditional belief in the soul's separation from the body at death.[97] At the final resurrection, the soul will receive back its "self-same body."[98] Based on this view of ensoulment, Calvin labeled abortion a "monstrous crime" of homicide.[99]

Given his views on ensoulment, resurrection, and abortion, one might expect Calvin to have formulated a clear position on the status of unborn bodies and souls in the afterlife. He did not. Perhaps if Calvin had penned a "Consolation for Women Whose Pregnancies Have Not Gone Well," Christians in the Reformed tradition might have a clearer sense of whether he thought a miscarried or aborted fetus in heaven was a theological possibility.

Miscarriages, stillbirths, and abortions happened in Protestant circles, from the time of the Reformation and forward.[100] Even when reproductive loss was mentioned by Luther and Calvin, those comments carried little if any doctrinal weight. The reformers were not just "cautiously agnostic" on the issue; they were apparently unable to conceptualize what the resurrection meant for those beings who died before birth with an undeveloped body.[101]

## Counterstories

History tells the narratives of victors and elites, but ordinary lived experience does not remain silent. Counterstories of everyday lives erupt through the surface of these *grands récits* and challenge their presumed dominance.[102] Fleeting, localized, and fragmentary, these nonelite voices, repressed experiences, and disregarded events contest the illusion of hegemony. No one notices in the moment. Power balances do not shift. Yet one can discern the traces, here and there, of an "insurrection of subjugated knowledges."[103] Women's reproductive experiences constitute subjugated counterstories.

Running alongside, underneath, and at the margins of theology's preoccupation with ensoulment and baptism were women's counterstories of pregnancy and birth. These stories were lived by women but rarely written by their own hand. The bodies of fetuses shaped their concerns, imagery, and experiences. Not ethereal souls but viscous uterine matter. Not baptismal fonts but birthing canals. Nothing about fetal bodies is abstract in women's counterstories. In women's tales, unborn bodies are experienced as linked to a woman's bleeding body, in an organic yet jagged continuum from menarche to menopause. Uterine beings, conceived in women's bodies, were conceivable to women.

Female believers who engage in the labor of bringing forth life do not credit theological pronouncements of a closed heaven. They have other sources of information. They await other annunciations. They receive them through the flutterings in their swollen bellies. From these epistemological quickenings arise their subjugated knowledges.

Even fetal death speaks a terrible truth. Women watch, helpless during a miscarriage, as the content of their wombs silently streams down their quivering thighs and pools at their feet. They bear

witness: the blood of this child is crying out to me from the ground![104]
Their words congeal, rise, and hover. Women see the apparition, which
is both trauma and truth. They are emboldened to importune God,
bereaved like widows demanding the judge for justice (Luke 18). In
the name of their blood and that of their children, women demand
resurrection. They tell their stories.

### Mary Conceiving and Birthing

Women know that actual conceiving and birthing bears little resem-
blance to the church's version of these realities. For the church, women
conceive in sin, tainted by their concupiscence. They birth in sin, tainted
by blood for which they must be purified.[105] In between these two sins
is the labor and pain of gestation and birthing, deemed by the church
as women's lot in life as Eve's daughters. Only Mary escaped it all: the
sin of Eve, sexual desire, the loss of maidenhood, the bloody birthing.

Counterstories about Mary circulate in the Apocrypha and the
skeptical minds of women. In women's minds, it is the same old story
they know only too well. Someone who thinks he is God's gift to
women impregnates a teenage girl but does not stick around to see
things through. The girl is lucky if she has the help of an older, wiser
auntie or cousin. If she is lucky, the girl finds a man to act as father of
her child. Too often, he is demanding and clueless about things like not
traveling close to her due date. Labor comes on suddenly, and she feels
the overpowering need to bear down. First birth, naive girl, all alone,
dirty floor. She will probably die trying to push that baby out on her
own. She has a slim chance of survival if she can find a good midwife.

This was Mary's story.[106] Women sitting around drinking their
coffee, nod, "Uh-huh, it's just like that." They shake their heads and tsk
when the male storyteller makes it all about her hymen.[107]

### Menstrual Meanings

People with ovaries and a uterus bleed with the moon's cycle. This
rhythm carries meaning that constitutes a counterstory to the church's

abjection of bleeding bodies. A twisted ecclesial logic links the blood taboo to Jesus's healing of the hemorrhaging woman (Mark 7). The church prides itself in understanding the true meaning of Jesus's beneficent act of overlooking her menstrual impurity. Namely, Jesus's example confers on the (male) apostolic church the authority to pronounce on the meaning of women's blood.

History suggests the presence of menstrual counterstories. These tales are barely known and little understood, especially when they are only available through texts that survive magisterial censorship. Yet evidence of women asserting authority over their monthly cycles can be glimpsed in the normative tradition. Although discussing such matters would have been considered beneath the dignity of any church focus, occasionally uppity women's practices caught the church's attention. The ecclesial behemoth paused and turned to see who in the crowd deigned to pull on its robes.

The third-century *Didascalia Apostolorum* notes a concerning activity taking place in some believing women's groups. Based on Jewish menstrual practice, Christian women were separating themselves from the community (and their husbands) during their period. The *Didascalia* chides the women for claiming they are "void of the Holy Spirit" during their monthly uncleanliness.[108] They must cease and desist from this silly practice.

It does not occur to the male theological mind that the presence and absence of a menstrual flow can have many causes and meanings. How these women understood the spiritual import of their act of ritual separation is lost to history. Women and girls know that an onset of bleeding can be the sign that a desired conception did not happen or a wanted pregnancy ended. In either instance, the bleeding would signify a spiritual void in her life. These women's acts of separation might have been evidence of a ritual recognition for a failed conception or a lost pregnancy. Almost no women-only rituals remain in the normative tradition.[109] Seeking separation in a community of supportive women after procreative challenges or disappointments makes every sense in the world. There is no reason to exclude these possible reasons to explain what menstrual separation might have meant for these women in the early church.

## Personhood in the Womb

The church made personhood in the womb all about the soul. Tertullian offered a traducian polemic for ensoulment at conception. A women's counterstory peeks through his *Treatise on the Soul* when he asks women, "the sex itself which is so intimately concerned" with uterine life, to give their testimony on the matter. He poses a rhetorical question about whether their experience of pregnancy—its movements, burdens, nausea, cravings—confirms the presence of a being with a "vital force" inside them. He assumes any woman would agree and goes on to mansplain that pregnancy is an event of "two souls in one person."[110] No women speak in Tertullian's text.

However, in the subjugated knowledges of women's experience, the movements, burdens, nausea, and cravings point not to an immaterial soul but to the embodied reality of pregnancy. A soul has nothing to do with swollen ankles. The dry heaves are not indications of the presence of an ensouled fetus. Heightened libido in pregnancy is hormones talking, not a uterine person.

## Surviving Pregnancy

The pregnant woman near her due date has one main thought: to get the baby and herself through this trial, alive and intact. How to express this thought in a way that slips by the church censors is tricky. Writing under the watchful eye of bishops, confessors, or pastors, women had to appear pious and compliant in addressing the meaning of pregnancy in light of Eve's curse.[111]

A 1652 devotional handbook by a well-educated German Lutheran noblewoman threads the needle of submissive piety and the agency needed to survive labor and birth. Having given birth to one son and having lost one newborn daughter, this noblewoman offers prayers, songs, and advice for pregnant women in "a voice that is identifiably female."[112] Her instructions are not about how to comply with the curse given to Eve but, rather, how to keep one's head during the long ordeal of sweating, bleeding, and being pulled apart during labor.

The devotional manual does not hide the scary risks facing pregnant women in the late seventeenth century. There is a real possibility that mother and child might find themselves together at death's door. The laboring woman is instructed to implore Jesus that she will not become her child's grave.[113]

At this liminal moment, the concern is not her child's soul, baptism, or election. The curse given to Eve is irrelevant in an obstructed birth. This woman's counterstory retells pregnancy as a matter of two bodies surviving an ordeal. For the baby to survive, she must survive. If she dies in labor or if the child dies within her, they will go together to the grave.

## Mothers Who Do Not Mother

Mothers sometimes demand to be freed from mothering and motherhood. Having birthed and raised children, those called by God to other vocations want to consecrate their bodies for lives apart from their children. These scandalous women can be found across the centuries. Two early church mothers, Perpetua and Felicitas, persisted in their desire to die as martyrs for the faith. Felicitas delivered her infant in prison and proceeded "from the blood and from the midwife to the gladiator."[114] She washed away the afterbirth and went out to spill her believer's blood in the arena.

Margery Kempe, fifteenth-century English mystic, wife, and mother of fourteen living children, begged to be released from her conjugal and mothering duties. She longed to answer Christ's call to follow him and become a spiritual mother to those who were not her natural children. Margery wanted to be loved by Christ as if she were "like a virgin."[115] She claimed that Christ did accept her as such. A repaired hymen had nothing to do with it.

Marie de l'Incarnation, a French seventeenth-century widow, abandoned her weeping eleven-year-old son so that she could enter an Ursuline convent and eventually become a missionary. Literate and driven by talent and ambition, she founded an Ursuline community in Canada and translated the catechism into several First Nations languages. She never returned for her son and accepted the epithet of "cruelest of all mothers" for the sake of Christ.[116]

These startling stories of a mother's abandonment of maternal duties are admitted into the church's religious canon because they can be used as testimonies about women's religious fervor. The male tradition makes these tales all about women leaving sex behind (their children are an unfortunate footnote). Women, however, see these narratives as fragmentary testimonies to the insurrectional truth of the demands and sacrifices of motherhood. Not all women want to become mothers or remain in their mothering roles. Religious callings—any callings—trump the claim of biology-is-destiny.

## Abortions

Women with an unwanted pregnancy pray for its ending. They always have. Not birthing and adoption. Not birthing and help from social service agencies or crisis pregnancy centers. They pray for an abortion. Apparently, some of these prayers were answered. The legend of miraculous abortions is one of the most suppressed in the historical tradition and is, ironically, found in hagiographies of saints.

The early sixth-century Irish saint Brigid of Kildare is said to have performed an abortion miracle for a woman who "fell prey to youthful lust" and got pregnant. The saint intervened and, miraculously, "what had been conceived in her womb disappeared."[117] Other legends tell of revered Irish saints performing similar miraculous pregnancy terminations. One hagiography gives a graphic account of a nun's abortion by a saint who "pressed down on her womb with the sign of the cross and forced her womb to be emptied."[118] This saint made a miraculous miscarriage happen.

These Irish legends carry the church's patriarchal filter. Along with their supernatural abortions, the women have their virginity restored and their fornication erased. The nuns can continue as representatives of the Virgin Mary, free from Eve's curse of sexual desire and labor pains. In other words, they can become like (the church's fantasy of) virgins. Having been rehabilitated enough by the church's censor, these abortion stories are domesticated. Their insurrectional power is all but ironed out. The abortionist saints do not go rogue in the Irish countryside, saving other desperate pregnant women. The saints' stories remain safely tucked in the pages of church tradition. These few women receive their abortion; all others are denied. All that is left are fragments of women's reproductive counterstories.

• • •

Christian history is dismal regarding infant salvation. The church historically never resolved the personhood status of beings in the womb and never committed to recognizing the death of fetal beings sacramentally. The eternal destiny of fetuses held great concern to grieving parents. Theologians from the early church through the Reformation, especially those who were fathers, were aware of and personally affected by reproductive loss. However, this existential awareness could not surmount a reticence in speaking about the unborn in heaven. The church did not storm those gates.

When beings in the womb died, they could not be theologically conceptualized or sacramentally acted upon as persons to be resurrected. Unborn bodies carried less theological weight than the tiny lump of flesh that fell into the midwife's open palms in a premature birth. That the theological dispensability of fetuses coincided with their location in bleeding female bodies did not occur to anyone. The woman, after all, was merely the supplier of blood to nourish the potential child—and both belonged, after all, to the father. The uterine being was undecipherable, because of its proximity to the sinful body of a daughter of Eve.

Women's counterstories contested the curse of Eve. Over the centuries women importuned God about the trials of gravidity and parturition, about their losses and hauntings. The church barely listened; God and the saints did not always respond. If their wombs could not be opened to be delivered of their baby, women implored that heaven's gates would be opened. They asked for this not on the basis of their own or their fetus's soul. They asked for their fetus's entry into paradise because it was inconceivable for them that their blood would have been spilled in vain.

Based on the *grand récit* of the Christian tradition, the resurrection of unborn bodies was and still is doubtful. If one asserts (as the church did for most of history) that any child of Adam must be cleansed of original sin, then heaven is closed to even an ensouled fetus who dies unbaptized. If one believes that the lack of baptism can be overcome by the parents' baptism of desire or by God's superabundant grace, then a fetus's soul has a possibility of attaining heaven, but reunification in the final resurrection with its nascent body seems inconceivable. Or, if because of delayed hominization, an embryo or fetus dies before receiving its soul, then not only are the gates of heaven closed to it, but it will simply perish out of existence.

# 3

## FINDING RESURRECTION
## IN BURIED GRAIN

THE SOUL PERVADES not only Christian theology but the imagination of Western culture. The soul imbues everyday idioms, saturates literature, and fills the lyrics of popular songs. Apologists take advantage of history's long love affair with the soul. They conclude that since the soul seems "to almost all people to be correct," it provides a solid basis for belief in the resurrection.[1] A soul that survives bodily death seems to offer the perfect bridge between the believer's life on earth and final destination in heaven. However, there is trouble in paradise. The soul idea has lost its luster. Less bedrock than baggage, this idea encumbers thinking about bodily resurrection.

Understanding the resurrection of the body has to begin with bodies. Prioritizing an immaterial substance called "soul" subordinates the value of bodies—always has. Christian thinkers today attempting to reclaim an embodied spirituality know this to be true. An embrace of the tactile richness of art, music, sexuality, daily domestic practices, the work of one's hands—this embrace requires a focus on bodies, not souls.[2] The soul as the privileged conduit to the divine seems destined to dip below the horizon of spiritual practices as the materiality of the body rises.

Even ancient and medieval thinkers, living in a soul-saturated culture, suspected that the soul hindered a deeper understanding of resurrection. Theological, poetic, and mystical minds in the early church and medieval era searched for other ways to speak of resurrection. They recalled the apostle Paul: "You do not sow the body that is to be, but a bare seed" (1 Cor 15:37). They dug deep and unearthed buried metaphors. Germinating grain. Sprouting seed. Bodies blooming again. These thinkers gathered around and nurtured these fragile metaphors that vibrated with hidden power.

At the theological table where resurrection is debated, the seed metaphor is not invited to mount the high dais and take a seat. The soul arrogates to itself the place of power at the head. The reigning assumption is that the soul holds the obvious key for overcoming death, given that it refers to the human person's immortal essence. Theologians, mistakenly, think this idea's referentiality is its power—namely, the power to unlock the meaning of resurrection. Like a bully, the soul thinks it can push metaphor aside. Not so. Rather, it is metaphor that holds the power.

Metaphors hold power. They are powerful because generative. They "retain the tension of the 'is and is not'"[3] that generates thought, emotion, imagination. Love is and is not a rose. War is and is not a chess game. Love blooms, having given the heart words to express itself. Kingdoms fall, once metaphor releases the catapult of an insurrectional imagination. Metaphoricity forecloses foreclosure of thought. The buried grain, having been found, finds the meaning of resurrection.

The soul has not always been a conceptual bully. It can be repurposed as metaphor. To sing "Be still, my soul: the Lord is on thy side" carries spiritual power because the soul is synecdoche for suffering. As an idea, however, the power of the soul is short-lived. Soul has to be continually reinvented and reinserted into the new system of thought that comes along: Stoicism, Neoplatonism, hylomorphism. The soul is only ever a gear in an ontology; it serves a useful purpose but generates nothing itself.

Returning to the metaphor of grain carries promise for rethinking resurrection in ways not dependent on the fading notion of an immaterial soul. Reconnecting with the power of metaphoricity opens the door for reimagining the materiality of bodily resurrection. The soul will always be part of the conversation, but the power dynamics are paradoxically reversed. The puffed-up soul has little to offer.

Theologians will have to lower their expectations about the soul's problem-solving capacities for finding the meaning of resurrection. Humble metaphor holds the imaginative power.

## Sprouting and Flowering — Root Metaphors for Resurrection

Metaphors that carry the power of "structuring and ordering experience" lodge deep in a culture's soil. These "root-metaphors" endure.[4] They generate thought and are "central to the meaning, ordering, and living" of a religion.[5] Christianity's root metaphor for resurrection is sprouting seed. The apostle Paul made waves in the ancient Christian communities when he wrote about the resurrection in terms of seeds, "perhaps of wheat or of some other grain" (1 Cor 15:37). That metaphor did for the Corinthian believers what metaphors do: provoke thinking. Grain became "the oldest Christian metaphor for the resurrection of the body."[6] This simple seed continued for centuries to generate thought about the materiality of resurrected bodies—until it was ignored or suppressed.

Despite Paul's intentional use of sown and germinating seed in 1 Corinthians 15, theologians chose to ignore metaphors of "organic growth,"[7] preferring instead to emphasize "stasis . . . permanence and impassibility" in the afterlife.[8] The church taught hope for acquiring a pristine body in heaven, not reuniting with the "disgusting vessel" that had been one's earthly body.[9] The heavenly saint's body was imagined in terms of a sparkling jewel, perfectly built temple, or divinely crafted "recast statue."[10] Augustine viewed the Pauline seed metaphor negatively, since he associated organic change with death, decay, and rot.[11] Metaphors of organic changeableness dimmed in importance.

A metaphor suppressed, however, does not necessarily remain buried. Seed will out. Paul had an inkling of this truth but, being no poet, he did not quite know what to do with his metaphor. Later thinkers more adept with metaphorical thinking saw the power in expanding the seed metaphor into parables about bodies blooming. Even with the church's entrenched hierarchical body-soul dualism, Christian thinkers used metaphor to affirm material flux and change in relation to the resurrection.

The second-century bishop Irenaeus analogized the resurrection in terms of germination: "And just . . . as a corn of wheat falling into the earth . . . rises with manifold increase . . . so also our bodies, being . . . deposited in the earth, and suffering decomposition there, shall rise at their appointed time."[12] He made no qualifications, nor did he voice embarrassment regarding the material processes of living bodies changing to corpses and then changing to risen bodies. Although substance dualist theologians today claim that only soul talk can support the notion of continuous personal identity, patristic-era thinkers employed the grain metaphor to make this very point: "You foolish one. Each seed will receive its own body. Have you ever sowed wheat and reaped barley? . . . No. . . . So, the body that is laid in earth, that very body shall rise again."[13]

The grain metaphor proved versatile. Its earthiness did not offend. On the contrary, it was used as "unambiguously appropriate to describe the journey toward heaven."[14] A twelfth-century Cistercian abbot mused that bodies in tombs would, like gardens, have their own "springtime" at the final resurrection when "their flesh will blossom again."[15] In a sermon for his deceased mother, one twelfth-century Benedictine monk wrote that her "bones . . . shall flower like an herb, rising to eternal life."[16] These thinkers did not reject the well-accepted notion of the immaterial soul. They held commonplace medieval attitudes about bodies as sites of filth and decay. Nevertheless, they found grain metaphors apt. Eschatological existence could be appropriately thought of as a divinely fructified sprouting.

The theological deck, however, was stacked against metaphors of germination, growing, and flowering.[17] By the high Middle Ages, "the Pauline seed was almost forgotten."[18] The fourteenth-century Scholastic and monastic schools of thought firmly refocused attention on the soul. Not only was the soul said to survive the body, but it would immediately begin experiencing beatitude in heaven or suffering in hell—even if only as a shade. The medieval and early Renaissance media blitz of this message was relentless, ranging from Benedict XII's dogmatic pronouncement in *Benedictus Deus* to the sublime Italian verses of Dante's *Divine Comedy.*[19] Metaphors are powerful but can lapse into banality from overuse. They drift off the cultural radar.

## Finding the Soul in the New Testament

Debates rage regarding whether substance dualism—the notion of the person as a body with an essential soul—is a Greek import to Christianity or a biblically based concept. One group of mostly Protestant thinkers insists that "a 'dualistic' anthropology is entailed by the biblical teaching of the intermediate state."[20] In other words, biblically committed Christians should be substance dualists.[21] However, it is unlikely that Paul or other New Testament writers assumed or promoted the interim existence of an immaterial soul. The biblical grounding of substance dualism is too tenuous to make it a necessary corollary of the core Christian belief in the resurrection.

The doctrine of bodily resurrection has deep roots in the New Testament. Paul challenged the nascent Christian community: "If there is no resurrection of the dead, then . . . your faith is in vain" (1 Cor 15:13, 14). The accounts of Jesus's resurrection appearances in the gospels solidified bodily resurrection as biblically central. For substance dualist thinkers, the soul is the key to understanding the Greco-Roman mindset informing biblical teachings on resurrection. This approach has gone seriously awry.

Substance dualist scholars make two mistakes. They interpret the presence of soul talk in the New Testament as the sign of a ruling ontology presupposed by the biblical writers. These scholars cannot be accused of a crass eisegetical planting of evidence; nevertheless, they read more conceptual coherence into biblical references to the soul than is merited by the texts. One also detects a hermeneutical literalism in biblical soul talk. Biblical writers used metaphor. Philosophers of metaphor have exposed the category mistake of assuming, for example, that when "the Bible says that God is 'father' then God is literally, really, 'father.'"[22] Sometimes the soul in the Bible is (just) a metaphor, not a term pointing referentially to some objective reality.

A typical pro-soul argument posits that the Old Testament bequeathed to the early Christian community a body-soul anthropology that assumed a distinction between individuals' earthly materiality and their God-given life and breath.[23] References to the dead in Sheol and to entities described as "departed spirits" (Isa 26:14)[24] are considered to be the "embryonic form" of what the New Testament writers later developed into the notion of an interim disembodied soul-state after death.[25] The soul's interim existence, found in an inchoate way in the Hebrew Bible, is affirmed in intertestamental Judaism and in the writings of Hellenistic Jews like Josephus.[26]

For substance dualists, the case for the soul gains momentum in the New Testament. References abound to the soul as distinct from the body.[27] The "literal meaning" of 2 Corinthians 5:6 ("we know that while we are at home in the body we are away from the Lord") implies a disembodied existence with God after death.[28] The interim state of souls after death is visually depicted in Revelation 6:9 ("I saw under the altar the souls of those who had been slaughtered for the word of God").[29] When Paul refers to the saints being "unclothed" when they leave their "earthly tent" at death (2 Cor 5:1–4), he gestures to an interim disembodied soul state.[30] Substance dualists ignore the glaring presence of metaphors and symbols in these verses (home, altar, tent). These thinkers conclude that Paul "simply presupposes a dualist soul-body distinction," even in the absence of the Greek term *psychē.*[31]

However, the issue is not whether New Testament writers sound dualistic. They understandably do at times, given their Hellenistic context. The more probing, and less anachronistic, question is this: When the New Testament writers sound dualistic, do they mean a literal, immaterial soul that survives death in the way substance dualists today are thinking of postmortem survival? If one consults scholars of the Bible and the ancient world, the answer to this question appears to be: unlikely.

It is unlikely that Paul had in mind a bodiless, "naked" soul existing in an interim period after death in 2 Corinthians 5:1–4.[32] Exegetes concur that Paul never suggested that resurrection faith meant a soul separated "from a decomposing body."[33] Paul showed no interest in a soul-like "existence between death and the parousia."[34] Given the accessibility of soul concepts for leaders of the new Christian community, if they had "wanted to teach that the 'soul' is the part of us which survives death and carries our real selves until the day of resurrection, they could have said so"—explicitly.[35]

Paul directed his most extensive resurrection teaching to the church at Corinth. Educated Roman citizen that he was, Paul would probably have been influenced more by "Stoic than Platonic concepts."[36] If so, Paul's use of dualisms related to personhood makes his teachings on the resurrection cryptic.[37] For Paul, what perdures after death is "a 'pneumatic body,'" composed of spiritual yet apparently not immaterial "stuff"—with the lower-level material of "sarx and psyche [soul/mind] having been sloughed off along the way."[38] When Paul declares that "flesh and blood cannot inherit the kingdom of God" (1 Cor 15:50), the terms "flesh and blood" refer to those parts of the earthly body that will not be carried over into the afterlife at all. The spiritual body will be made up of incorruptible pneuma-stuff—but stuff nevertheless.[39] Paul's eclectic even mystical Hellenistic soul/spirit concept seems a far cry from the soul of substance dualism today. Pauline scholarship is fairly unified: Paul did not promote or suggest a disembodied soul state after death.

Substance dualists can point to a seeming affirmation of the interim soul in the gospels. Perhaps the gospel writers had time to refine Paul's teachings. A gospel passage that should "carry great weight" in support of the interim soul theory is Jesus's promise to the thief who was crucified alongside him ("I tell you the truth, today you will be with me in paradise").[40] The exegetical jury is still out on this enigmatic passage. The meaning of "today" is ambiguous.[41] Luke may have had in mind a resurrection that transcends chronological time.[42] Even different punctuation with the temporal adverb changes the sentence's entire meaning: "Truly to you I say *today*, with me you will be in paradise."[43] Biblical references to individuals miraculously brought back to life or rising from their tombs in the gospels and Acts make no mention of their souls having survived their death.[44] Finding modern substance dualism in the gospels seems a stretch.

The soul has its place in the New Testament. But contrary to the assertions of Christian substance dualists, finding a convincing biblical basis for the soul's interim postmortem existence is doubtful. Hellenism may have instilled in Paul a soul-body hierarchy, but when push came to shove, Paul tried to raise "the status of the soma," in order to convince skeptical Hellenized Christians to accept the resurrection of the body.[45] Paul affirmed that each person has a soul, but soul was not his privileged concept for personal postmortem survival in the way substance dualists speak of it today. Substance dualism seems too anachronistic a label to slap on the apostle's back. The same holds true for the gospel writers. Perhaps because they lack compelling biblical backing for their ontology, substance dualist scholars turn instead to the Christian theological tradition to promote the centrality of the soul and its postmortem survival.

## Finding the Soul in Christian History

The soul in Christian history is an embarrassment of riches. The soul appears in abundance in the writings of the early church, the councils and creeds, Roman Catholicism, the Eastern Orthodox tradition, the Protestant reformers, and up to the present day. Substance dualist scholars tout an "overwhelming consensus" about the immaterial soul.[46] Church authorities are said to "affirm with one voice" this understanding of the soul.[47] A quick squint at history seems to back up these claims, but on closer examination, the soul idea stands on shaky historical ground.

Scholars mistake the ubiquity of the soul in Christian sources for explanatory power and consensus. The soul was everywhere but more as a cacophony of ideas than a consensus. If consensus existed, it was on the soul's superiority over the body, particularly the female body. The claim of univocity regarding the soul crumbles with the challenge of hylomorphism. To deny this challenge would be analogous to looking slack-jawed at the sky and saying that Copernicus was not a revolution of Ptolemy.

## A Multiplicity of Souls

The soul, while ubiquitous in the early church, was never a one-voice idea. The Greco-Roman soul was a philosophical coat of many colors. What early church and patristic figures meant by the soul was influenced by an almost cacophonous assortment of philosophies and religious myths of the ancient world. The soul (in life and after death) meant something radically different in Origenist, traducian, and creationist understandings of ensouled personhood. The various views of the soul might additionally have been inflected with Platonic, Aristotelian, Stoic, Manichean, or Galenic understandings of the body.

The first centuries are devoid of consensus on the soul and its role in bodily resurrection. Irenaeus thought in Platonic terms of the soul as immortal, which meant that only the body needed to be saved.[48] If Jesus had to wait three days to ascend to heaven after his death, it was fitting, Irenaeus reasoned, that ordinary believers' bodies should lie in their graves until reunited with their immortal soul at the final judgment.[49] Someone influenced by Stoicism, such as Tertullian, thought in traducian terms of the soul as "subtle" matter passed down to one's offspring during sexual intercourse.[50] Tertullian rejected the notion of the soul's interim state after death and, instead, insisted on the resurrection as an embodied event "where the whole person can be either rewarded or punished."[51] A follower of Origen (if not denounced first as a heretic) might have thought of the soul as a preexistent incorporeal entity.[52] Origen believed the soul left the earthly body at death and was given an "ethereal" body.[53]

Augustine toyed with Manichean, traducian, and creationist views of ensoulment, eventually leaning toward the latter.[54] He thought of the soul as a "special substance, endowed with reason, adapted to rule the body," and he could say without equivocation, "I myself am my soul."[55] Augustine accepted the Platonic assumption that "the soul's relationship to a body is *contingent*," meaning one has to have a body to live, but one's particular body is not "some essential necessity."[56] At the resurrection, God would gather together all the bits of one's decomposed body and reassemble them. Miraculously, one's "own flesh . . . shall be restored,"[57] molded by God into a perfected body marked by "weightlessness, beauty, impassibility, and incorruption," now worthy to be reunited with the rational soul.[58]

In the Eastern empire, Gregory of Nyssa developed an innovative take on the soul, based on the ideas of Plotinus and Origen and the medical knowledge of the second-century physician Galen.[59] Galen thought of the soul as a tripartite substance located in the brain, the heart, and the liver, in order of importance.[60] Galen's materialism influenced Gregory's view of the resurrection. At death, the soul does not leave the body but remains connected to the "fleshly glue" of the disintegrating body until such time as the soul is called upon to re-form the dissolved parts into a resurrected body.[61] Presumably, that meant head, heart, and the humble liver too.

How souls were re-embodied, who would be resurrected, and when—these issues were also up for grabs. At least some Christians embraced the idea of souls transmigrating to new bodies, since Clement of Alexandria argued so strongly against it.[62] The *Didache* suggests that only believers would be resurrected.[63] The most elite among the faithful, those who suffered martyrdom, were said to be taken bodily, exultant with their wounds, immediately to heaven. This martyrology put pressure on Christian leaders to affirm that for all other Christians, only souls rose at death. The corpses of ordinary believers remained in the grave until the final judgment, because "if everyone ascends to heaven at death, the exaltation of the martyrs is decidedly less remarkable."[64]

The soul in the patristic era was a mishmash of ideas. The ancient thinkers could not agree if it was corporeal or immaterial or something in between; whether it was a single substance or perhaps tripartite; whether it hovered near the decomposing corpse, transmigrated to a new body, or ascended in the martyr's body to glory in heaven. Any number of other soulish options were also possibilities.

## The Soul Denigrating the Body

A wide consensus existed on the soul-body hierarchy. Vaunting the nobility of the soul ended up denigrating the body—especially the female body. Influenced by streams in Greco-Roman and other ancient philosophies, the church privileged the intellectual soul and viewed bodily processes negatively: "eating, growing, giving birth, sickening, aging," and ultimately dying and putrifying were an "ontological scandal."[65] A soul-body hierarchy was reflected in the church fathers' general cultural aversion to bodily flux, decay, and sensual temptations. The church elevated the soul as the unchanging spiritual core of the person and pictured the body as a tedious weight.

This negative view of the body expressed itself in the asceticism of the desert fathers and mothers and in religious orders. Monks and nuns, who already had taken vows of poverty, chastity, and obedience, took on practices of fasting, sleep deprivation, and self-flagellation in order to pacify the body. These practices were a direct outgrowth of a soul-body hierarchy in which subduing the body—that "recalcitrant 'other'"—was necessary to enable the soul's spiritual ascent.[66]

The female body was a notable site of leaking and disgusting fluids and "sexual humors."[67] Only the most devout female believer, like Gregory of Nyssa's sister Macrina, was considered to have the ascetic discipline sufficient for transforming her female body's "gross and heavy texture . . . into something more subtle and ethereal."[68] The goal of asceticism generally was to mortify the unruly flesh; the female ascetic attempted to transcend the signs of her very femaleness.[69]

So prevalent and effective was the Platonic-inflected denigration of bodies, that the early church had to contend with the pendulum swinging too far in an anti-body direction. Church leaders suppressed heresies that denied bodily resurrection and issued edicts categorically rejecting that heaven would be an abode of disembodied souls. The fifth Ecumenical Council of 533 combated Neoplatonic tendencies by anathematizing anyone who asserted that the saints will be given "ethereal" bodies at the resurrection.[70]

Across the centuries, the theological pendulum would swing back and forth between affirming a resurrected body and shying away from a too-fleshly body in heaven. In his typically earthy way, Martin Luther described heaven to his sixteenth-century congregants: "You will not eat, you will not sleep, digest, or defecate, or take a wife, or bake or brew."[71] One detects a faint sigh of regret in Luther's by-the-book denial of sensual pleasures in heaven.

Body and soul have been an enduring pair in Christian history. However, the patristic panegyrics to the immaterial soul become less appealing when set in the context of the fathers' visceral abhorrence of the body—its earthly needs, appetites, and pleasures. When one adds the misogynous attitude toward female bodies,[72] then the embarrassment of riches of the soul in early Christianity becomes, simply, an embarrassment.

## The Medieval Challenge to Substance Dualism

The definitive challenge to the Neoplatonic soul can be said in a word: Aristotle. The Aristotelian paradigm shift in medieval Scholastic theology instigated a theological revolution.[73] Aristotle promoted a hylomorphic ontology in which the body was informed and shaped by its soul as a "first actuality."[74] The soul-body connection was necessary, not contingent. Aquinas flatly rejected the Neoplatonic idea that "I am my soul" and insisted that "my soul is not me."[75] The person is a unified whole: a body informed by its soul.

The rise of Aristotelian hylomorphism presented a fork in the ontology road. Catholic thinkers and later Protestant reformers had to choose between two incommensurable views of ensouled person-hood. Martin Luther largely accepted a Scholastic anthropology.[76] John Calvin remained committed to a Platonic model.[77] In a dig at Aquinas, Calvin wrote that he saw no need "to seek a definition of 'soul' from philosophers" and affirmed that "hardly one, except Plato, has rightly affirmed its immortal substance."[78] The battle for the soul— hylomorphic or dualistic—has continued in this vein.

Contemporary substance dualists, mostly Protestants, try to dis-count that hylomorphism is a real philosophical competitor.[79] They suggest that Aquinas and Calvin meant the same thing when they referred to the soul as a simple immaterial substance,[80] which is a stretch. Or they brush aside as "obscure" the Aristotelian-influenced views of Aquinas.[81]

Even if substance dualists could succeed in sweeping hylomor-phism under the rug (unlikely), they would still be faced with the massive heterogeneity of soul talk in church history. The soul took on various personae in ancient dualist systems of thought from Man-icheanism to Galenism. The fact that the soul appears in the guise of so many different characters in so many systems of thought undercuts the claim of its power as a referential idea. The soul was a versatile thespian who assumed many roles. Christianity accorded this tal-ented actor with greater significance than it deserved. The church used the soul's renown to denigrate the body, spread misogyny, and extol body-deadening asceticism. There is no reason for theology today to retrieve this soul or to continue to overinflate its power.

## Saving the Soul and Losing Orthodoxy

Substance dualist philosophers are eager to claim doctrinal orthodoxy. However, in making the soul the key to resurrection, their position falters. Substance dualism promotes two ideas that make the body irrelevant to the afterlife: the body is accidental to one's identity; after bodily death, the disembodied soul can experience God's presence. In saving the soul from annihilation and granting it beatitude, substance dualism flouts the logic for a doctrine of bodily resurrection. This ontology sells the body for a mess of soulish pottage.

When personal identity is said to reside in the soul essentially, the body is contingent. In technical jargon, a person remains herself over time by virtue of "the persistence of a simple immaterial substance" (read: her soul) that has "no necessary connection to a particular physical or psychological career" (read: her body).[82] This type of dualism is commonly called simple substance dualism.[83] Whatever its sobriquet, dualism emphasizes that while a body is obviously important for life, one's essential self has no necessary connection to the body or any embodied property. The soul alone is "ontologically fundamental"; any particularities from the individual's life are contingent, changeable, and dispensable.[84]

Simple substance dualism sees death as the event when the soul leaves its nonnecessary body behind. The Christian substance dualist, wishing to display creedal orthodoxy, adds a codicil: the soul will reunite with the body in the final resurrection. This imagined reunion, however, is a peculiar one. The soul need not and most likely will not be reunified with the particular body it had at the point of death, or at any point in the person's past life. One need not even posit that the soul will reacquire the person's mental contents and characteristics. Substance dualism asserts that the soul will be given "*a* new resurrected body,"[85] reunited with "*a* new glorified body."[86] The problem the church fathers faced—namely, figuring out how God might round up and reattach all the bits and bobs of long-decomposed corpses—goes away. Because substance dualism puts all the postmortem continuity eggs into a soul basket, any bodily container will do in the afterlife.

Simple substance dualism claims to secure sufficient orthodoxy. The individual (soul) will continue to exist after death, and there will be bodies in the afterlife. However, it is a theological sleight of hand that fools no one concerned with a robust doctrine of bodily resurrection. This account of the survival of the soul is only loosely connected to orthodoxy's insistence on individual bodily resurrection. In substance dualism, the very element that frees the soul to survive—its contingent relation to its body—becomes the impediment to claiming the necessity or even the fittingness of the soul's reunification with that body. My body in the grave? It seems the soul can take or leave it, metaphysically speaking.

Advocates of simple substance dualism are unconcerned with the contingency of bodies and do not see it as a serious problem for Christian faith. Quite the contrary. Because dualism apparently "resonates with ordinary people," and because one should strive to make Christianity intelligible "for the masses," substance dualism has much in its favor, religiously speaking.[87] The polling data on this point, however, is inconclusive, indicating that beliefs range from not needing a body in the afterlife to being supplied with a perfect one in heaven.[88] Cost-benefit analyses of Christianity's mass appeal to the side, the fact remains that simple substance dualism is unwilling (because it is conceptually unable) to assert that one's very own body will be resurrected.

For this reason, other Christian philosophers try to work out a less contingent, more holistic link between the soul and the body. These philosophers enlist Thomas Aquinas in an attempt to construct a "neo-Aristotelian or hylomorphic" type of substance dualism.[89] Called "Thomistic substance dualism,"[90] this approach attempts to merge simple substance dualism and hylomorphism.[91] Even though the name changes, Thomistic substance dualism changes little from simple substance dualism when it comes to postmortem continuity. After death, the person continues as a separable soul.[92] Body and soul, which are necessarily related in life, assume a contingent relationship in death. The soul is saved, but the body is left behind.

In both types of substance dualism, the bodiless soul does not just drift sleepily through space and time. In its interim state, the believer's soul retains capacities of higher consciousness and passes immediately into a state of "enjoyment of the presence of Christ."[93] Thomistic substance dualism is particularly aware of the image problem here. The soul's apparently contented and bodiless communing with God makes a resurrected body superfluous.[94] These philosophers try to counteract the image of a dispensable body with hylomorphic theological claims that having a body in heaven is the soul's "telos,"[95] or that the soul has a "natural exigency for embodiment even while disembodied."[96] They insist that the "body is a mode of the soul," as if repeating this hylomorphic-sounding claim will make the body seem less irrelevant for the soul in the afterlife.[97]

One might understandably suspect other motivations for hanging on to the soul so tenaciously. The soul is not just key to life after death but a right to life. A number of soul-oriented scholars endorse "a robust ethic of life" that secures for a fetus "the highest metaphysical status that is possible"—namely, ensouled personhood in utero.[98] From this perspective, it is the soul of an embryo or fetus that will enjoy eternal life.[99] Little regard is given to its undeveloped body, which is accidental to its essential personhood.[100] That this soul-based solution to fetal resurrection has already been considered and rejected ever since Augustine seems to escape the prolife contingent among substance dualist philosophers.

Whether in a simple or Thomistic form, a substance dualist approach to postmortem survival may save souls, but it does not resurrect bodies. In an effort to maintain orthodoxy, this approach insists that souls, who have been perfectly happy in their body-free heavenly existence, will be perfectly happy to submit to re-embodiment. This soul story is only convincing to someone who has already committed to the soul's interim existence after death. For all others, that dog won't hunt.

Substance dualism offers a dubiously Christian version of resurrection. As thinkers increasingly abandon the soul ship, a viable alternative appears on the philosophical horizon: materialism. Proposals for resurrection without a soul offer new possibilities for conceptualizing an embodied afterlife, with some unexpected echoes to Christianity's root metaphor of seed.

## Materialist Resurrection without a Soul

Christian materialist thought presupposes that persons are organisms living in and as their bodies and that the resurrection should be thought of in these terms. Materialism rejects as logically unnecessary and metaphysically "troublesome" any entity that might exist independently of an organism's bodily "physical-structural states."[101] Materialist thinkers reference scientific (especially neurobiological) research in support of a materialist basis for self-awareness, higher consciousness, and personal identity.[102] Much of what the Christian tradition has attributed to the soul can be coherently explained in terms of the brain and neuroanatomy. Souls are not needed for selfhood; bodies, however, are.

Substance dualism will not go down without a fight. Its supporters suggest that materialism's dispensing with the soul is a childishly "recalcitrant" and "stubborn refusal" to acknowledge the power of transcendent realities—namely God.[103] For all their finger-wagging at those theologians who do not jump on the soul train, the fact remains that substance dualism faces a significant challenge from materialism. Substance dualism's attempt to play the God card fails. It is not God who is excised from Christian materialism—only the soul. God is central to each of materialism's three fundamental principles for bodily resurrection.

First, death is real. Materialist Christian thinkers argue that appealing to a soul's interim existence suggests that there is no real death, just "mere disembodiment."[104] Basic to a materialist ontology is the premise that "if persons are physical things, then—in the actual world—they die and their death results in their ceasing to exist."[105] When materialists take seriously the reality of the cessation of existence, they draw a contrast between the mortal creature and the immortal Creator.

Second, persons are embodied subjects with some persistent capacity within themselves for maintaining their existence. Philosophers call this the "*immanent* causal" condition for preservation of life over time.[106] Even granting that being resurrected from the dead necessitates divine intervention, there must be some immanent causal continuity that is maintained to be able to say that the same person has passed from death into new life. One's identity cannot simply be miraculously carried over by "God's free decree" alone into the afterlife (and still be considered human).[107] If God resurrected an individual by fiat, bypassing all "natural processes" of human existence, "the thing such an action of God's would produce would not be a member of our species."[108] Divine intervention plus immanent causality are needed to secure personal identity continuity for a human organism.

Third, a materialist approach insists on spatiotemporal continuity between death and the resurrection. An embodied subject cannot fall out of existence at one point in time and then come back into existence later at the final judgment and still be considered the same person. Without having recourse to an interim soul state, Christian materialism must find a way to conceptualize bodily resurrection happening immediately at death. Unless one can conceive of *something* continuing at the point of death, one is confronted with the insuperable problem of what philosophers refer to as gappy existence.[109] A substance dualist or a Thomist does not need to "mind the gap" between death and resurrection.[110] However, in materialist thought, immediate bodily resurrection is required to uphold immanent causality and spatiotemporal continuity. Immediate bodily resurrection is a tall order, but they have a God for that.

If one accepts the materialist dictum that there is no person without that person's immanently causal bodily existence, then the necessary (though not sufficient) condition for resurrection is the continuous presence of some physical matter upon which that person's homeostasis depends. However, this materialist position faces challenges—for example, if my body is resurrected immediately at death, then whose corpse is lying in the coffin? Or in the case of prenatal death, whose body lies dead in the womb?

A spate of materialist thinkers have experimented with various imaginative and much-discussed thought projects to address this problem. God can miraculously make an exact replica of the person at death that will appear in another world.[111] God might perform a miraculous body switch so that the real body is resurrected, and a "simulacrum" is put into the grave—without anyone knowing the difference.[112] The now-famous "falling elevator" model appeals to the fantastical "'physics' of cartoons" to explain how resurrection might be like jumping out of a falling elevator just in time before the car comes crashing to the basement floor. The jump from the corpse would actually have to be a miraculous process of "fission" where all or at least the minimum crucial parts of the body split off just at the moment of death.[113] Other materialist philosophers who work with the fissioning notion also see it as a whole body event. One set of basic bodily particles (or "simples," in technical metaphysical language) "would immediately cease to constitute life and come instead to compose a corpse, while the other [set] would . . . constitute a body in heaven."[114] Whatever the theory, the body that appears instantly in the afterlife is thought to be the same (or very close to the same) as the one at the moment of death.

All these proposals assume God's intervention to effect bodily resurrection, whether via replication, body snatching, or fissioning. That said, it is important for materialist philosophers that the resurrection happens in a particular causal way (immanently), at a particular moment (at death), and in a particular mode (corporeally). These elements must be in place to affirm that the deceased person and the resurrected one are the same human person.

By skirting the soul, Christian materialism provides a metaphysical alternative to soul-based resurrection. There are, however, strings attached. This alternative works for some bodies but not for others. The above-mentioned materialist models are unsuited for conceptualizing the resurrection of an undeveloped body in the womb. These materialist philosophers assume that the matter that reconstitutes immediately in the afterlife is that of a fully formed person.[115] The sample individuals whom materialist thinkers reference in their sometimes playful thought experiments are adults.[116]

Materialist resurrection is body focused but does not imply ongoing organic growth in the afterlife. This assumption has implications for embryonic or fetal resurrection, since bodies that die prematurely in the womb would need ongoing processes of maturation.[117] While materialist resurrection in theory does not rule out a process of growth for a resurrected embryonic or fetal body, this issue has not been explored.[118] However, if embryos and fetuses are also "physical things . . . in the actual world" that die, then Christian materialism should address their resurrection possibilities.[119]

A materialist model for the resurrection of unformed, even microscopic, unborn bodies is possible, but it would need some creative imagining. Dean Zimmerman plants the seed for such an alternative materialist imaginary when he suggests that one might think of the resurrection event as a kind of "budding." He speculates that just at the moment of death, instead of fissioning, perhaps the body's "atoms do something . . . more like 'budding', producing exactly similar offspring in the next world."[120] That is, God would invest each "atom within the corpse" with its own "miraculous 'budding' power . . . to produce *new* matter in a distant location."[121]

The speculative idea of budding at death is thought provoking. Thought crosses the Rubicon from analytic philosophy to the is/is not of metaphorical theology. The body buds but does not bud. Budding as a tensive metaphor pulls speculative thought further toward the possibility of conceptualizing fetal resurrection.

The budding metaphor also reconnects speculative philosophy with Christianity's root metaphor for the resurrection: seed. Neither substance dualist nor hylomorphic approaches to resurrection cared a fig for sprouting seeds. Big mistake. While substance dualism and Thomism have been battling over what type of soul should carry the self into the afterlife, believers have been singing hymns at Easter and funerals.

> *Now the green blade riseth, from the buried grain,*
> *Wheat that in the dark earth many days has lain;*
> *Love lives again, that with the dead has been:*
> *Love is come again, like wheat that springeth green.*[122]

The pervasiveness of the soul apparently never buried the seed metaphor. Resurrection as sprouting grain has continued to inspire resurrection faith. Theology would do well to tap into the power of this metaphor.

• • •

The soul has taken hits on all sides. Scholars who find the soul in the Bible mistake it for revelation when, in fact, they are only seeing the ripple-effect of a mishmash of Greco-Roman philosophies. The soul shines most strongly in the Bible—as metaphor. There never was one reigning soul concept in Christian history.

The orthodoxy of a substance dualist view of resurrection is questionable. While the sheer volume of soul talk "has encouraged many to suppose that the victory over death is the escape of the soul from the dead body," orthodoxy hangs its hat on the idea (popular or not) of resurrection as "the defeat of death."[123] Whatever explanatory power the soul once had has waned under the barrage of materialist critiques.

When Paul lamented rhetorically, "Who will rescue me from this body of death?" (Rom 7:24), he had a paradigm shift in mind for an answer. That revolutionary paradigm came in a very small package: a seed husk. Thinkers today concur: only metaphor has the "power of *redefining reality*."[124] Death in life, life after death—the soul has little to say about this paradox, never having died. Paradox is metaphor's thing. A good metaphor enables the "reduction of the shock between two incompatible ideas."[125] Resurrection is (and is not) wheat that springs up green.

That budding resurrection echoes Christianity's root metaphor of seed suggests that this organic image, which never died out in Christian history, can be brought back into play in a new type of materialist approach. A budding materialist approach has the potential to find resurrection again in buried grain.

# 4

## EMERGING
## INTO RESURRECTED LIFE

THE SOUL RUNS deep in Christianity. It buoys the heartbroken and moves the pens of poets. The soul has led soldiers to battle and the penitent to their prayers. The soul has vaulted over every obstacle in life—the most formidable one being death itself, so the story goes. If the materialist view of life is right, however, the soul never was the comforter, muse, or guide. The body—it was the body all along, the plodding, stalwart mule of our creaturehood. The Christian God in ancient times conferred on this lowly creature, against all credible expectations, life eternal. The idea stuck. The church's liturgies, catechisms, and creeds affirm "that creatures do not lose their creatureliness in the after-life."[1]

Grounding the belief in creaturely resurrection has proven to be daunting for materialist Christian thought. Resurrection hope rubs up against the prickly materialist assertion that there is no soul to escape death. Materialism accepts the sting of death (1 Cor 15:56) and wagers on a God loving and powerful enough to resurrect actual bodies.

Materialist resurrection anticipates elbows bumping in the after-life. Creatures will stand before God and face-to-face unashamed. The Other will be recognized as flesh of my flesh, my wounded neighbor, my brother whom I slayed, my famished prodigal son, my friend who betrayed me for pieces of silver, the lover whom my right hand embraced—with all the deep restitution, repentance, forgiveness, acceptance, healing, and pleasure that such recognition will entail. Heavenly peace may take time. If uterine beings have a share in this unruly communal shalom, then they will need bodies to participate.

The move beyond bland platitudes about heaven and vacuous hand-wringing about fetal demise must dare the risks of speculative theology, and do so without the soul. A materialist approach to the resurrection has the possibility of wrapping its arms around the undeveloped bodies of uterine beings who die. However, to do so, Christian materialism will need to eschew quick fixes of bodies replicating or fissioning at the moment of death. Bodies need time to resurrect. They need an ontology that gives bodies time.

Emergence metaphysics is dripping with time. Emergence tracks the history of archaic humans evolving across eons. The microscopic and minute changes during embryonic and fetal development testify to the measured emergence of each human life. Emergence tells the story of body and mind interacting over a lifespan, until both enfold back into each other at death. If the human person is an emergent mind-body interactive reality over time—evolutionarily, gestationally, during life—then an account of postmortem personal survival should reflect that reality.

Developing a doctrine of resurrection using an emergence metaphysics is a delicate operation. Emergence, a shy and slow-moving metaphysics, cannot be forced from its conceptual shell by the pokings and proddings of analytical theology. Emergence must be coaxed and enticed. Theology drops a few metaphors—grain, seed, blossom—hoping for a reaction; emergence is interested. When the apostle Paul inserted these metaphors in his letter to the believers in Corinth, he got a reaction. Word spread and created a buzz. From buried seed, the green blade riseth. The metaphor's simplicity entices.

In the soil of such a metaphor, doctrine can take root—a doctrine of budding materialist resurrection that leaves corpses in their graves while emergence vigils. Cellular matter disperses. Spiritual bodies germinate from these seeds into a bloom of resurrection. In time, these bodies take their place in the heavenly procession. No souls hurry on ahead. Emergent resurrection tarries, entrusts itself to a distant eschaton, to that last "uncertain hour before the morning/ Near the ending of interminable night."[2]

## Emergent Materialism and Death

Science stands on the shoulders of decades of research in evolutionary theory, genetics, and neurobiology. Emergence thought translates this science into ontology.[3] Combining science with materialist philosophy, emergence unearths the corporeal processes of personhood, setting the ontological stage for a new understanding of bodily resurrection.

Humans emerged in prehistory. The forerunners of the human species crept, crawled, lumbered, then stood erect in evolutionary emergence. Hominids and ultimately *Homo sapiens* evolved to acquire complex intelligence as an adaptive biological and anthropological reality. Emergence stands at odds with the model that dominated Christian thought until the modern period: creationism. Old-style creationism hawks the idea that God one day (on the sixth, specifically) created the first human beings. New-style creationism concedes a Darwinian point that God perhaps waited until a particular era in prehistory to endow more evolved *Homo sapiens* with "the requisite soul with its advanced capabilities."[4] Emergence philosophy demurs. No offense to the Creator, but human consciousness developed naturally. When certain genetic, corporeal, social, and other elements coalesced in human evolution, mental capacities emerged "as a natural consequence of the elements in their combination and relationship."[5] Early hominid brains and bodies underwent incremental organic changes over millions of years until—wait for it, wait for it—higher consciousness emerged.

Persons also emerge gestationally. The human organism in the womb takes nine months to coalesce from fertilized ovum to a being with lungs ready to take in air and a brain able to "cause and sustain emergent mental phenomena."[6] Brain capacity progresses for most born people into various degrees of complex cognitive function, such as self-awareness, intentionality, and moral consciousness. The soul tries to take all the credit. Science indicates otherwise. Primates (near-evolutionary kin to humans) exhibit cognitive and social capacities that far outstrip a human fetus, without anyone attributing souls to them.[7] Give credit where credit is due: natural emergence. The individual self emerges gestationally—not when it acquires a soul, but when it achieves "the right configuration and functioning of the brain" in a body that can support it.[8]

Persons function as complex, emergent mind-body systems. Materialist emergence echoes the mantra of other types of materialism: no "non-mental substance that is dual to the body."[9] In a materialist emergence ontology, the mind never lacks the presence of organic bodily matter out of which it emerges and upon which it supervenes. Body and brain emerge and survive as a dynamic system together, or not at all.[10]

Over a lifetime persons-as-systems perdure. Lacking a soul concept, emergent materialism configures other ways to account for an "enduring yet changing" self.[11] What accounts for the unique self that continues over time turns out to be not an immaterial soul but, rather, a process.[12] Persons are the "continuing manifestation of smoothly evolving emergent" mind/body interactions.[13] Once begun, the person continues in dynamic homeostasis, until interrupted by some greater force that brings death.

By construing the self as an interactive bodily process (not an immaterial entity), emergence names death as the definitive counterforce of life. If a person's mind-body system screeches to a halt at death, resurrection must provide a complete ontological reboot. Emergent materialism casts about for a good idea for postmortem survival. It settles on the materialist proposal for immediate, full body fissioning at death.[14] When the person dies, "God miraculously confers causal powers" on their unified body system, enabling it immediately to fission. For a brief moment, two bodies exist: "the dying state of the body remaining on earth" and "the newly generated one" in the afterlife. Awkward. The twoness, however, does not last. In the twinkling of an eye, my particular "unity-conferring emergent features" go where my living bodily system goes: into the afterlife.[15] Death descends like a sword, and the body escapes in the nick of time, sustaining not a scratch.

This depiction of resurrection adheres to materialist dictums,[16] yet something in this picture does not ring true for life understood as an emergent process. In this type of materialism, the resurrection process marches forward, double time, as a unified bodily event; however, emergence has seemingly dropped out of the band. This materialist approach rushes to get the body transported into the afterlife, forgetting that emergence is a process, and a slow one at that.

Organic things need time to grow. If human creatures emerge (in evolutionary history and in utero) over time, then creaturely resurrection should reflect that reality. Thinking of death and resurrection as extended processes slows down the metaphysical metronome. Emergent materialism needs to linger longer over death and allow a different, more organic ontology to germinate.

## Emergent Budding Resurrection

The imagination grasps at straws in an effort to conceptualize bodily resurrection. The apostle Paul fumed in frustration trying to explain: "Fool! What you sow does not come to life unless it dies" (1 Cor 15:36). His unlikely idea invigorated a medieval imaginary of corpses budding and blooming into the afterlife. The metaphor of death as germination provoked thought for the premoderns, and it can again today.

Speculative thinking about organic budding into the afterlife begins at the all-too-real physical event: death. Science speaks of death as an irreversible event but also one that separates two "biological processes of dying and bodily disintegration."[17] Just as biologists insist that conception is not a momentary event, they also are careful to explain that death itself is not a momentary event. Death lingers, even after the body has definitively passed the threshold from which it cannot return. Science recognizes the irreversible state of death as a "window of time." In this period after death and before decomposition begins, the person is not alive, but there is living activity. Cells and parts of cells are active, and some chemical processes even accelerate until, finally, all cellular life ends, and decomposition commences. This "twilight of death" can last anywhere from hours to days.[18] Poetry speaks similarly of "Being between two lives—unflowering, between / The live and the dead nettle."[19] Death concatenates.

The evidence of death together with the Pauline seed metaphor elicit theological speculation. If some minute biological activities of the body continue after the person is irreversibly dead, then theology has a material basis for imagining how living matter might emerge from a corpse into resurrected existence. A corpse might slough off minute seeds of matter that could be divinely enabled to bud emergently after death. Analytic philosophy toys with a similar idea.[20] Still living cellular matter from a dead body might pass over the threshold of death to form the organic substrate out of which a "spiritual body" develops (1 Cor 15:44). Science and metaphor provoke the idea of a budding materialist emergent resurrection.

As a speculative eschatology, budding materialist emergent resurrection, no doubt, has some explaining to do, especially to skeptical metaphysicians.[21] Esoteric theology is sometimes all about the numbers. Medieval Scholastic theologians debated about angels on the head of a pin. Metaphysicians count numerical identity: one person in life and that numerically same person after death. Substance dualism does simple math: one soul here, one soul there. QED.

Christian materialism has to contend with the numbers not adding up in hypothetical resurrection disaster scenarios. If fissioning happens while the person's body lingers alive on earth, there is a two-person problem: my about-to-die body on earth and my replica body that has already arrived in the afterlife. Or, something might get lost in the fissioning transition (analogies to Star Trek transporter malfunctions abound), resulting in a less-than-complete person arriving in heaven.[22] Or, if the replication process goes haywire, too many me-replicas might materialize in the hereafter. These theoretical problems are dubbed the "closest continuer" issue where the numerically identical postmortem person is difficult to identify.[23]

Budding materialist resurrection seems to escape these disaster scenarios and the closest continuer problem. Emergent budding resurrection happens *after* the person is definitively dead, so there is no risk of a competing survivor on earth. Moreover, since cells from my corpse could not pass into the afterlife without divine assistance, God would presumably ensure that the one or many cells that survive my death would be coordinated, so as to form just one emergently resurrected body. Divine power precludes a closest continuer issue in resurrection.[24]

A budding emergence approach can also rely on the science of genetics to fend off the closest continuer problem. In soul-based ontologies, it is an immaterial substance that guarantees identity continuity. In materialist emergent resurrection, genes create a material link between the body that died and the body in heaven. In budding resurrection, the body that begins its emergent resurrection in the twilight of death carries that person's genetic material into the afterlife.[25] Paul could only imagine a "*gumnos kókkos* (a naked kernel: 1 Cor 15:37), which will be sown in corruption and raised in incorruption."[26] Emergent budding invests that kernel metaphor with the idea of genetic continuity.

Genes and metaphors, however, are fragile. Humans are complex. People find it hard enough holding themselves together in the day-to-day of living. Explaining how personal identity might be held together into the afterlife is a daunting task. Budding emergent materialism needs an account of divine power and a robust theory of personal identity.

## God's Will and the Creature's Story

What God wills, God accomplishes. Any doctrine of bodily resurrection affirms God's ability to accomplish the miracle. The devil is in the details of how a resurrected person will still be the same person in the aftermath.

Begun in twilight death, budding emergence remains in penumbra without divine causal and sustaining intervention. God coaxes and cradles the body's matter across the threshold of death so that it can emerge into resurrection. That the Supreme Being could accomplish such a feat is no surprise. God opting not to contravene all previously normal biological processes during an emergent resurrection—that surprises. Miracle is grace wrapped in nature. Once the budding process is divinely begun, grace works with nature, respecting some degree of the body's immanent causality.[27] Eventually, the emergently resurrected body can take its own steps on the path toward eschatological glorification. Emergence traces the *longue durée* of resurrection's miracle.

The idea of a body being emergently resurrected comes into focus. What remains fuzzy is the basis for claiming that the same *person* has been resurrected. An emergent budding approach to resurrection needs more than an appeal to miracle for a plausible account of identity continuity.

## Thomism and Incipient Persons

The unnaturalness of the soul's postmortem existence, pending the Parousia, has vexed hylomorphic models for personhood. Aquinas preached that there is never a person without a body informed by its soul. The soul-actualized-body idea clashes with the claim of the disembodied soul communing with God after death. A body without its soul, or a soul without its body, is only an incipient person. Scholastic theology squares the circle by allowing for an exception to the hylomorphic rule. In one and only one instance—death—the self persists as a disembodied soul, unnaturally, imperfectly, and temporarily. This truncated personhood discomfits Thomist scholars.[28] The category of unnatural soulish existence strikes materialist thinkers as an unwarranted case of metaphysical special pleading.[29]

Emergent budding resurrection avoids special pleading and circle squaring. This resurrection view takes the hylomorphic idea of an unnatural interim soul state and translates it into a materialist emergent key.[30] After death what emerges from the corpse is not a disembodied soul self but, rather, the organic seeds of a self—still incipient but not *un*natural. The emergently budding self cannot enjoy the beatific vision of God—at least not for a very long while. Unperturbed, God waits patiently for the process to unfold.

Budding emergent resurrection, thus, reconfigures incipiency. Matter from an individual body passes—incipiently but naturally— from death into a new life process. But emergent budding promises even more. Emerging into resurrection are not just cells, muscles, and bones but the brain itself. Weighing in at about three pounds (mostly water), the adult brain is a mushy bowlful of cognitive properties and neural events called mind. The self sloshes in the brain. To explain how God resurrects that self, without a single drop lost, speculative theology needs a theory of the self.

### Narrative Selves

To preserve the self in the afterlife, do not drink the water—of Lethe, that is.[31] Unlike Greek mythology, Christian resurrection demands embodied selves with memories in the hereafter. At the final judgment, people must give an accounting *coram Deo* of their own past deeds (Matt 25:34–56). Accountability implies cognitive awareness, such as memories, self-consciousness, personality, a sense of oneself as a moral being, and experiences of relationality.[32] Resurrection without memory would churn out not beings drunk with the waters of forgetfulness but, rather, zombies.

Dualism battles zombiehood with an immaterial soul. In Christian materialism, bodies escape the zombie apocalypse by fissioning into heaven at the moment of death. Other resurrection models, such as constitutionalism,[33] do it by divine fiat.[34] Armed only with the Pauline metaphor of buried seed, budding emergence appears to lack a theory robust enough to fend off zombies.

Emergent resurrection requires a supporting theory of personal identity continuity after bodily death. *Doctrine of resurrection with*

*organic interests seeks companion theory: must enjoy process and respect the*
*passage of time, no dualisms need apply.* A theory of narrative identity fits
the profile of this job description.

Philosophies of narrative identity define the person as a changing
but ongoing life story. In written stories, narrative drenches characters
with a past, present, and future. The protagonist materializes so concretely on the page that the reader catches a *soupçon* of her perfume.
Stories birth a self. Narrativity is a dynamic not just in books but in
life. Having been given a story at infancy, persons grow to "weave"
their own autobiographies. A narrative identity feeds the ego (in a
good way) so that individuals can "think of themselves as persisting
subjects," in an "unfolding story."[35]

The doctrine of the resurrection stands outside the purview of
secular philosophies of narrative identity. Indeed, if selfhood depends
on a story that I tell or that others tell on my behalf, then a narrative
approach forecloses all talk of personal postmortem survival. At death,
we all become "human nonpersons."[36] This secular narrative view of
persons leaves unaddressed "how a self which is inscribed through narrative can persist beyond death."[37]

Narrative theology reads things differently. No person's life story
unfolds apart from divine presence. God's book holds "all the days that
were formed for me, when none of them as yet existed" (Ps 139:16).
Persons are embodied stories, whose fullest telling lies hidden in God.
At death, when I lose the capacity for self-narration, God preserves my
story, not only as a past narrative but as an unfolding future. In death,
I am never a nonperson. An abbreviated life that ends in utero, before
anyone even knew it had begun, has a story known to and preserved by
God. To say that God carries forward each person's story into the afterlife does not mean that selves are mere novellas nestled in the divine
memory.[38] God storicizes, so to say, the risen self until the body can
remember and speak its own mind.

How an emergently resurrected body regains its story cannot be
known. Budding emergent resurrection can no more delineate how

this process might transpire than Thomism or substance dualism can delineate how a disembodied soul and its body reunite in the final resurrection. The reinscribing of one's story into one's emergently resurrected body would have to entail something more than God downloading memories for the emergent brain to scroll through, akin to using photos and home videos to jog an amnesiac's memory. A sense of self depends on the amnesiac not just having memories but regaining the capacity emotionally to "own" those memories again.[39] The amnesiac's reacquiring of personal identity cannot be done by psychiatric fiat. Neither can resurrected selfhood be generated by divine fiat. The miracle has to nurture nature.

Nature: the emerging organism develops a brain and acquires human cognitive capacities. Miracle: God returns to that brain the memories and life story of the person who died. The two entwine. Nature awaits miracle. Miracle beckons nature. The emergent self grows into its body, and the body remembers and recaptures the person it was. This miraculous and mysterious *pas de deux* needs no additional entity—a soul. The principle of parsimony directs thought away from an additive metaphysical solution. A theologically necessary and sufficient doctrine of the resurrection postulates God alone as safeguarding one's storied identity until one's resurrected body is formed. At that point, the self can take up again weaving its story. The warp and weft of a self that unraveled in death can now unfold in heaven, like threads of purple in which the divine is pleased to be held captive.[40]

A theory of narrative identity serves a theology of budding emergent resurrection. A tale of re-membered bodies in the afterlife that remember. A person dies. Still living cells are sloughed off the corpse. Those particles are divinely enabled to germinate like seeds. From the shed bits of cellular matter, a body emerges into resurrection. Brain re-forms. Slowly. The creature looks around in bewilderment at the glories of heaven. Miracle lays its hand upon the furrowed brow. Synapses snap. The mind begins to remember its own story.

Narrative identity after embryonic and fetal death is another matter. These beings reside in liminality, with barely a layer of narrative to
shield them from ontological obscurity. Augustine's words about those
who die before birth haunt. Will there be in heaven "souls without
bodies though they once had them,—only in their mother's womb"?[41]

## The Resurrection of Emergent Unborn Bodies

The historical church struggled with the idea of fetuses, not to mention embryos, in heaven. Theology still lacks a suitable ontology for
imagining the unimaginable. Line up all the usual philosophical sus-
pects: substance dualism, hylomorphism, materialism, emergent dualism. Not a one speaks adequately to the conundrum of an afterlife for
a being that dies before birth.[42] Budding emergence theory offers an
ontological opportunity to take up Augustine's dilemma. The place to
begin this thought process is at the end—with death.

### Embryonic and Fetal Demise

Death in the womb is sui generis—the death of one human organism
within the body of another. Death and wombs make an odd but recurring couple dating back to human prehistory. The Neolithic world rit-
ualized the arc of life, from the maternal body to burial in the womb
of the earth.[43] The ancient myth of the return to the Mother in death
has a curious echo in current scientific research on the phenomenon of
microchimerism. After early pregnancy loss, the maternal body reab-
sorbs embryonic or fetal cellular matter. With the advent of genetic
testing, scientists have found chimeras of fetal DNA decades after the
fact in the mother's brain and other organs.[44] When nascent uterine
beings die, no corpse remains. Their demise may go unnoticed because
they were never known to have existed at all.

Conceptualizing embryonic or fetal resurrection must take into
account death with a corpse and death without bodily remains visibly
present. Emergence theory offers ontological clues. The notion of cells

being sloughed off and divinely enabled to emerge into resurrection can apply to embryonic or fetal beings. A uterine being dies in a dark womb and is resurrected during the twilight of death. The gears of this organic-yet-miraculous process might engage at the time of a miscarriage or an abortion. Or the emergent process might initiate as late as the time of death of the mother (given microchimerism). The cells of mother and child go together into their emergent future. The age or size of the deceased's remains is no matter. God does not count cells, weigh tissues, or watch the clock.

Budding resurrection approximates, in a miraculous and novel organic way, the emergent processes that the born deceased person's body already underwent. With a uterine being, however, budding emergence into the afterlife completes a process the embryo or fetus never passed through. The muscles of speculative theology are stretched to the maximum in attempting to grasp resurrection as a novel emergent phenomenon.

Science might lend some aid to the imagination. For human bodies to develop ex utero (again or for the first time after death in the womb), special conditions and processes are needed. Speculative theology can turn to clinical precedents for the use of artificial wombs in the science of mammalian gestation.[45] Seeing pictures of artificial womb bags used in lab experiments with animals makes the analogue for a doctrine of bodily resurrection hard *not* to visualize.[46] To disallow the idea of a special gestational-like environment for the emergent resurrection of embryonic and fetal bodies would be to deny that a creator God can miraculously accomplish for the unborn in the next life what biomedical technology is on the verge of creating for near-term fetuses on earth. A too-reticent theology prematurely clips the wings of the miraculous.

A being developing in utero never dies alone, whether its gestating mother knows of its existence or not. Some mothers tragically die along with their unborn child. An emergent budding resurrection model can address the event of fetal and maternal death better than other ontologies. When a pregnant woman dies, her body continues, for a few moments or minutes, to sustain the fetus. If emergency measures are not available to continue gestation or to remove a viable fetus after the mother's death, it soon dies within its mother's womb. In a materialist model, the pregnant woman's body would fission, at the moment of her death, into the afterlife and leave her still-living fetus behind in a replica maternal body. That fetus dies alone. An emergence ontology avoids this horrendous scenario.

A pregnant woman dies, and her budding emergence begins. Her dead, though still warm, body gently harbors her fetus until it too meets death and begins emergence. The cells from mother and fetus embark on their budding emergent resurrection together. Even death does not part them.

Death in pregnancy highlights the connection between mother and fetus as well as the differences in their paths to emergently resurrected selfhood. Her personhood is renarrativized in the afterlife. However, a fetus, not to mention an unknown embryo, does not have much of a story to renarrativize. Its storied selfhood has to be thought of differently.

## Embryonic and Fetal Narrative Identity

The idea that I, after a long life, might pick up again my personal storyline in heaven is a radical enough idea. Narrative personal identity for the unborn in the afterlife is even more challenging. The unborn being's story is not a self-narrated one. That uterine being does not tell but is told about.

Some analogies exist for the narrative personhood of individuals unable to tell their own story. A neonate who tragically dies has a birth and life story, however short, now sadly recounted by parents and family. Losing, temporarily or permanently, the neurological means for consciousness does not erase a person's past story or prevent any ongoing narration done at their bedside by loved ones. Someone born with severe cognitive disabilities can be given a story by attentive caretakers.

That person acquires meaningful selfhood beyond mere existence as a passive recipient of care.[47] God remembers all these individual stories.

Death in the womb, however, leaves a very thin basis for narrative personhood. That story is entirely told by others and projected onto a uterine being, who was only seen on an ultrasound, if at all. The tales of these unborn beings are written by the hand of God in a script beyond human comprehension. Faith affirms that God wills to preserve even the trace of an unknown embryo's story. Bestowed by others (if at all) with the briefest of stories or imagined futures, an unborn being's narrative identity is diaphanous.

Existing theories of selfhood are poorly equipped to address uterine beings. Narrativity theory in secular philosophy highlights how stories spring from and enhance personal agency. Individuals self-constitute when they "organize their experience"—past, present, and future—in acts of "self-narration."[48] The person makes stories which make the person. This agency-focused theory has little to no applicability for the unborn. In Christian materialist models, one fissions with an intact brain; one's story continues in heaven with barely a comma's pause. However, fissioning does no good for unborn beings with little to no brain and whose own storytelling never began. In substance dualism, the soul makes the self; a functioning brain and storytelling capacities are irrelevant. In all these theories, personhood is the prerequisite for postmortem personal continuity. First personhood, then resurrection. No personhood, no resurrection.

An emergence approach reverses the order—with better prospects for embryos and fetuses in the afterlife. If one can secure the plausibility of the resurrection of liminal unborn bodies whose personhood is in doubt, then one dispenses with personhood (however it is theorized) as a requirement of resurrection. An embryo or fetus is resurrected not because it *is* a person but because God wills to bring that nascent being into personhood in the afterlife. An unformed body and brain and the lack of a soul pose no impediment for emergent budding into the afterlife. Budding resurrection only requires some human organismal matter and some storied identity known, at least, to God. Embryonic and fetal bodies and brains emerge and quicken in heaven under a slow divine tutelage that will eventually include a storied identity.

## Emergent Resurrection and the Christian Tradition

Substance dualism touts the orthodoxy of the soul, any "deviation" from which wavers on doctrinal "heresy."[49] The theological weaknesses of soul talk aside,[50] budding materialist emergence should prove its own doctrinal and scriptural mettle.

### Doctrinal Grammar and Budding Emergence

The doctrinal soundness of emergent resurrection depends on how well it coheres with key tenets of Christian faith. Doctrine, however, is slippery. Historically, the quest for doctrinal consensus too often devolved into cat-herding at ecumenical councils.[51] What worked in one era was anathematized in another. Doctrinal truth becomes whatever sticks when thrown at the ecclesial wall in a particular geography, denomination, or moment in history. A postliberal regulative approach to the "grammar" of doctrine simplifies the process of assessing doctrinal orthodoxy across time, context, and tradition.[52]

According to the theory of regulative doctrine, orthodoxy consists of the *regula fidei*—formal rules of faith, codified in creeds, catechisms, and liturgical practices—which Christians assent to and live by, to some degree. Theology teases out the truth of these tenets using a vast array of philosophical constructs and metaphors. One need not slavishly follow any particular philosophical schema or systematic idea to articulate orthodox belief.[53] The church fathers wrapped doctrine in Neoplatonic garb. The tradition has worn bespoke cloaks of many philosophical cuts and colors over the centuries. Styles do change. Nothing substantive of the grammar of Christian faith need be lost or distorted when philosophical paradigms shift.

Budding emergent materialism can be tailored to fit the doctrine of the resurrection, and vice versa. Even creeds, catechisms, and liturgies with the most soul-laden language can be reformulated using an emergent materialist grammar, with no loss of orthodoxy. Doctrine will not be left naked. The creed will still speak its truth to human experience.

Substance dualism, for example, judges that the Heidelberg Catechism's use of soul terminology "reflects the standard" Christian view of the resurrection.[54] Case closed. An emergence theology disagrees with this literalism and appeals this decision on the grounds of grammar. The catechism states, "Not only will my soul be taken immediately after this life . . . but also my very flesh will be raised by the power of Christ, reunited with my soul, and made like Christ's glorious body."[55] Regulative theory parses the doctrinal grammar, separate from the dualist ontology. Subject: each person. Verb: will be raised and remade. Object: a resurrection body like Christ's. Adverb: immediately. The grammar dictates the bones of orthodoxy. The bones hold the doctrinal structure together. Soul is not bred in the bone.

Emergent budding materialism retains Heidelberg's grammar but rewrites the catechism, using a different metaphor and philosophical paradigm:

> *Not only will the seeds of my body be taken immediately after this life to begin rising like Christ, the first fruits of glory, but also my very story, remembered by God, will be retold to my risen self, which will emerge in everlasting joy.*[56]

An emergent budding formulation does not breach orthodoxy or diminish the "comfort" of this catechism's teaching on the resurrection.[57] Seed imagery, emergence ontology, and narrative theory drape lightly on the basic doctrinal structure. The bones hold.

The notion of a developing organic postmortem body raises the issue of whether emergent materialism coheres with belief in life everlasting. The *regula fidei* has a narrow remit regarding the grammar of eternal life. Individual bodily resurrection is a requirement for the stated primary purpose of meting out individual justice, based on one's deeds in life. All "shall rise again with their bodies; and shall give account of their own works" (Athanasian Creed). The creed specifies that divine justice requires bodies, with memories, standing before God. An emergence budding resurrection model coheres with this rule of faith by envisioning an eschatological time of individual embodied reckoning.

A grammatical approach to doctrine can specify the purpose of resurrection (reward or punishment) but cannot parse the metaphysics of life everlasting. Everlastingness evades every theological attempt to pin it down. Budding emergence endorses a long and winding road to eschatological perfection but lacks the ability to pronounce on the physics of eternity. Emergence into the afterlife might mean another time/place/dimension of suffering, remorse, repentance, and renewal in the ascent to perfect divine communion.[58] One can only speculate whether individuals also will enjoy other activities such as meeting and embracing lost loved ones, growing in wisdom, or recreating in God's creation, itself now "set free from its bondage to decay" (Rom 8:21).[59]

A believer can easily (hence this view's popularity) claim that an unchanging immaterial soul exists forever—but an organic body, not so much. An organic, emergently resurrected person implies significant bodily processes and cycles of growing that would include the ongoing assimilation of biological matter, for some unknown period of time, in a dimension of our physical universe, or one like it.[60] The raft of speculative theology drifts into the rough currents of theoretical physics here.

Pulling on the two oars of common sense and regulative doctrinal theory, theology can stay on course in the vast sea of metaphysics. Common sense says anything that grows eventually has a natural end, even the longest-living known organisms. A scientific understanding of the world says organic entities cannot continue in homeostasis forever.

Thus, it makes sense to think of emergently resurrected bodies having a gloriously long yet also time-limited existence in a human material form.

Imagine one has faced and passed through the process of divine judgment in one's emergently resurrected body. One has communed with the saints and progressed toward eschatological glorification. One might then morph into a new form of existence in God's presence. Perfected "eschatologically glorified bodies" may eventually be freed from their "carbon-based biochemistry" as we currently know of it.[61] This eventuality implies that corporeal individuality itself will be transformed. The Bible hints in this direction.

The apostle Paul states (cryptically) that at the end of Christ's rule, God will be "all in all" (1 Cor 15:28). In an effort to explain, theology has to mumble something in Greek or Latin about the *totus Christus*, the *koinonia* in heaven, or a *perichoresis* with the Trinity.[62] In order to untangle this complex theological teleology, one has to do the grammar. Find the rule in the creed. The ultimate end for each creature is to commune with God, the "eternal . . . uncreated and immeasurable being." The rule of orthodox eschatology is to confess this paradox: for the creature "born in time" there will be an endless end in a timeless God.[63]

Emergent eschatology upholds the apophatic paradox of life everlasting.[64] Carbon-based beings emerging into resurrection will participate in the Trinity's eternal perichoretic dance. Bodily emergence in heaven may go on and on, or it may only be a prequel to a more incomprehensible union with the vastness of a divine being beyond any imaginable embodiment.

### Emergent Resurrection and the Bible

The Bible knows nothing of emergent materialism. New Testament scholarship warns against "cherry-picking" any particular aspect of Jesus's resurrection accounts, especially his "physicality."[65] Whether the gospel writers invested the risen Christ's eating, walking, and touching[66] with more theological import than his almost ghostly appearances, dis-appearings, or ascension,[67] one cannot say. Theology cannot discover a cohesive materialist, soul-based, or any other anthropology in the New Testament. In using the New Testament to ground doctrinal interpretations, one should apply Hippocrates's dictum: do no harm. A doctrine of the resurrection should not harm the plain sense of scripture, which is supposed to communicate something revelatory, even when cryptic.

The apostle Paul's expression "raised a spiritual body" (1 Cor 15:44) is cryptic. Paul might have meant an immaterial-soul-joined-af-ter-an-interim-disembodied-existence-with-its-glorified-body. Or Paul might have meant that persons are raised, as bodies, into a new spiritual reality with the divine. Neither interpretation is easily conceptualized. Both interpretations assume that Paul's listeners needed to be won over to his novel religious message. The materialist interpretation, however, is less encumbered with added metaphysical concepts. Sometimes less is more.

Paul did not celebrate the body. He tended toward a Hellenistic hierarchical dualism in his preference for *pneuma* over *soma*. One has to take Paul's dim view of the flesh with a large grain of salt. The later gospel accounts of Jesus's resurrection can be seen as correcting any overspiritualizing in Paul's anthropology.[68] Paul spoke about resurrection in the abstract; the gospels recount Jesus's actual dying. Jesus's bones, blood, and breath are pivotal to these narratives.

The gospels do not discuss Jesus's soul. Luke mentions Jesus commending his spirit to God but says nothing about it being separated from his body at death.[69] The crucifixion narratives would have been a perfect opportunity to clarify this point once and for all. But an argument from absence cannot establish much. The gospels say nothing of Jesus's resurrection in terms of seeds sown and rising either.

Emergent materialism would have much stronger biblical grounding if Jesus had said to the thief crucified alongside him, "Truly I tell you today, you will be sown like a seed and will rise with me into Paradise." However, if one follows the principle of less-metaphysics-is-more, then it is better not to bulk up the "you" in Luke 23:43 with too much Hellenistic baggage of immaterial souls.[70] Materialism offers a simpler model of the thief's journey to heaven. At death, the emergent resurrection of his body, sagging on a cross, began. The thief cried out upon dying, "Jesus, remember me" (v. 42). God remembers his storied identity.

A key passage that militates against an emergence view of the timing of resurrection is 1 Corinthians 15:52: "In a moment, in the twinkling of an eye, at the last trumpet . . . the dead will be raised imperishable, and we will be changed." Literal or metaphorical—that is the question. The biblical writers anticipated a transformative eschatological event marked by archangels and trumpets. Christ will descend from the clouds and sneak in unannounced at the gates (1 Thess 4:16; Matt 24:29–33). Soul-based anthropologies read a literal soul state into this time before the Parousia. Budding emergent materialism reads things like seeds and trumpets as metaphorical. A budding resurrection process begins at death, *akin* to seeds sprouting. A transformative, perhaps culminating, resurrection event will happen, *as if* announced by a final trumpet's blast. Revelation wraps itself in metaphor and simile.

The New Testament offers a mixed bag of resurrections. Jesus and other New Testament individuals rose from the dead with their whole bodies intact, and in fairly short order. Jesus appeared in full bodily form three days after death; Lazarus arose, not too worse for wear, after four days.[71] These resurrections do not suggest twilight death or a lengthy budding emergence. The apostle Paul may have missed the (oral tradition) memo read by the gospel writers about how to describe resurrection. Paul avoided equating the final resurrection with Jesus's resurrection or that of any other people raised from the dead in Paul's lifetime (e.g., Acts 9:40; 20:10). When members of the Corinthian church queried Paul, "How are the dead raised?" (1 Cor 15:35), he did not answer: "Just like Jesus, Lazarus, Tabitha, and Eutychus." Instead, Paul's go-to explanation was metaphorical.

Paul's audience struggled to find a hermeneutical key to decipher the metaphysics and temporality of the resurrection. Paul turned to metaphors. They multiply and cascade in 1 Corinthians 15: "Sow . . . sow . . . bare seed . . . wheat . . . grain . . . to each kind of seed its own body. . . . What is sown is perishable . . . sown . . . sown" (vv. 37–44). Those who have ears will hear. Paul implied "an organic *continuity* with the mortal body that preceded" and the resurrected one in the after-life.[72] He did so, through the use of metaphor.

Unless one reads Paul as a clueless rhetor, he knew what metaphors do. They are expansive and provocative linguistic images that work by a process of "surprise and reversal."[73] To understand resurrection, do not look for literal souls drifting up to heaven. Look down into the soil where metaphors are germinating in the twilight of death. Resurrection is and is not a seed.[74] Another word for biblical surprise and reversal: revelation.

Biblical teachings on the resurrection lead the interpreter on a circuitous path with switchbacks, dead ends, and precipices. *Pneuma*, no, *soma*. Lazarus, no, the thief on the cross. Christ in the clouds, no, Christ at the gates. In this biblical maelstrom of meaning, budding emergence offers a hermeneutical lens that does not harm the plain sense. Emergence offers resistance to the New Testament's own sub-text of Hellenistic hierarchical dualism. Most important, a budding emergence view of the resurrection understands that metaphors are not extraneous trimmings. Metaphors are, perhaps, the most pivotal vehicle for scripture's revelatory truth.

•  •  •

Budding emergence comes late onto the stage of Christian philo-sophical approaches to the resurrection. A cousin of materialism and younger sibling of emergence ontologies, budding resurrection is a wild child, philosophically and theologically. Budding emergence fid-gets over the fusty interim state of the soul or sci-fi bodies fissioning into the afterlife. These ontologies gaze endlessly into the heavens.

Budding emergence runs outside to play in the dirt. Looking down at the soil, one can imagine how "flesh will blossom again."[75]

The grain metaphor inspires speculative thought; however, emergence theology would be nowhere without science. From gill and fin to lung and hoof, species emerged and morphed over eons. From blastocyst to brain, a human emerges from amniotic waters to breathe air. In death, the corpse cools and releases its hold; its cells drift away like silent monks after compline. Within each dying cell, DNA vibrates at decibels only heard by God, and perhaps angels. Believers long to know what happens next. The angels are not talking.

Soul talk is touted as having all the answers, until someone starts asking uncomfortable questions. What about a fetus before it receives its soul? What about an embryo with no body? A budding emergence approach answers with metaphor, image, and simile as guides: imagine sowing seed. Think of being knit together, as if in a mother's womb. The self is a story.

Budding emergence is not meant to be arcane or mystifying. This approach to the resurrection aims to speak concretely—because metaphorically—to the reality of death, including the death of unborn beings. Budding emergence provides no flash metaphysical fix. Instead, it plants a familiar earthy image, out of which resurrection hope can grow.

# 5

## ENVISIONING DISABLED BODIES IN HEAVEN AND REPRODUCTIVE AGENCY ON EARTH

PREGNANT PEOPLE AND their families today search for ways to plan their childbearing in the face of obstacles, such as infertility, miscarriages, and pregnancy complications. Medical science and technology accompany expectant parents on the road to conceiving, managing a pregnancy, and birthing. Knowledge can be superficial: a blue or pink baby blanket. Knowledge also opens a door to power and, with power, moral complexity and a plethora of decisions. Diagnostic ultrasounds can detect conditions needing risky prenatal surgery. Genetic testing looks deep into embryonic and fetal DNA to expose a missing chromosome, a genetic mutation, or an inherited lethal disease. For some couples, the path from prenatal screening to selective abortion can be a direct one.[1]

Disability theology challenges the morality of selective abortion.[2] Having a disability is not a flaw to be avoided but manifests "the mystery of the human being with all its dignity and nobility."[3] For disability theology, selective abortion acts at cross-purposes with a God-given right to life because "aborting a human fetus because he or she is disabled is not substantially different from aborting a human fetus for other reasons."[4] A prolife and prodisability position asserts, with very few exceptions, the moral obligation of parents-to-be "to welcome and nurture any child."[5] Prodisability theologians affirm the intrinsic value of the unborn, including those affected by anomalies.[6]

An eschatology that envisions affected unborn beings in heaven would seem to follow from, and also to underscore, this prolife stance.[7]

If God welcomes fetuses with prenatal anomalies into the next life, then a pregnant woman should commit to welcoming into this world any unborn being—including those with disabilities. God confers an inviolable right to be born upon every conceptus, overruling any contrary reproductive choice, including selection abortion based on disability.

However, there is another way of coming at the issue of disabled bodies in heaven and the moral authority for selective abortion on earth. Which is to say, there is another way of understanding how God acts providentially and eschatologically. Emergence theory provides a lens.

An eschatology of budding emergence addresses bodies that die, affected fetal bodies included. Heaven's gates are open to all such liminal human beings who emerge in the hereafter. Their cellular matter passes over the threshold from death to new life, carrying the marks of their disability. These emergent resurrected beings are welcomed by God as such.

The womb and its working have long proven difficult to theologize. The male gaze and the myth of maternal instinct encumber theological insight. Emergence theology's focus on actual bodies displays pregnancy's unique, intimate, and vulnerable entwinement. Two emergent bodies but only one moral agent. The numbers do not add up, and God knows it. However the conception came about, the pregnant person must make all the decisions for them both. Her moral responsibility is immense. Precarity prowls around her swollen ankles.

Miscarriage or uneventful birth, lethal anomaly or robust newborn—no pregnant person ever knows what lies ahead. God confers on each pregnant person a unique embodied agency but reveals barely a fig of what any particular pregnancy or pregnancy outcome means morally. The believer turns to God's word for guidance, but attempting to discern God's will for pregnancy is like entering a shadowy hall of mirrors. Theodicy skulks in the dark corners.

Something else also moves in the dimness of divine silence. Moral reasoning lifts its head. Lacking a transcendent God's-eye view, moral reasoning sniffs among the shadows for the scent of the good, the spores of righteousness. Ethical judgment tries to flush out a good answer amid uncertainty. The good that emerges is not always beautiful. The lesser of two evils may be the quarry moral reasoning carries home from the hunt.

Christian theology inflects this human reasoning process with pneumatology. God so loved the creature's moral agency that God sent the Paraclete. The Holy Spirit speaks to the heart of the believer with sighs "too deep for words" (Rom 8:26). An emergence theology sees no way through the moral maze of pregnancy decision-making other than Spirit-guided choice. Faith in God's everlasting regard for unborn beings and for pregnant people's agency charts a path for moral understanding. The value of emerging unborn life and the value of the believer's agency—never one without the other. Together, these values underscore the divine affirmation of emergent life and serve as an antidote to patriarchy's deeply engrained suspicions about pregnant women's ethical gravitas and spiritual authority.[8]

## Disabilities and Bodily Resurrection

Prodisability theologies diverge on the nature of heavenly existence, with the afterlife seen in two mutually exclusive ways. Either all disabilities and diseases will be eliminated, or bodies will retain the marks of their disabilities, just as Jesus rose with his scarred hands. This elimination/retention debate has stalled. In addition, both models hit a wall on the question of bodily resurrection because of their dependence on a soul-based anthropology. A budding emergence approach offers a better prodisability vision of the afterlife beyond the stalemate of elimination versus retention.

A Thomistic elimination viewpoint invokes Aquinas's hylomorphic view of the person. The immaterial soul survives death but retains a "natural inclination to be united to the [glorified resurrected] body." Affirming a healed resurrected body does not entail "pejorative" implications about disabled persons.[9] One's essential self resides in "the *esse* of the soul."[10] Disabilities, technically, constitute a "privation" or an accidental property of the person; they are not "directly willed" by God.[11] Complete healing will occur in heaven not because disabilities are flaws God wishes to eliminate but because resurrected existence means arriving at one's "true homeland freed from all limitations of the fallen world."[12]

This elimination model speaks especially to those parents or siblings caring for someone with a disability and who hope for a better life for their loved one in the hereafter. One can affirm in a prodisability way that one's disabled child is created in the image of God while still "at the same time grieve what he cannot do."[13] The differently abled ways in which some people live can be affirmed, even while recognizing that many opportunities for flourishing are cut off because of physical and mental limitations.[14] It would be enough if disabled persons held the memory of their disability on earth while they enjoy their glorified bodies in heaven.[15] People with severe intellectual disabilities "must be healed in heaven," or communion with God has no apparent meaning.[16]

However, an elimination position might have potentially negative, ableist implications for persons living with disabilities. The notion of healed resurrected bodies "threatens the continuity between their present identities and that of their resurrected bodies."[17] Heaven, seen as an Edenic place with perfect bodies and minds, does not take seriously the self-understanding of many disabled persons. A child with an intellectual disability asks her parents, "Will I be retarded when I get to heaven?" When they answer no, she then asks, "But how will you know me then?"[18]

A retention-oriented disability theology affirms that one cannot "eradicate the disability without eliminating the person."[19] Disability theologian Nancy Eiesland insisted that if she were to enter heaven purged of her degenerative disability, "I would be absolutely unknown to myself and perhaps to God."[20] A retention model contends that the disabled in heaven should be thought of as retaining many, perhaps all, of their identity-marking conditions but without suffering and without impediment to their enjoyment of God.

Disability theologies probe new imaginaries. Some scholars search for how to theorize heaven populated by both healed and disabled resurrected bodies.[21] Others pivot away from eschatology and focus on the life on earth that affirms and includes disabled persons.[22] Living with and caring for a disabled family member "can proceed quite well without knowing what he will look like in heaven."[23]

Feminist disability theologies reject both a romanticized view of disabilities in heaven and visions of "compulsory able-bodied Edenic restoration." These theologies reframe eschatology in terms of the "perfection of mutual care, interdependence, and vulnerability."[24] This type of reframing of eternal life can spark ethical responsiveness in the present context. That said, frames are not resurrected, bodies are. Visions of a heavenly future rest on theological anthropological assumptions about the materiality of bodies crossing the threshold of death. This aspect of the puzzle remains largely unaddressed in disability eschatologies, in part because of their dependence on the soul.

Both retention and elimination views assert the centrality of the soul for identity continuity into the afterlife.[25] "The soul remains in relationship with God when our brains deteriorate" or are otherwise impaired.[26] Appealing to the soul grounds the claim that people retain spiritual responsiveness when injury or ageing affects brain capacity. A soul-based eschatology seems at first glance promising for conceptualizing postmortem identity continuity for disabled persons. Upon closer examination, however, it presents a now-familiar conceptual problem. Namely—why a soul already experiencing God in heaven would need to be reunited with its body. Disability theologians see the conundrum. Take the case of infants who die with severe brain incapacities such as microencephaly. Even the retention model recognizes that child's need for a "glorious and powerful resurrection body" with a brain healed to the point of being able at least to perceive God's presence.[27]

Budding emergence takes seriously the materiality of disabled bodies, including unborn ones. Human life emerges in a long gestational process within the body of a woman who faces dangers on all sides. Unborn beings know nothing of that. Their cells divide and bones fuse. Anomalies sometimes emerge. When an affected unborn being dies, the God of emergence enables its microscopic particles to cross over the threshold of death—with chromosomal variants intact. Divine grace acts upon the last seeds of fetal cellular life that emerge as a resurrected body.

Retention and elimination are compatible with an emergence model. Disabled persons emerge into the afterlife, affirmed and recognizable to themselves and others.[28] A person with Down syndrome emerges in the afterlife with a spiritual body marked in some way by trisomy 21, but without suffering or stigma. Hence, retention. An embryo or a fetus affected with a condition incompatible with life is enabled to participate in budding emergent resurrection. Its body is graced with the ability to achieve homeostasis in the afterlife. Hence, elimination.[29]

It makes sense to think of the endless glorified existence toward which all resurrected persons emergently move as eventually reaching a satisfactory conclusion. One cannot theologically rule out the possibility that processes of growth and deepening beatitude will perfect all bodies and minds. The degree to which the God of emergence sees fit to change, mitigate, or heal any bodily imperfections or disabilities in the afterlife transcends the binary of retention or elimination.

The nature of ultimate human "imperishability" (1 Cor 15:53) has no description in Scripture or the creeds. Imperishable existence would have to be transformative. If corporeal individuality eventually disappears in an experience of a perfect union with the other saints and the divine, then any personal markers (disability, sexed identity, race) will also eventually fade away. Emergence can affirm (with the retention model) that disabilities are present in heaven. Emergence can also affirm (with the elimination model) that eternal life means eventually morphing into other glorified forms. Emergence can affirm—with eschatologies thinking outside the retention/elimination binary—that heaven will not erase but will deepen corporeal interdependence.[30]

## Virtuous Acts and Divine Providence

God wills for embryos and fetuses to be emergently resurrected. To say otherwise provokes a theodicy dilemma of why God would permit so many uterine beings afflicted with genetic anomalies to miscarry and disappear out of existence. It might seem that this view of divine providence designates a singular moral path for pregnancy. If God welcomes into the next life any fetus that dies prematurely, then *surely* God wills for every pregnant woman always to welcome her fetus into this world, no matter what her circumstances. However, faced with a deeper understanding of virtue and providence, this moral surety wobbles. An obligation to bring every being to birth need not and should not follow from the premise that embryos and fetuses are resurrected. Such a conclusion misunderstands pregnancy as a virtuous act and entails a theologically questionable notion of divine providence.

### Pregnancy and Virtue

Asserting God's regard for all uterine beings might motivate some Christian women to continue an unplanned pregnancy or to welcome the birth of a disabled child. There is no fault and much virtue in such actions. However, to take one woman's or even many women's virtuous efforts at mirroring heavenly divine hospitality and impose it as a moral requirement on all other pregnant women misunderstands virtue, in general, and the virtue of pregnancy, in particular.

Procreation is not a prima facie duty or a prioritized virtue for female bodied persons. Christians, except perhaps fundamentalist followers of the pronatalist Quiverfull movement,[31] do not take the biblical phrase "be fruitful and multiply" (Gen 1:28) literally as a divine command to have children. To mandate or encourage procreation or to remove or denigrate the exercise of reproductive control commodifies fertile bodies. Black feminist scholarship has driven home the horrors of forced impregnation and gestation during chattel slavery.[32]

Pregnant people and the emergent life they carry should be valued, but birthing is not a prima facie "value to be preserved."[33] Nor is having a baby the just deserts for having sex. Avid antiabortion positions recognize the nebulous morality of imposed pregnancy by trying to lessen the sting of pregnancy and birthing. Pregnancy is mansplained as a mere nine-month task, during which "some women report feeling even better than normal."[34] The physical risks of "mood swings, irritability, low libido, and weepiness" are manageable.[35] Apparently pregnancy constitutes no onerous burden, except perhaps for the husband who has to put up with his wife's crankiness. Far from being virtuous, pregnancy is a normal and relatively safe nine-month matter. Scientific studies and the testimony of postpartum people would beg to differ.[36] The biblical writers would give this view of easy pregnancy the side-eye.

The Bible speaks of pregnancy as fraught and often dangerous. God allowed pregnancy to become, after the fall (Gen 3:16), a precarious (and painful) corporeal reality for mother and baby. God's chosen people face miscarriage and barrenness (Exod 23:26).[37] Biblical wives afflicted with difficulty in conceiving are depicted as desperate for children. Sarah finally produces an heir by arranging a surrogacy relationship with Hagar (Genesis 16)—a mistress–slave relationship that disturbs womanist scholars to this day.[38] Rachel competes with her sister and fertile co-wife Leah to produce children for their husband Jacob, again with both wives resorting to the use of surrogacy. At one point Rachel begs Jacob, "Give me children, or I shall die!" (Gen 30:1). Ironically and tragically, when she finally conceives her second child, Benjamin, she dies in childbirth (Gen 35:16–19). Only in a few biblical pregnancies does God express a direct preference for a pregnancy outcome.[39]

There is little indication in the Christian tradition that these special callings of notable biblical fetuses should be universalized and seen as ontologically determinative.[40]

Pregnancy, itself a sui generis precarious bodily state, creates an opportunity for a particular type of virtuous act. Gestating a uterine being is a corporeal gift, a generous offer of intimate bodily hospitality.[41] An "extraordinary physical enmeshment," pregnancy pushes the envelope of self-giving to the limits.[42] The gestational sustaining of another life is a supererogatory act—but only when the pregnant person is allowed to consent.[43] The concept of virtue barely encompasses the physical reality of the risky bodily self-sacrifice of pregnancy and birthing.

The concept of virtue does, however, capture the interplay of goodness and uncertainty in pregnancy. Virtue acts to pursue a good in light of uncertainties or obstacles. Virtue results when someone is moved by grace to do the good.[44] The believer hopes to have chosen a good path, whose perfect end is known only to God. Because "even the very wise cannot see all ends," humans must exercise "epistemic humility" when decision-making in the midst of a morally complicated world.[45] In the absence of receiving a direct revelation from God (and even there, one should be circumspect), humans have to find their moral way in the world without knowing clearly what God's will is.

Epistemic humility should make anyone cautious about pronouncing on the relative virtue of one's neighbor's actions. Virtue can be a cudgel used to bring one's neighbor into line with a particular moral position. Disability theology notes how appeals to virtue and God's will get entangled in ways that harm:

> *It is one thing for an individual to come to accept his or her disability as the result of God's intentions . . . ; it is quite another for others to be told by well-meaning and able-bodied people that God has basically chosen to inflict their disabilities for God's own reasons.*[46]

Analogously, it would be one thing for me to forego selective abortion because I perceive giving birth as God's will and my own virtuous maternal calling. It would be quite another thing for me to tell other parents considering selective abortion what God's intention is for that affected fetus and their family. The pregnant person depends on their sense of God's will to sustain their decision either way.

Pregnancy is a virtuous act. One pregnant person is moved by grace to consent to it, amid physical demands, obstacles, and moral uncertainties. Another believer may be moved by grace not to birth her fetus with a genetic anomaly. This possibility cannot be ruled out as a virtuous act as well. Strict prolife morality sees only a narrow path with no morally justified detours: give birth to each and every baby. God's will, however, is not a one-way street.

## Providence and Human Finitude

The doctrine of providence has "fallen on hard times" in our modern world.[47] The definition given in the Heidelberg Catechism only partly rings true with many believers today:

> *God's providence is his almighty and ever present power,*
> *whereby . . . he still upholds heaven and earth and all*
> *creatures, and so governs them that leaf and blade, rain and*
> *drought, fruitful and barren years, food and drink, health*
> *and sickness, riches and poverty, indeed, all things, come to us*
> *not by chance but by his fatherly hand.[48]*

This cosmology strikes modern people as somewhat quaint. Much of what grows, dies, or prospers in our universe is governed by physical laws. Moreover, realities like climate change show that the human community is to blame for much of what goes wrong with leaf or blade, rain or drought. There is a disconnect between the catechism and modern science.

Christian faith depends upon the beneficence of God's providence. Theology thus faces the challenge of how to affirm divine care of creation without falling off of two equally unpalatable theological cliffs. One cliff sends theology tumbling toward a "superlatively able-bodied" divine being who asserts control over the universe.[49] This archaic cosmology attracts few modern believers. Another cliff descends into a Dostoevskian scenario where all is permitted. Even if there is a powerful and good God, no one can know the divine mind.[50] In the latter case, the crux of the issue is epistemological, and it is thorny.

Regarding a doctrine of providence, theology must not overstep its epistemological bounds. Discerning God's will entails knowing who God is. As the doctrine of God goes, so goes the doctrine of providence and vice versa. An emergence approach is epistemologically cautious about the divine. The God of emergence creates and sustains not by fiat but by the unseen enabling of emergent processes.

In the beginning was emergence. Sky and stars, time and tempests, wind and wing, seas and cities emerged. Immersed in the world's processes, God swirled unseen and immanent in the eddies of earth's ancient evolutions. Layer upon layer of goodness and evil evolved. The human world became a massive rock, striated with love, hate, tenderness, cruelty, and acts of mercy. Life continues to emerge, gulping for air, gulping for the breath of God.

The currents of human history pull at the hem of divine transcendence. God's garments are weighed down with the waters of human tears. The God of emergence does not impose providential power to reverse the whirlpool of human or natural cataclysms. The pious and the resolute hope for ultimate beneficence and divine power in the long arc toward justice.[51] In the meantime, befuddlement about God's providence pervades many prayers.

Nowhere is providence more perplexing than in pregnancy. Affirming the intrinsic goodness of lives developing in the womb is basic to a Christian ethos, but knowing God's providential will regarding their disposition and care is another matter altogether. All beings are bestowed with the goodness of existence, but God does not intervene to preserve all that is. Nor does God reveal what parts of God's good creation the creature should devote energies and resources to protect.

The biblical question "Who is my neighbor?" echoes through the ages. The vulnerable "Other becomes my neighbor precisely through the way the face summons me."[52] However, our neighbors are legion, and it is not possible to respond to every "face." Samaritanism regarding the needs of one's vulnerable neighbor stands in a tensive relationship with human finitude—a situation that is complicated even more by patriarchal, classist, and other inequities affecting those upon whom most of society's caretaking labors fall.

Feminist disability theology understands creaturely limits. Seeing limitedness as "unsurprising" and ubiquitous breaks down the binary of abled and disabled.[53] A "theology of limits" opens the door to a broader understanding of interdependent creaturely finitude. Bumping up against each other's limits and needs directs us away from equating the good with the perfect or the normal. God did not create a perfectly normal world but, rather, an emergent, impermanent, vulnerable, and mutually dependent one.[54] Accepting the reality of limits orients people to a realistic view of giving and accepting care.

Finite creatures, individually or together, cannot care for or maintain in existence all that is. God's justice would never require what is impossible. The biblical God has designated humans as stewards of a good and vulnerable creation—a recipe for both virtue and tragedy. Human acts of caring always take place under the conditions of the "ambiguities of an incomplete, open-ended world."[55] Uterine life is one of many goods about which the pregnant believer has to exercise moral discernment. In the real world, acts of valuing and preserving unborn beings are necessarily contingent, finite, and discretionary.

A strict prolife disability theology would not include selective abortion in the category of discretionary actions where there is epistemic uncertainty regarding God's will. If one claims that "*every* human in existence is good because they are *created by God exactly as they are*," then to arrest the development of an affected fetus would be directly to thwart God's will.[56] From this perspective, even trying to ascertain the presence of a genetic disability comes under suspicion of ableism.[57] Succumbing to extensive prenatal testing risks devaluing a fetus with a genetic anomaly.[58] A selective abortion amounts to a refusal to accept "a sign of benevolent divine involvement in human affairs" and God's providential intention for "human variation" in the species.[59]

The notion of God desiring variation in creation raises no theological red flags. Variation infuses an emergence metaphysics. However, implying that whatever happens in creation is God's will flirts with a problematic view of providence. Very little of God's providential will is revealed by the presence of HCG in a woman's urine.[60]

An Augustinian view of creation affirms that whatever is, is good.[61] The goodness of created being flows from a good Creator. However, applying this notion to disabilities—without an appropriate caveat—leads to theological distortions. "That a child born with, say, Tay-Sachs disease is good is for Christians beyond dispute; that it is good for a child to be born with this condition is a different question altogether."[62] Tay-Sachs is an emergent consequence of the joining of recessive genes from both biological parents. The love of God and the family encircle the child born with Tay-Sachs. Yet nothing of God's will is revealed when this genetic event happens.

Theology demurs at claiming that whatever is *is* God's will and counsels against asserting "too tight a fit between contingent events and the divine will."[63] To avoid the dubious theological move of linking God's will to biological events, theology asserts the inscrutability of providence. This idea of epistemic uncertainty in reproductive matters is not just some newfangled modern skepticism. In 1542 Protestant reformer Martin Luther (himself a husband and father) penned a perceptive and compassionate pastoral letter on miscarriage, writing, "We may not and cannot know the hidden counsel of God" regarding why "God did not allow the child to be born alive." Luther's point is not that one knows that the miscarriage was God's will but, rather, that one does not know God's will regarding pregnancy outcomes.[64]

Just as theology should not overstate the providential meaning of whatever has come to be, theology must take care not to overstate the revelatory function of whatever has come to be. A prodisability theology might claim that disabilities function as God's "revelatory annunciation."[65] Poetic language like this challenges believers to see marginalized persons with new, more compassionate eyes.[66] The suffering Other reveals the face of Christ. God's preferential love is bestowed on the poor and downtrodden. Yet theology should hesitate before suggesting, even poetically, that a disabled person, or the discovery of a disability through prenatal testing, serves to announce God's will.

The signs of God's providence are more "like a small rash: patchy, intrusive, and unpredictable."[67] The believer cannot know indubitably, or sometimes even plausibly, how any event or human action might advance the divine good and just plan. Belief in beneficent providence does not eliminate doubts about God's will; rather, belief in providence goes hand in hand with the unanswerable questions that arise in life. Even devout parents who accept *that* the disability of their newborn is God's will may also admit that they do not understand *why* God willed that child to have a disability.[68] The divinely intended path of any pregnancy remains shrouded. Epistemic uncertainty about providence opens the door for the work of the Holy Spirit.

## The Holy Spirit and Self-Trust

The Holy Spirit hovers over each emergent being, each swelling womb, each anxious expectant mother, each wailing infant. Prolife disability theology invokes the Spirit to foster acceptance and guide the understanding when parents discover that their newborn is affected by a disabling condition.[69] An emergence theological approach to pregnancy appeals to Spirit-guided understanding and self-trust not just after but also before birth when the outlines of uterine life and God's will are blurry.

## Self-Trust and Decision-Making

Significant parental decision-making happens during gestation. Pregnancy demands the day-to-day labor of micro and macro decisions. Prenatal testing can precipitate an agonizing medical and moral choice. Knowledge is power—and pain.[70] The facts and statistics offered by genetic counselors inform but cannot determine moral choice.[71] Self-doubt and antidisability bias prevent parents from making a courageous choice to trust God and welcome a disabled child into their family. Self-doubt and antiabortion stigma prevent pregnant people from trusting God and their own moral competence. When the voice of providence is undetectable, the pregnant person must take steps, even if her willpower wobbles. Decisions about her pregnancy rest on her shoulders, even though the world has not always seen women as competent moral agents.

In the long (mostly male) history of philosophy, the moral agent was defined as rational, autonomous, and endowed with free will. Feminist philosophy rebuts those definitions because they inadequately take into account human relationality, embodiment, and societal power imbalances.[72] Longstanding feminist arguments for reproductive rights invoke principles of bodily autonomy, the right to consent, and equal protection under the law.[73] However, these rights have no traction if women lack the capacity to enact moral agency. To be an agent requires self-trust.

Self-trust is a necessary but fragile aspect in reproductive decision-making. The embodied aspects of pregnancy and birthing render women vulnerable in various medical, psychic, economic, corporeal, and other ways. Feminism calls on women "to stand up for our own interests" and cultivate "an attitude of optimism about our own competence."[74] Self-trust develops in someone who is supported to think and act as a moral agent.[75] Often mistaken for solipsism, libertarianism, or Enlightenment individualism, self-trust grows relationally in a "nonoppressive social environment that builds or fosters autonomy skills."[76] It takes a village to build self-trusting agents.

The zeitgeist in North America regarding abortion, however, is not conducive to fostering women's self-trust. In a society marked by pervasive sexist attitudes, "trusting women to make good decisions for themselves and their families is a hard sell."[77] Trust erodes even more as racism paints women of color as "sexually promiscuous" and "bad mothers" and ableism paints disabled mothers as inadequate.[78] Women are expected to justify their reproductive decisions in the court of supposed revealed or natural moral law. The deck is stacked against them.

Self-trust battles the bias that pregnant people are inept or morally untrustworthy. In pregnancy, moral complexities loom. The reality of an unborn being living in and dependent on the body of a born person is as morally complex as things come. Neither God nor even the best medical science promises easy conception, carefree gestation, painless birth, live baby, or healthy mother. Maternity tugs uninvited at heartstrings, and adoption is unimaginable.[79] Good outcomes are hard to predict and impossible to ensure. Mystery shrouds pregnancy, obscuring God's benevolence.

The corollary to a willingness to accept the mystery of God's counsel is the willingness to trust one's fellow believers to "live 'wisely in the darkness.'"[80] Self-trust for the pregnant person is not a fast track to self-evidently good or divinely ordained outcomes. Self-trust only disposes the agent toward decision-making that she hopes will maximize the good. The good is not always the beautiful.

Choosing may come from the gut, as when a woman blurts out, "I can't have this baby!" In this cry, she articulates her own assessment (however it is arrived at) that she lacks the resources, will, or desire required to go through with that pregnancy and mother that child well. There may very well be disability biases or less-than-saintly motives mixed in with her other supposedly valid reasons. Indeed, if she does harbor negative views about disability, then she has competently determined that she is not a good candidate to gestate and raise a disabled child. A prodisability ethics wishes she would just "rise cheerfully to the occasion," show some backbone, or do her duty.[81] However, one cannot say she is exhibiting a "defect of judgment" regarding her mothering situation.[82] The opposite is the case. A decision for selective abortion arises from her assessment of her own situation and capacities. Such a decision instantiates self-trust within a "theology of limits" and the obscurity of divine providence.[83]

## Stigma and the Spirit

Societal attitudes about disabled people need to change. Countries with almost universal prenatal testing have high selective abortion rates for conditions like Down syndrome.[84] With noninvasive prenatal testing techniques (NIPT), fetal anomalies can be screened for as early as the tenth week of pregnancy with a high rate of accuracy for detecting the risk of Down syndrome.[85] This technological advance causes pro-disability advocates to claim that NIPT will increase selective abortion rates.[86]

Disability stigma is real, even when unintended. This dynamic, termed expressivism, means that disability bias inundates and is expressed in societal attitudes and structures—even when there is no intention to promote this bias. The widespread use of prenatal testing may privilege so-called normal, fully functioning bodies over those requiring certain types of care.[87] Selective abortion may express and propagate a eugenicist attitude, even if the parents choosing this option in their private family life have good personal reasons and the best of intentions.[88] The very act of aborting an affected fetus may contribute culturally to marking disabled persons as not worthy to have been born. At the extreme are claims that prenatal screening technologies contribute, in effect, to eliminating disabled populations[89] and even steepen a slippery slope to "infanticide and euthanasia" of born children.[90]

Misogyny is also real. To say that a woman who terminates a pregnancy because of a detected disability is locked in "sinful routines of self-isolation" is misogyny talking in religious terms.[91] To say that prenatal testing "presents mothers with a bewildering set of social pressures" condescends.[92] This viewpoint replays old sexist patterns of assuming that too much information bewilders women, who are somehow cognitively or morally incapable of processing complex information when managing their reproductive and mothering responsibilities. A paternalistic distrust is woven into laws requiring women to jump through various restrictive hoops before they are allowed, if at all, to terminate a pregnancy.[93]

Declaring abortion to be an immoral, antimaternal, or selfish act injures pregnant women who have had or even are considering having an abortion. Speaking disparagingly about pregnancy termination expresses a message to all pregnant women: I do not recognize *your* sense of your own precarity; I only recognize the precarity of your fetus and *my* sense of your obligation to that fetus. This "misrecognition is more than misunderstanding; it entails a moral injury," which may also threaten a woman's health and possibly her life.[94]

A commitment to self-care, self-trust, and an acceptance of one's parenting limits are not sins of selfishness or signs of moral incompetence. A selective abortion may be sad or even tragic, but that does not mean it was not an ethical act of a reliably competent moral agent. Deciding whether or not to gestate a fetus diagnosed with a disability inevitably entails trying to envision that fetus as one's actual future child with particular care needs. Prolife disability extremism mobilizes this thought process in order to assert a moral equivalency between affected fetuses and born disabled children. This kind of equivalence leads to spurious and cruel claims that a decision to abort an affected fetus is the same as deciding to "kill their toddler if they learn that she will be less intellectually capable than other children."[95] Filicide rhetoric stigmatizes families who selectively aborted or whose affected fetus died unexpectedly. This rhetoric demeans families who do decide to raise a disabled child out of love, not fear of a murder charge.

Anecdotal accounts provided by parents lovingly and gratefully raising a disabled child are importance sources. Data-driven studies document high levels of satisfaction among parents raising a disabled child.[96] Nevertheless, to mandate, coerce, or even coax a woman to birth a child she does not want, including when there is a disability—these acts should instill moral horror. A birthing mandate is neither a practical nor an ethical way of rooting out the stigma in societal attitudes on disability.[97]

Studies of couples facing prenatal testing show how seriously they grapple with their responsibilities and options after genetic testing.[98] Women voice gratitude for their born disabled child, but when asked hypothetically about future pregnancies, they say they wish to avoid any future pregnancy.[99] One woman with a Down syndrome child said she would not abort if she received another such diagnosis because, in her words, "I know now that having a child with a disability wasn't all bad."[100] Nevertheless, she planned not to have any more children in order not to face that decision in actuality.

Few women approach an abortion decision blithely or think that they have done something trivial in ending a life that was developing within their own body.[101] It does not make theological or moral sense to ascribe to women—especially the believing women who have selective abortions—unholy motives of "refus[ing] to praise the Trinitarian Creator for fertility and new life."[102] Christian women say "they 'turned to' prayer for guidance" before their abortion.[103] In one study, the factor that most influenced women in making their decision to have a Down syndrome child was listening to their "inner voice."[104] High value is set on the freedom to make "reproductive choices with conscience and faith as our guides, without having to also negotiate laws."[105]

People of faith meet the silence of God with prayer. They trust the whisperings of their own heart. They exercise "pneumatological imagination." That is, they attempt "to seek out, listen to, and discern the presence and activity of the Holy Spirit."[106]

A key feature of pneumatological imagination is its performativity: not just knowing but doing.[107] Reproductive discernment, by definition, entails intensive and intimate corporeal actions: either committing to the responsibilities and risks of pregnancy, birthing, and, most likely, childrearing; or preventing a being from coming into the world "to whom such questions of parental responsibility and emotional attachment" would apply.[108] Disability theology has pneumatology wrong when it suggests that deciding not to birth a disabled child displays an "*atrophied pneumatology*" born of a "*sinful attraction to the promise of an easier life.*"[109] How and where God sends the Holy Spirit into the world and for what purpose remains a mystery. One cannot rule out that a pregnant believer's self-assessment regarding her selective abortion is Spirit-guided. A robust pneumatology (Acts 2:17–18) implies that the Spirit *is* at work in her life, fostering self-trust, honing her mind, and helping her to discern the good.

This pneumatology rejects the "transcendent omnipotence of Spirit" that heals and reveals all from afar.[110] The Spirit does not remain safely ensconced in the perfect love of the trinitarian divine communion. The Spirit moves in and among human brokenness and pain and operates under cover of human frailty. Not triumphal and distant, the Spirit journeys alongside humanity "limping and unhinged."[111] Clinging to the Spirit, the creature limps.

The church prays for God to pour out the Spirit. However, being filled with the Holy Spirit does not necessarily mean the tongues of angels but also the tired sigh of the mother sitting at her kitchen table after a long day of work. She and her children survived to face another day. Women, people of color, the poor, and marginalized groups value survival as a moral, even biblical virtue.[112] Approbation of survival engrafts self-trust onto the pregnant person weighed down with society's stigma and injustice. Those who have had an abortion await the church to hear the Spirit's call to trust those who choose to survive.

• • •

An eschatology of budding emergence and the mystery of God's providence form the basis for valuing disabled fetal life as well as affirming women's reproductive moral agency. Severely disabled uterine bodies rarely see the light of day. Heaven is open to these unborn beings who are welcomed by God. Embryonic or fetal value is not grounded in a principle of the right to life or being declared an ensouled person but, rather, in a God-given eschatological destiny.

Danger hovers around pregnant bodies. God seems to hover far away. Both realities disturb and frustrate moral decision-making for the pregnant believer. The degree to which theology absorbs the reality of pregnancy as precarious will determine the clarity of theology's recognition of the virtue of pregnancy in light of God's silence. Virtue is the child of epistemic uncertainty regarding God's providence.

God has deigned not to reveal—with very few biblical exceptions—the divine plan for each being that comes into existence in the womb. For whatever unknowable reasons, the Creator allows many embryos to be affected by lethal anomalies and allows pregnancy and birthing to be risky events. The God of emergence leaves wombs in moral dimness. The lack of pristine moral clarity about reproductive decisions cannot simply be attributed to human ignorance, finitude, or sinfulness. Moral uncertainty is a factor of the complexity and demands of pregnancy and birthing in a fallen world. The obscurity of divine providence does not nullify women's reproductive agency but rather requires it.

The Spirit blows over the dark waters of epistemic reticence and moral ambiguity. Sexism and paternalism paint the woman who decides not to give birth to a disabled child as incompetent, selfish, and stubbornly refusing to trust in God. A theology of limits counsels us to recognize human finitude and to value women's acts of survival. Pneumatology insists that the Spirit speaks to complex moral decision-making. Pregnant women can be trusted to listen. The believer's moral agency is not primarily grounded in the secular principle of her right to choose or to bodily integrity but in being Spirit-filled. God's enabling of a pregnant woman's pneumatological imagination is what constitutes the spiritual basis for her self-trust and moral authority.

That one is not able to see how God's will can encompass both Spirit-guided reproductive choice and the welcoming of fetuses into

heaven is a factor of seeing "through a glass, darkly."[113] That epistemological limitation, however, should not be leveraged to stigmatize or
impede the exercise of a pregnant person's moral agency. The Spirit's
comings and goings are veiled. No one should pronounce that they
know the signs of God's will for their neighbor's uterus.

Every born child should be welcomed into the loving arms of
parents, family, and community. Every woman who experiences an
ended pregnancy—whether in the form of a miscarriage tragedy that
befalls her or her own reproductive choice—deserves to be consoled
and supported, not brought low with words of mistrust and condemnation. She deserves a Pentecost of self-trust.

Christian theology has always struggled to recognize the complicated interconnectedness of eschatological hope, reproductive endings, fetal value, disability ethics, and women's reproductive agency.
No wonder. At the very heart of coming to terms with these inter-
connected realities and experiences lies the nature of God. A God of
emergence does not imprint an indubitable divine plan onto the minds
of certain rightly guided church leaders. The Creator's will manifests
ambiguously in the creature's tentative, messy, but earnest attempts
at virtue. Grace perfects nature, but in infinitesimal ways. The God
of emergence coaxes the truth and rejoices when the creature has the
courage to self-trust and attempt the good.

The Spirit blows with ubiquity; the epistemically reticent crane
their necks to catch a glimpse. Emergence offers a glimpse of divine
truth: bodies can be resurrected without souls. Unborn beings are valued by God and will participate in bodily resurrection. Pregnancy is
a virtue because of its precarity. Forced pregnancy is a moral outrage.
Spirit-guided moral agency is the birthright of all people. These truths
are but seeds, pressed into the soil of the theological mind, with the
hope that they will spring up green.

# CONCLUSION

DOCTRINE MATTERS. IT matters, not more than the lived experience of the community of believers, but because the deposit of faith is like a caged wild thing. One should not turn one's back to it. Faith seeking to understand this wild thing is dangerous business. Someone has to do it. The resurrection of the body is a particularly unpredictable doctrine. It hovers over the "bloody act" at Golgotha.[1] Resurrection looks to the heavens, promising light and life, but blood drips from its talons. Theology, like a falconer, needs gloves when handling the resurrection.

Pregnant bodies matter. In pregnancy, a human life emerges, dependent on the body of its gestating mother who must negotiate her place in a society that does not recognize her value or needs. Precarity dogs them both. Faith seeks to understand reproductive vulnerability. Theology too often gets it wrong.

Theology confuses the blood of crucifixion with the blood of giving birth, as if both are divinely required forms of sacrifice—one from a God-Man, one from womankind. "This is my body," says Jesus to the disciples. Women are supposed to read from the same script. Their assent to a "burdensome pregnancy" becomes a eucharistic and cruciform sacrifice in kind.[2] The gory events of the cross or birthing-gone-wrong are palatable because the story will always have an ultimate happy ending: resurrection. The resurrection, however, is not a divine clean-up operation. Theology should explain why not, by clarifying what is at stake when pronouncing on the meaning of pregnancy, unborn life, death, and the afterlife.

## What Is at Stake

Women die from pregnancy. Maternal mortality has not disappeared, even in the developed world. Even before the repeal of *Roe v. Wade*, the rate of women dying from pregnancy and birthing was on an alarming rise.[3] Pregnant women of color in the US die from pregnancy and birthing complications at a rate four to five times higher than white women.[4] The well-being and the lives of pregnant persons are at stake during pregnancy. God mourns these women's deaths, most of them preventable. The Paraclete is sent to whisper a warning to each pregnant person: take care, for you are now sheep among wolves.

Pregnancies fail—often. Early pregnancy loss happens at a higher rate than ob/gyns reveal to their anxious patients. Researchers conservatively estimate that 30 percent of embryos die unnoticed prior to implanting in the uterus, and another 30 percent expire after implantation.[5] After age twenty-five, miscarriages "are the norm rather than the exception."[6] God mourns these tiny beings, like so many sparrows falling to the ground. Their limp weightlessness is beloved by God. Personhood has nothing to do with it. God cradles each tiny clump of humanity and wills its emergent resurrection.

Feminists say that God holds these deaths, and the women who mourn them, within the compassionate arms of a trinitarian embrace.[7] But on the question of why these deaths happen—the Trinity is keeping its own counsel. The silence of God and the precarity of pregnancy throw decision-making onto the pregnant woman's shoulders. She has no choice but to choose. Hers is the corporeal labor, hers the weighty moral authority.

Patriarchy and demonarchy have never accepted this reality but, instead, granted to fathers and masters ownership over their progeny.[8] The law of the father tramples underfoot the reproductive agency of women. Yet still they rise.[9] Fierce in their self-knowledge, wise as serpents, pregnant believers lay claim to God's guidance on their journey toward procreation or not, birthing or not, mothering or not. Women read with uncanny accuracy the signs of what lies ahead for each birth, each armful at the breast. Maids or matrons, slave or free, poor or rich, cisgender or genderqueer, they have always made in their heart of hearts the solemn choice about conferring or denying life—whether they have been allowed to implement that choice or not. When the choices of pregnant people are thwarted, their hearts are pierced.

Theology may think that dilemmas of ethics and politics can be avoided by retreating to the safety of doctrinal reflection. The resurrection, however, will not go gently into that good night of dogmatic domestication.[10] Theology will need to wrestle it to the ground and risk being pinned. Such a contest of faith seeking understanding is not for the faint of heart. Doctrinal construction means holding on and letting go.

## Holding On and Letting Go

Constructive theology does not abandon ship. It holds on to the *regula fidei* of the tradition and cuts loose worn concepts. The notion that doctrine changes while maintaining continuity can be called a development[11] or a regulative grammar[12] or faith seeking understanding in new contexts.[13] Whatever the name, the notion implies that new thinking, questioning, and debates are possible while maintaining a connection to the tradition's historical norms.

This work of doctrinal reconstruction is a delicate mining operation. It is faith seeking understanding deep into the tradition's mother lode. Belief in the resurrection of the body is an important vein theology has mined these many years. This core Christian belief sparkles in scriptural stories of an empty tomb, the dead rising from their sick beds, visions of ascension, the sounds of trumpets, the New Jerusalem. But all that glitters is not gold. Resurrection belief has only ever been mixed with glittery conceptual impurities and contradictions. Clear away this dross, and the bare creed remains: "Christ has been raised from the dead, the first fruits of those who have died" (1 Cor 15:20). This verse designates a way of thinking about dying and rising: death is real, but it will be overcome. Theology holds on to this doctrinal nugget and lets go of the dross.

The concept that tarnishes Christian belief is the soul. In the normative tradition, the soul has ever had but one ultimate goal: to pacify bodies. Promising heaven, the soul entices bodies to the pews, to their hymns and hallelujahs. Threatening hell, the soul brings bodies to their knees, penitent. Little did the faithful know that in buying into the soul-body hierarchy, the real essence of their humanity was leaching away. The poets know this. A person is not a soul; persons are bodies. That is their God-given pathos.

Poems of the afterlife show the pathos of souls without bodies. Virgil's Aeneas, traveling through the underworld, finds his beloved deceased father in the Elysium Fields. Overcome, he tries three times to embrace him, but his father's shade, "vainly clasped, fled from his hands, even as light winds, and most like a winged dream."[14] The same failed embrace occurs in the *Divine Comedy*. As the pilgrim exits the darkness of hell, he sees his dear friend, the poet Casella, who welcomes him into the light of purgatory. But their joy of meeting can have no physical expression. The flesh-and-blood pilgrim cries out, "O shades—in all except appearance—empty! Three times I clasped my hands behind him."[15] Like one hand clapping, no flesh touches flesh. Virgil's and Dante's verses capture the pathos of loss through the trope of never again feeling the warm solidity of the beloved's body.

The immaterial soul of substance dualism and hylomorphism is without pathos. This soul has no soul. It peddles an eschatology only slightly more sophisticated than Hollywood. In some ways, it is slightly less sophisticated, since the soul of this retrograde Christian spirituality renders bodies superfluous. The soul ignores, because not essential to personhood, the vulnerabilities of bodies. How they succumb to shame, trauma, and vanity; how they strive to make a noble gesture; how they drown helpless in love's deep waters. In truth, humanity's vulnerabilities are where the Spirit enfolds itself into the human condition. Virgil and Dante wrote of shades because they understood the body's frailty and necessity.

Those who do not heed the poets can find the same message in materialist and feminist thought. Materialist philosophy cuts personhood free from the decrepit and deceptive moorings of the

immaterial soul. It's the body, stupid.[16] Feminist theologies wage gue-
rilla warfare, blowing up heteronormatively sexy personhood, ruled
by the soul as superego. From the ashes of these explosions arise new
subjectivities, genders, desires, and bodies—even the earth as God's
body.[17] Soul-based views of the person lead theologies like lemmings
ever closer to a doctrinal precipice of irrelevance and injustice. For
too long theology has thrown its arms around the soul and come up
empty. Let it go.

The soul is a drag on bodily resurrection. Church history and
popular piety have long told the story that at death, one's soul survives
disembodied. But the question of why a soul in heavenly bliss would
need to be reunited with its body—especially a fetal or disabled one—
stops soul defenders in their tracks. Darling of Greco-Roman philosophy, interloper to Second Temple Judaism, the immaterial soul turns
out to be a theological cul-de-sac. Let it go.

A doctrine of the resurrection of uterine bodies is an orphan
looking for a theological dwelling place. Fetal or embryonic resurrection needs more bodily heft than what substance dualism or Thomism
can provide. It needs more time and space for growth and organic
change than what materialist philosophy envisions. Resurrection takes
time. Bodies are slow, fickle, and mistimed things. Poets know this.
Some bodies might reach heaven in "the uncertain hour before the
morning," others "in May, with voluptuary sweetness," and still others
"at night like a broken king."[18]

Sometimes the apostle Paul waxed poetic about the resurrection, writing "to each kind of seed its own body" (1 Cor 15:38). The
image inspired medieval friars and abbesses who found the truth of the
resurrection buried in the metaphor of sprouting grain. The mystics
saw everything, including resurrection, encompassed in "a littil thing,
the quantitye of an hesil nutt in the palme of my hand."[19] Emergence
understands the hazel nut. Emergence understands the potentiality of
small beginnings, the dynamism of organic growth, the burgeoning of
new life. The nut holds not a soul but more nut.

Resurrection is not the soul rising like a ghostly mist from the corpse. Let that cinematic image go. Emergence drops a new idea into theology's palm. God carries the cellular matter of the just-deceased person over the threshold of death, and out of these seeds, a slow blooming resurrection.

Emergent resurrection is not old but new. It fits in a modern age of embryological science that knows a conceptus is not some kind of soulish homunculus. Emergence makes sense in light of the science of twilight death. This approach to resurrection affirms how the material relationality between the mother and fetus is never completely severed, according to the science of microchimerism.[20]

Emergent resurrection is not new but old. Emergence attends to, while redirecting, Augustine's still-haunting question about whether there be in heaven "souls without bodies though they once had them,—only in their mother's womb."[21] Emergence directs attention away from souls and toward emergent mind-body processes. This ontology allows theology to let go of the soul and embrace emergent resurrection. The embrace is speculative but not empty.

Emergence echoes ancient traditions, such as this eschatological vision of an obscure fourth-century theologian:

> One who dies in the womb of his mother and never comes
> to life, will be quickened at the moment [of the resurrection]
> by [Christ] who quickens the dead; he will then be brought
> forth as an adult. If a woman dies while pregnant, and
> the child in her womb dies with her, that child will at the
> resurrection grow up and know its mother; and she will
> know her child.[22]

This extraordinary passage indicates, at the very least, the fruitfulness of thinking of the resurrection of the body as a dynamic process. Women throughout the centuries nurtured an unruly desire to hope in a God who resurrects after death in the womb. But after so much spiritual travail, they are wary of toxic promises of the afterlife. An emergence doctrine of resurrection offers a model upon which such wild hope can rest.

For some pregnant people, survival and self-care mean terminating a pregnancy. Abortion ends a unique type of relationality. How that ended relationship might or might not be taken up again in the hereafter is something many believing women think about after miscarriage or abortion. If emergently budding resurrection turns out to be a reality, then that fetus's and that woman's stories (which were for a period of days, weeks, or maybe even months intertwined) will be taken up into divine communion after death. If God does return storied identities to the emergently resurrected bodies of fetuses and their mothers, there will be no recrimination, guilt, or sorrow but acceptance and a peace that "surpasses all understanding" (Phil 4:7). If theology dares to wrestle with this resurrection, then there is hope that bodies holding bodies in heaven will be more than a winged dream.

# NOTES

## Introduction

1 "Flowers" was a euphemism for menstruation. Some emmenagogues may have been used as abortifacients. Sara Read, *Menstruation and the Female Body in Early Modern England* (New York: Palgrave Macmillan, 2013), 24–25. Menstruation, pregnancy, and birthing also happen in bodies of those who do not self-identify as female or as a woman. My use of terms such as *female* and *woman* indicates my focus on the role and status of persons deemed as such in traditional Christian discourses.

2 Pew Research Center, "Belief in Heaven" (2015), https://tinyurl.com/bdcrc7y8.

3 Trenton Merricks, "The Resurrection of the Body," in *The Oxford Handbook of Philosophical Theology*, ed. Thomas P. Flint and Michael C. Rea (New York: Oxford University Press, 2009), 482.

4 See "Why a Body in a Resurrection?," *Closer to Truth*, created by Robert Lawrence Kuhn, season 14, episode 1407 (2015), https://tinyurl.com/yc7dd7ru.

5 Jeff McMahan, *The Ethics of Killing: Problems at the Margins of Life* (New York: Oxford University Press, 2002), 26.

6 John F. MacArthur, *Safe in the Arms of God: Truth from Heaven about the Death of a Child* (Nashville: Thomas Nelson, 2003), 99.

7 For some helpful introductions to the issues see Ted Peters, Robert John Russell, and Michael Welker, eds., *Resurrection: Theological and Scientific Assessments* (Grand Rapids: Eerdmans, 2002); Georg Gasser, ed., *Personal Identity and Resurrection* (Burlington, VT: Ashgate, 2016); Jerry L. Walls, ed., *The Oxford Handbook of Eschatology* (New York: Oxford University Press, 2007).

8 H. L. Mencken quoted in McMahan, *The Ethics of Killing*, 10–11.

9 Helen Keane, "Foetal Personhood and Representations of the Absent Child in Pregnancy Loss Memorialization," *Feminist Theory* 10, no. 2 (2009): 163.

10 Keith Ward, "Bishop Berkeley's Castle: John Polkinghorne on the Soul," in *God and the Scientist: Exploring the Work of John Polkinghorne*, ed. Fraser Watts and Christopher C. Knight (London: Ashgate/Routledge, 2012), 129.

11 "No more shall there be in it an infant that lives but a few days" (Isa 65:20).

12 For an account that claims a univocal prolife early church, see Michael J. Gorman, *Abortion and the Early Church: Christian, Jewish and Pagan Attitudes in the Greco-Roman World* (Eugene, OR: Wipf and Stock, 1998), 50–51. For a critique of this position, see Margaret D. Kamitsuka, *Abortion and the Christian Tradition: A Pro-choice Theological Ethic* (Louisville: Westminster John Knox, 2019), ch. 1.

13 The Vatican finally issued a theological commission's statement approving the "strong grounds for hope" regarding unbaptized infant salvation. International Theological Commission, "The Hope of Salvation for Infants Who Die without Being Baptized," the Vatican, January 19, 2007, §103, https://tinyurl.com/3anx6mhy.

14 Augustine, *Enchiridion*, 23.85, in *Confessions and Enchiridion*, trans. Albert C. Outler (Philadelphia: Westminster, 1955), 275.

15 Zubin Mistry, *Abortion in the Early Middle Ages, c. 500–900* (Woodbridge, Suffolk, UK: York Medieval, 2015), 267. *Abortivi* (Latin plural of *abortivus*) included "the stillborn infant, the fetus dead in the womb, the premature newborn, the product of abortion (deliberate or otherwise)" (265).

16 The condemnation was as much if not more directed to the sexual sin that produced the unwanted pregnancy. Beverly Wildung Harrison, *Our Right to Choose: Toward a New Ethic of Abortion* (Boston: Beacon, 1983), esp. ch. 5.

17 Theresa Bonopartis, "The Souls of Aborted Babies and the 'Hope' of Heaven," *Reclaiming Our Children* (blog), November 2, 2018, https://tinyurl.com/3anx6mhy.

18 Tina Beattie, *God's Mother, Eve's Advocate* (New York: Continuum, 2002).

19 Karen O'Donnell, *The Dark Womb: Re-Conceiving Theology through Reproductive Loss* (London: SCM, 2022), 115.

20 Grace Ji-Sun Kim and Hilda P. Koster, eds., *Planetary Solidarity: Global Women's Voices on Christian Doctrine and Climate Justice* (Minneapolis: Fortress, 2017).

21 International Theological Commission, "The Hope of Salvation for Infants."

22 Hans W. Frei, "The 'Literal Reading' of Biblical Narrative in the Christian Tradition: Does It Stretch or Will It Break?," in *The Bible and the Narrative Tradition*, ed. Frank McConnell (New York: Oxford University Press, 1986), 72. Frei wrote of the "realistic or history-like quality" of the crucifixion-resurrection narratives in *The Identity of Jesus Christ: The Hermeneutical Bases of Dogmatic Theology* (Philadelphia: Fortress, 1975), 143.

## 1. Leveraging Heaven When a Pregnancy Ends

1 Karen O'Donnell, "Theology and Reproductive Loss," *Modern Believing* 60, no. 2 (2019): 126. See also Susan Bigelow Reynolds, "From the Site of the Empty Tomb: Approaching the Hidden Grief of Prenatal Loss," *New Theology Review: An American Catholic Journal for Ministry* 28, no. 2 (2016): 51–52.

2 I reiterate that I am mostly using terms such as *female* and *woman* because of my focus on the construction of persons deemed as such in traditional Christian discourses. Some of my analyses may be relevant to the research of nongender binary and transmen scholars of religion writing on reproductive issues.

3 Judith Butler, *Bodies That Matter: On the Discursive Limits of Sex* (New York: Routledge, 1993), 17.

4 Michel Foucault describes the discursively constituted subject as "the product of a relation of power exercised over bodies . . . movements, desires." *Power/Knowledge: Selected Interviews and Other Writings, 1972–1977*, trans. and ed. Colin Gordon et al. (New York: Pantheon, 1972), 74. For an application of these concepts in feminist theology, see Margaret D. Kamitsuka, *Feminist Theology and the Challenge of Difference* (New York: Oxford University Press, 2007), 72–73.

5 Feminist solidarity is complicated. See Kamitsuka, *Feminist Theology and the Challenge of Difference*, ch. 6. That said, feminism is

like a family; we members can fight among ourselves, but woe to the patriarchal outsider who attacks one of our own.

6 Prolife activists in the African American community invoke black babies as threatened by a racist abortion industry in the billboard campaign "TooManyAborted." Monique Moultrie, "#BlackBabiesMatter: Analyzing Black Religious Media in Conservative and Progressive Evangelical Communities," *Religions* 8, no. 11 (2017): 255.

7 Theresa Bonopartis, "The Souls of Aborted Babies and the 'Hope' of Heaven," *Reclaiming Our Children* blog (November 2, 2018), https://tinyurl.com/44pj7sk7.

8 See Shrine of the Holy Innocents, Saugerties, NY, https://tinyurl.com/368xekm5.

9 Bonopartis, "Souls of Aborted Babies."

10 Charles K. Bellinger, *Othering: The Original Sin of Humanity* (Eugene, OR: Cascade, 2020), 160.

11 Francis J. Beckwith, "Taking Abortion Seriously: A Philosophical Critique of the New Anti-abortion Rhetorical Shift," *Ethics & Medicine* 17, no. 3 (2001): 162. For an analysis of racial politics in hardline antiabortion rhetoric and imagery, see Amaryah Shaye Armstrong, "Surrogate Flesh: Race, Redemption, and the Cultural Production of Fetal Personhood," *Journal of Ecumenical Studies* 55, no. 4 (2020): 518–43.

12 Center for Reproductive Rights, "The World's Abortion Laws," Feb. 23, 2021, https://tinyurl.com/32w76wce.

13 Sydna Masse, "Abortion: Heaven's Hope," Ramah's Voice: Abortion Recovery Blog, Mar. 28, 2016, https://tinyurl.com/544ckayr.

14 Kathryn Gin Lum, *Damned Nation: Hell in America from the Revolution to Reconstruction* (New York: Oxford University Press, 2014), ch. 1.

15 Peter Kwasniewski, "King Herod and the Martyr-Children" and Brian Harrison, O.S., "Aborted Infants as Martyrs: Are There Wider Implications?" in *Abortion and Martyrdom: The Papers of the Solesmes Consultation and an Appeal to the Catholic Church*, ed. Aidan Nichols, O.P. (Leominster, Herefordshire, UK: Gracewing, 2003).

16 See the website of the organization called Prayer League of the Holy Innocents and St. Stylianos: https://tinyurl.com/ewdk9n64.

17 Harrison, O.S., "Aborted Infants as Martyrs: Are There Wider Implications?," 114.

18 Michele M. Schumacher, "The Martyr Status of the Aborted Child: A Share in Christ's Witness to the Father of Mercies," in Nichols, *Abortion and Martyrdom*, 73.

19 Archimandrite Nektarios Serfes, "The Massacre of 14,000 Holy Innocent Infants, in Bethlehem and Its Borders," *Orthodox Christianity*, January 29, 2011, https://tinyurl.com/f742x5c6.

20 These are quotes from three stories posted on the Silent No More Awareness website. Jacqueline, "It's Not Simple to Live with Yourself After," https://tinyurl.com/bdcw4nx2; Laura, "2020 March for Life Testimony," https://tinyurl.com/2k6kvhpv; Christina, "The Unspeakable Word," https://tinyurl.com/bdd6vr8r.

21 David C. Reardon, "A Defense of the Neglected Rhetorical Strategy (NRS)," *Ethics & Medicine* 18, no. 2 (2002): 24.

22 Kimberly Kelly, "The Spread of 'Post Abortion Syndrome' as Social Diagnosis," *Social Science & Medicine* 102 (2014): 21.

23 Some rituals use a "bereavement doll" that the parents can place in a cradle to symbolize laying their aborted child to rest and to be with God. Rachel's Vineyard, "Memorial Service," https://tinyurl.com/2jsty45r. See Donna Krupkin Whitney, "Emotional Sequelae of Elective Abortion: The Role of Guilt and Shame," *Journal of Pastoral Care & Counseling* 71, no. 2 (2017): 101.

24 Linda Ellison, "Abortion and the Politics of God: Patient Narratives and Public Rhetoric in the American Abortion Debate" (ThD diss., Harvard Divinity School, 2008), 121.

25 Rachel's Vineyard, "FAQ: What Is the Benefit of a Group Setting?" https://tinyurl.com/bdmwndb7.

26 See the website for the National Day of Remembrance for Aborted Children, https://tinyurl.com/2xpd2y4u.

27 Judith Samson, "The Scars of the Madonna: The Struggle over Abortion in the Example of an American Post-abortion Pilgrimage to Mary," *Journal of Ritual Studies* 28, no. 2 (2014): 42–44.

28 Jack W. Hayford, *I'll Hold You in Heaven: Healing and Hope for the Parent Who Has Lost a Child through Miscarriage, Stillbirth, Abortion or Early Infant Death* (Ventura, CA: Gospel Light, 2003), 9.

29  Reputable scholars refute this notion. Gail Erlick Robinson et al., "Is There an 'Abortion Trauma Syndrome'? Critiquing the Evidence," *Harvard Review of Psychiatry* 17, no. 4 (2009): 268–90.

30  See Lynn S. Neal, *Romancing God: Evangelical Women and Inspirational Fiction* (Chapel Hill: University of North Carolina Press, 2006). For more on abortion in Christian romance novels, see Margaret D. Kamitsuka, "Prolife Christian Romance Novels: A Sign That the Abortion-as-Murder Center Is Not Holding?," *Christianity & Literature* 69, no. 1 (2020): 36–52.

31  Frank E. Peretti, *Tilly* (Wheaton, IL: Crossway, 1988).

32  Peretti, *Tilly*, 68.

33  Peretti, *Tilly*, 99–100, 113.

34  For an argument against accommodating families who request baptism of a dead infant, see Martin Leever et al., "'Baptizing' Deceased Infants? Is There a Catholic Ritual That Chaplains Can Perform to Relieve Grieving Parents?," *Health Progress* 85, no. 6 (2004): 44–49.

35  The Vatican finally issued a statement specifically disabusing people of the notion that baptism is a necessity for salvation. International Theological Commission, "The Hope of Salvation for Infants Who Die without Being Baptized," the Vatican, January 19, 2007, https://tinyurl.com/3anx6mhy.

36  United States Conference of Catholic Bishops, *Ethical and Religious Directives for Catholic Health Care Services*, 6th ed. (2018), 19, ¶ 17, https://tinyurl.com/4a5a3vfc.

37  Puneet Singh, Kearsley Stewart, and Scott Moses, "Pastoral Care Following Pregnancy Loss: The Role of Ritual," *Journal of Pastoral Care & Counseling* 58, nos. 1–2 (2004): 45.

38  Singh, Stewart, and Moses, "Pastoral Care Following Pregnancy Loss," 49.

39  Elette Gamble and Wilbur L. Holz, "A Rite for the Stillborn," *Word & World* 15, no. 3 (1995): 350. See also Gareth E. Williams, "Stillborn Funeral Liturgies in Theological Perspective," *Whitefield Briefing* 3, no. 4 (1998).

40  See Ewan R. Kelly, *Marking Short Lives: Constructing and Sharing Rituals Following Pregnancy Loss* (Oxford: Peter Lang, 2007), 189.

41  See Thomas Moe, *Pastoral Care in Pregnancy Loss: A Ministry Long Needed* (New York: Routledge, 2014, originally 1997), 104. "Grievers will need to work through their imagery of what their child would look like when they meet in heaven" (132).

42  Moe, *Pastoral Care in Pregnancy Loss*, 42. Moe does not offer his own views on infants in heaven. He does telegraph a prolife stance in his use of select quotes from early church writers supposedly affirming personhood from conception (65–66).

43  From the Episcopal Church's Standing Commission on Liturgy and Music, "A Rite for Mourning the Loss of a Pregnancy," in *Enriching Our Worship 5: Liturgies and Prayer Related to Childbearing, Childbirth, and Loss. Supplemental Liturgical Materials* (New York: Church Publishing, 2009).

44  See "Abortions Welcome" resources provided by the Religious Coalition for Reproductive Choice, https://tinyurl.com/38jxj354.

45  Carol M. Norén, *In Times of Crisis and Sorrow: A Minister's Manual Resource Guide* (Minneapolis: Fortress, 2020), 78. The author offers sample liturgies and prayers for miscarriage and stillbirth but not abortion (231–32, 238–39, 247).

46  Rosemary Radford Ruether, *Women-Church: Theology and Practice of Feminist Liturgical Communities* (San Francisco: Harper & Row, 1988), 161–63; Diann L. Neu, "Women's Empowerment through Feminist Rituals," in *Women's Spirituality, Women's Lives*, ed. Judith Ochshorn and Ellen Cole (New York: Hawthorne, 1995), 185–200; June O'Connor, "Ritual Recognition of Abortion: Japanese Buddhist Practices and U.S. Jewish and Christian Proposals," in *Embodiment, Morality, and Medicine*, ed. Lisa Sowle Cahill and Margaret Farley (Dordrecht: Kluwer Academic, 1995), 93–111; Hannah Ward and Jennifer Wild, eds., *Human Rites: Worship Resources for an Age of Change* (London: Mowbray, 1995), 148–51, 216–18, 241–42; Rev. Darcy Baxter and Colleagues, "Regeneration & Loss: Honoring Our Reproductive Lives," Side with Love, https://tinyurl.com/ysez55ja.

47  Maureen L. Walsh, "Emerging Trends in Pregnancy-Loss Memorialization in American Catholicism," *Horizons* 44, no. 2 (2017): 374. Naming rituals are often used in this regard; however, one study found that after a termination due to fetal anomaly, few parents wanted to name their deceased fetus. F. Susan Cowchock

et al., "Spiritual Needs of Couples Facing Pregnancy Termination Because of Fetal Anomalies," *Journal of Pastoral Care & Counseling* 65, no. 2 (2011): 7.

48  Standing Commission on Liturgy and Music, "A Rite of Repentance and Reconciliation for an Abortion," in *Enriching Our Worship* 5, 27.

49  "Compassionate God, I have ended the life briefly held in my body. . . . Forgive my sins." (Standing Commission on Liturgy and Music, "Prayers Surrounding the Termination of Pregnancy: Following an Abortion," in *Enriching Our Worship*, 5, 61.

50  Tish Harrison Warren, "What Happens When We Bury Our Unborn?" *Christianity Today* 62, no. 9 (2018): 43–44.

51  Leslie J. Reagan, "From Hazard to Blessing to Tragedy: Representations of Miscarriage in Twentieth-Century America," *Feminist Studies* 29, no. 2 (2003): 359.

52  See Leslie J. Reagan, *When Abortion Was a Crime: Women, Medicine, and Law in the United States, 1867–1973* (Berkeley: University of California Press, 1997).

53  Elizabeth Cady Stanton, "On Marriage and Divorce" (1871); https://tinyurl.com/y85hvbvu.

54  Parley Ann Boswell, *Pregnancy in Literature and Film* (Jefferson, NC: McFarland, 2014), 89–90.

55  Holly Cave, "The Miscarriage Taboo," *Atlantic*, March 2, 2016.

56  Kate Greasley, *Arguments about Abortion: Personhood, Morality, and Law* (Oxford: Oxford University Press, 2017), 7–8.

57  Judith Butler, *Frames of War: When Is Life Grievable?* (New York: Verso, 2009), 19–21.

58  Lynn Marie Morgan and Meredith W. Michaels, eds., *Fetal Subjects, Feminist Positions* (Philadelphia: University of Pennsylvania Press, 1999), 4.

59  Deborah Lupton, *The Social Worlds of the Unborn* (New York: Palgrave Macmillan, 2013), 35.

60  Helen Keane, "Foetal Personhood and Representations of the Absent Child in Pregnancy Loss Memorialization," *Feminist Theory* 10, no. 2 (2009): 163.

61  Linda Layne, "Troubling the Normal: 'Angel Babies' and the Canny/Uncanny Nexus," in *Understanding Reproductive Loss: Perspectives on Life, Death and Fertility*, ed. Sarah Earle, Carol

Komaromy, and Linda Layne (Farnham, UK: Ashgate, 2012): 135–36.

62 The website Shout Your Abortion works to normalize abortion and lessen stigma. See https://tinyurl.com/sy48wk67.

63 Kate Parsons, "Feminist Reflections on Miscarriage, in Light of Abortion," *International Journal of Feminist Approaches to Bioethics* 3, no. 1 (2010): 2, 3.

64 Ann J. Cahill, "Miscarriage and Intercorporeality," *Journal of Social Philosophy* 46, no. 1 (2015): 56.

65 Martin Luther, "Consolation for Women Whose Pregnancies Have Not Gone Well, 1542," introduction by Kristen E. Kvam, in *The Annotated Luther,* vol 4: *Pastoral Writings,* ed. Mary Jane Haemig, Hans J. Hillerbrand, Kirsi I. Stjerna, and Timothy J. Wengert (Minneapolis: Fortress), 422.

66 One nationwide miscarriage survey in the United States found that over 40 percent of women who had a miscarriage "reported feeling that they had done something wrong." Jonah Bardos et al., "A National Survey on Public Perceptions of Miscarriage," *Obstetrics and Gynecology* 125, no. 6 (2015): 1313.

67 Judith L. M. McCoyd, "Women in No Man's Land: The Abortion Debate in the USA and Women Terminating Desired Pregnancies Due to Foetal Anomaly," *British Journal of Social Work* 40, no. 1 (2010): 142.

68 McCoyd, "Women in No Man's Land," 143–44. I will discuss selective abortion in more depth in ch. 5.

69 Shaw James Paterson, "How Might Parish Ministers (and Other Pastoral Caregivers) Better Support Women Who Have Experienced an Early Miscarriage?" (PhD diss., University of Glasgow, 2020), 142.

70 One woman in the study remarked that "if you use that terminology then you feel you are guilty" (Paterson, "How Might Parish Ministers," 146).

71 See these sites at Planned Parenthood: "What Is a Miscarriage?" https://tinyurl.com/3n7fcmf3; "What Happens during an In-Clinic Abortion?," https://tinyurl.com/58r7zj43; "How Does the Abortion Pill Work?" https://tinyurl.com/ycxvdh3m.

72 For research into the effects of being denied an abortion, see the "turnaway" study project run by the Advancing New Standards

in Reproductive Health research program of the University of California, San Francisco, https://tinyurl.com/2p8nxdvd.

73  See Aalap Bommaraju, Megan L. Kavanaugh, Melody Y. Hou, and Danielle Bessett, "Situating Stigma in Stratified Reproduction: Abortion Stigma and Miscarriage Stigma as Barriers to Reproductive Healthcare," *Sexual & Reproductive Healthcare* 10 (2016): 62–69; Kate Cockrill, Ushma D. Upadhyay, Janet Turan, and Diana Greene Foster, "The Stigma of Having an Abortion: Development of a Scale and Characteristics of Women Experiencing Abortion Stigma," *Perspectives on Sexual and Reproductive Health* 45, no. 2 (2013): 79–88.

74  See Jasveer Virk, Jun Zhang, and Jø Olsen, "Medical Abortion and the Risk of Subsequent Adverse Pregnancy Outcomes," *New England Journal of Medicine* 357, no. 7 (2007): 648–53.

75  Carla Dugas and Valori Slane, "Miscarriage," National Center for Biotechnology Information, June 29, 2021, https://tinyurl.com/44effnrc.

76  Brian Brock, *Wondrously Wounded: Theology, Disability, and the Body of Christ* (Waco, TX: Baylor University Press 2019), 95.

77  Norman Brier, "Anxiety after Miscarriage: A Review of the Empirical Literature and Implications for Clinical Practice," *Birth* 31, no. 2 (2004): 138–42.

78  Shannon Dingle, "I Was in the Pro-Life Movement. But Then, Widowed with 6 Kids, I Prepared for an Abortion," *USA Today*, Opinion, Oct. 11, 2020, https://tinyurl.com/49rwyfza.

79  Dingle, "I Was in the Pro-Life Movement."

80  Lisa Isherwood and Elizabeth Stuart, *Introducing Body Theology* (Sheffield, UK: Sheffield Academic, 1998).

81  Heather Eaton, "An Earth-Centric Theological Framing for Planetary Solidarity," in *Planetary Solidarity: Global Women's Voices on Christian Doctrine and Climate Justice*, ed. Grace Ji-Sun Kim and Hilda P. Koster (Minneapolis: Fortress, 2017), 40.

82  Neomi De Anda, "Miscarriage Matters, Stillbirth's Significance, and the Tree of Many Breasts," in *Parenting as Spiritual Practice and Source for Theology*, ed. Claire Bischoff, Elizabeth O'Donnell Gandolfo, Annie Hardison-Moody (Cham, Switzerland: Palgrave Macmillan, 2017), 175.

83 Monica A. Coleman, "Sacrifice, Surrogacy and Salvation: Womanist Reflections on Motherhood and Work," *Black Theology* 12, no. 3 (2014): 206.

84 Beverly Wildung Harrison, "The Power of Anger in the Work of Love: Christian Ethics for Women and Other Strangers," in *Making the Connections: Essays in Feminist Social Ethics*, ed. Carol S. Robb (Boston: Beacon, 1985), 4.

85 See Mary Daly, *Gyn/ecology: The Metaethics of Radical Feminism* (Boston: Beacon, 1978); Rosemary Radford Ruether, *New Woman, New Earth: Sexist Ideologies and Human Liberation* (New York: Seabury, 1975); Katie G. Cannon, *Black Womanist Ethics* (Atlanta: Scholars, 1988); Carter Heyward, *Touching Our Strength: The Erotic as Power and the Love of God* (San Francisco: Harper & Row, 1989).

86 See n46 above.

87 O'Donnell, "Theology and Reproductive Loss," 126.

88 Nadine Pence Frantz and Mary T. Stimming, eds., *Hope Deferred: Heart-Healing Reflections on Reproductive Loss* (Cleveland: Pilgrim, 2010), 9.

89 Janice Allison Thompson, "Making Room for the Other: Maternal Mourning and Eschatological Hope," *Modern Theology* 27, no. 3 (2011): 399. Thompson recounts her own shattering experience of neonatal loss.

90 Mercy Amba Oduyoye, "A Coming to Myself: The Childless Woman in the West African Space," in *Liberating Eschatology: Essays in Honor of Letty M. Russell*, ed. Margaret A. Farley and Serene Jones (Louisville: Westminster John Knox, 1999), 116. Oduyoye, a Ghanaian theologian from the Methodist tradition, writes of her miscarriages in an African context.

91 Reynolds, "From the Site of the Empty Tomb," 48.

92 Prov 29:18 KJV.

93 Nicole Johnson, "Invisible Grief? Theological Reflections on Miscarriage," *Other Journal* (March 17, 2014), https://tinyurl.com/ycxeth72.

94 See Serene Jones, *Trauma and Grace: Theology in a Ruptured World* (Louisville: Westminster John Knox, 2009), 127–28.

95 Thompson, "Making Room for the Other," 406.

96 Shelly Rambo, *Resurrecting Wounds: Living in the Afterlife of Trauma* (Waco, TX: Baylor University Press, 2017), 148.

97 Jones, *Trauma and Grace*, 145.

98 Ada María Isasi-Díaz quoted in Emily Pennington, *Feminist Eschatology: Embodied Futures* (New York: Routledge, 2016), 68. Liberation theologies have long protested that "eschatology has been severed from historical hope." Rosemary Radford Ruether, *Sexism and God-Talk: Toward a Feminist Theology*, with a new introduction (Boston: Beacon, 1993), 245.

99 Karen O'Donnell, *The Dark Womb: Re-Conceiving Theology through Reproductive Loss* (London: SCM, 2022), 115.

100 O'Donnell, *The Dark Womb*, 116.

101 Rosemary Radford Ruether, "Eschatology in Christian Feminist Theologies," in *The Oxford Handbook of Eschatology*, ed. Jerry L. Walls (New York: Oxford University Press, 2007), 332.

102 Grace Jantzen, *Becoming Divine: Toward a Feminist Philosophy of Religion* (Bloomington: Indiana University Press, 1999), 141.

103 Sallie McFague, *The Body of God: An Ecological Theology* (Minneapolis: Fortress, 1993), 102, 174.

104 Ruether, *Sexism and God-Talk*, 257.

105 Joan M. Martin, "A Sacred Hope and Social Goal: Womanist Eschatology," in Farley and Jones, *Liberating Eschatology*, 220.

106 Emilie M. Townes, *In a Blaze of Glory: Womanist Spirituality as Social Witness* (Nashville: Abingdon, 1995), 70.

107 Townes, *In a Blaze of Glory*, 122.

108 Ada María Isasi-Díaz, "Mujerista Narratives: Creating a New Heaven and a New Earth," in Farley and Jones, *Liberating Eschatology*, 228.

109 Ruether, *Sexism and God-Talk*, 251.

110 Some feminist thinkers address how imaginaries of the afterlife might counteract the anti-body and antisexuality themes. See Patricia Beattie Jung, *Sex on Earth as It Is in Heaven: A Christian Eschatology of Desire* (Albany: State University of New York Press, 2016); Margaret D. Kamitsuka, "Sex in Heaven? Eschatological Eros and the Resurrection of the Body," in *The Embrace of Eros: Bodies, Desires, and Sexuality in Christianity*, ed. Margaret D. Kamitsuka (Minneapolis: Fortress, 2010).

111 Simone de Beauvoir, quoted in Judith Butler, *Gender Trouble: Feminism and the Subversion of Identity*, 10th anniv. ed. (New York: Routledge, 2002), 3

112 See Anne Stensvold, *A History of Pregnancy in Christianity: From Original Sin to Contemporary Abortion Debates* (New York: Routledge, 2015); Clare Hanson, *A Cultural History of Pregnancy: Pregnancy, Medicine and Culture, 1750–2000* (Houndmills, Basingstoke, Hampshire, UK: Palgrave Macmillan, 2004); Dorothy E. Roberts, *Killing the Black Body: Race, Reproduction, and the Meaning of Liberty* (New York: Vintage, 1999); Lynn O'Brien Hallstein, Andrea O'Reilly, and Melinda Vandenbeld Giles, eds., *The Routledge Companion to Motherhood* (New York: Routledge, 2020).

## 2. Closing Heaven to the Unborn

1 Michel Foucault, "Two Lectures," in *Michel Foucault Power/Knowledge: Selected Interviews and Other Writings 1972–1977*, trans. and ed. Colin Gordon et al. (New York: Pantheon, 1980), 81–82.

2 Zubin Mistry, *Abortion in the Early Middle Ages, C.500–900* (Woodbridge, Suffolk, UK: York Medieval, 2015), 41.

3 Tertullian quoted in John J. O'Keefe, "The Persistence of Decay: Bodily Disintegration and Cyrillian Christology," in *In the Shadow of the Incarnation: Essays on Jesus Christ in the Early Church in Honor of Brian E. Daley, S.J.*, ed. Peter William Martens (Notre Dame, IN: University of Notre Dame Press, 2008), 233–34.

4 Peter Brown, *The Body and Society: Men, Women, and Sexual Renunciation in Early Christianity* (New York: Columbia University Press, 1988), 352.

5 Alexandra Cuffel, *Gendering Disgust in Medieval Religious Polemic* (Notre Dame, IN: University of Notre Dame Press, 2007), 35.

6 Mistry, *Abortion in the Early Middle Ages*, 257. Mistry gives an extensive discussion of the various literal and metaphorical meanings (mostly negative) for *abortivi* in medieval Christian discourses (262–95).

7 Jacqueline Tasioulas, "'Heaven and Earth in Little Space': The Foetal Existence of Christ in Medieval Literature and Thought," *Medium Aevum* 76, no. 1 (2007): 29.

8  Tasioulas, "Heaven and Earth in Little Space," 30.

9  See Petr Kitzler, "Tertullian and Ancient Embryology in *De carne Christi* 4, 1 and 19, 3–4," *Zeitschrift für Antikes Christentum/Journal of Ancient Christianity* 18, no. 2 (2014): 207–8.

10 See Eliezer Gonzalez, "Anthropologies of Continuity: The Body and Soul in Tertullian, Perpetua, and Early Christianity," *Journal of Early Christian Studies* 21, no. 4 (2013): 483–84. Tertullian wrote, "The embryo therefore becomes a human being in the womb from the moment that its form is completed." *A Treatise on the Soul*, in *Ante-Nicene Fathers*, vol. 3, trans. D. D. Holmes, ed. Alexander Roberts and James Donaldson (New York: Scribner's, 1899), XXVII, available at https://tinyurl.com/mtp7y999.

11 Tertullian, *A Treatise on the Soul*, LVI.

12 Tertullian, *A Treatise on the Soul*, XXXVII.

13 See Margaret D. Kamitsuka, *Abortion and the Christian Tradition: A Pro-choice Theological Ethic* (Louisville: Westminster John Knox, 2019), 40–43.

14 I. L. S. Balfour, "The Fate of the Soul in Induced Abortion in the Writings of Tertullian," *Studia Patristica* 16, no. 2 (1985): 127–31.

15 See Marie-Hélène Congourdeau, "Debating the Soul in Late Antiquity," in *Reproduction: Antiquity to the Present Day*, ed. Nick Hopwood, Rebecca Flemming, and Lauren Kassell (Cambridge: Cambridge University Press, 2018), 118.

16 *Enchiridion* 23.86, in Augustine, *Confessions and Enchiridion*, trans. Albert C. Outler (Philadelphia: Westminster, 1955), 276; https://tinyurl.com/efcc86yk.

17 *Enchiridion*, 23.85, 275. Augustine distinguished between "formed fetuses (*formati*)" and "unformed abortions (*informes abortus*)." Mistry, *Abortion in the Early Middle Ages*, 268–69.

18 Eusebius in the fourth century implied something similar in explaining that the verse "let them vanish like water that runs away" (Ps 58:7) refers to the destiny of a fetus who "will have [no] part in the resurrection." Danuta Shanzer, "Voices and Bodies: The Afterlife of the Unborn," *Numen* 56, nos. 2–3 (2009): 351.

19 Mistry, *Abortion in the Early Middle Ages*, 270.

20 Augustine, *City of God*, 22.13-14, in *The Nicene and Post-Nicene Fathers*, vol. 2, trans. Marcus Dodd, ed. Philip Schaff

and Henry Wace (Grand Rapids: Eerdmans, 1972), 494–95, https://tinyurl.com/5areazke.

21 Augustine "saw salvation as the crystalline hardness not only of stasis but of the impossibility of non-stasis." Caroline Walker Bynum, *The Resurrection of the Body in Western Christianity, 200–1336* (New York: Columbia University Press, 1995), 97.

22 Shanzer, "Voices and Bodies," 350.

23 See Benjamin P. Blosser, "The Ensoulment of the Body in Early Christian Thought," in *A History of Mind and Body in Late Antiquity*, ed. Anna Marmodoro and Sophie Cartwright (Cambridge: Cambridge University Press, 2018), 218–19.

24 Pelagius represented an opposing contingent that promoted baptism but rejected the notion of infants born with original sin. See Everett Ferguson, *Baptism in the Early Church: History, Theology, and Liturgy in the First Five Centuries* (Grand Rapids: Eerdmans, 2009), 809–16.

25 In the Eastern churches infant baptism was encouraged but not seen as a requirement for salvation. Stephen Morris, "Words in the Face of Unspeakable Tragedy: Eastern Christian Preaching at the Funeral of a Child," *Greek Orthodox Theological Review* 51, nos. 1–4 (2006): 73–80. Jane Baun, "The Fate of Babies Dying before Baptism in Byzantium," *Studies in Church History* 31 (1994): 119.

26 "The souls of children who have been reborn by the same baptism of Christ . . . if they die [will] immediately (*mox*) after death . . . be with Christ in heaven." Pope Benedict XII, "Benedictus Deus: On the Beatific Vision of God" (1336), the Vatican, https://tinyurl.com/2xx6c3jj.

27 Ferguson, *Baptism in the Early Church*, 376–77.

28 Madison Crow, Colleen Zori, and Davide Zori, "Doctrinal and Physical Marginality in Christian Death: The Burial of Unbaptized Infants in Medieval Italy," *Religions* 11, no. 12 (2020): 13–14.

29 Steven Bednarski and Andrée Courtemanche, "'Sadly and with a Bitter Heart': What the Caesarean Section Meant in the Middle Ages," *Florilegium* (2011): 47.

30 A separate women's sphere of fertility and birthing rituals, charms, and incantations existed alongside what little medieval churches

had to offer. Roberta Gilchrist, *Medieval Life: Archaeology and the Life Course* (Woodbridge, Suffolk, UK: Boydell, 2012), 222–23.

31 Gilchrist, *Medieval Life*, 220. Archaeologists determined the age range of the skeletal remains to be from fetal stage to six-month-old infant (221).

32 David F. Wright, *Infant Baptism in Historical Perspective. Collected Studies* (Milton Keynes, UK: Paternoster, 2007), 86.

33 Bednarski and Courtemanche, "Sadly and with a Bitter Heart," 33–69; Rosemary Keupper Valle, "The Cesarean Operation in Alta California during the Franciscan Mission Period (1769–1833)," *Bulletin of the History of Medicine* 48, no. 2 (1974): 265–75. Crow, Zori, and Zori, "Doctrinal and Physical Marginality in Christian Death," 8.

34 Archaeological evidence from church cemeteries shows "women's skeletons containing full-term fetuses" lodged in their abdomen area. Maaike van der Lugt, "Formed Fetuses and Healthy Children in Scholastic Theology," in *Reproduction: Antiquity to the Present Day*, ed. Nick Hopwood, Rebecca Flemming, and Lauren Kassell (Cambridge: Cambridge University Press, 2018), 172.

35 The procedure would have been a medical option under Jewish or Muslim law. See Ron Barkai, "A Medieval Hebrew Treatise on Obstetrics," *Medical History* 33, no. 1 (1989): 109n68.

36 The church's interference in the delivery room may have "saved some babies, but lost many mothers." Y. Michael Barilan, "Abortion in Jewish Religious Law: Neighborly Love, Imago Dei, and a Hypothesis on the Medieval Blood Libel," *Review of Rabbinic Judaism* 8, nos. 1–2 (2005): 23.

37 Bednarski and Courtemanche, "Sadly and with a Bitter Heart," 48.

38 Bednarski and Courtemanche, "Sadly and with a Bitter Heart," 48.

39 A survey of Irish Catholic women's views on infant death reveals that "belief in Limbo and the associated fears for the eternal welfare of the unbaptized infant persisted into the 1960s." Liam Kennedy, "Afterlives: Testimonies of Irish Catholic Mothers on Infant Death and the Fate of the Unbaptised," *Journal of Family History* 46, no. 2 (2021): 246.

40 See "Traditions," Archdiocese of Chicago, https://tinyurl.com/3k5ywarx.

41 Attempting a baptism in the case of miscarriage or premature birth was mandated in the 1917 and again in the 1983 Code of Canon Law. "If aborted fetuses are alive, they are to be baptized insofar as possible." *Code of Canon Law* (1983), bk. IV, ch. III, can. 871, the Vatican, https://tinyurl.com/3xxy67pj.

42 See United States Conference of Catholic Bishops Committee on Doctrine, *Ethical and Religious Directives for Catholic Health Care Services*, 6th ed. (2018): 11.

43 Kennedy, "Afterlives," 241, 243–44. Catholic mothers giving birth as late as the 1990s in the Netherlands speak of how their miscarried or stillborn infant was whisked away at birth and buried anonymously. Laurie Faro, "Monuments for Stillborn Children and Disenfranchised Grief in the Netherlands: Recognition, Protest and Solace," *Mortality* (2020): 1–20.

44 See Lori R. Freedman, Uta Landy, and Jody Steinauer, "When There's a Heartbeat: Miscarriage Management in Catholic-Owned Hospitals," *American Journal of Public Health* 98, no. 10 (2008): 1774–78. Jaime Lowe and Stephanie Sinclair, "What a High-Risk Pregnancy Looks Like after Dobbs," *New York Times*, Sept. 13, 2022.

45 Augustine quoted in Francis A. Sullivan, "The Development of Doctrine about Infants Who Die Unbaptized," *Theological Studies* 72, no. 1 (2011): 3.

46 Shanzer, "Voices and Bodies," 340.

47 Mistry, *Abortion in the Early Middle Ages,* 271.

48 See Brian Harrison, O.S., "Aborted Infants as Martyrs: Are There Wider Implications?" in *Abortion and Martyrdom. The Papers of the Solesmes Consultation and an Appeal to the Catholic Church*, ed. Aidan Nichols, O.P. (Leominster, Herefordshire, UK: Gracewing, 2003), 116.

49 *The Aeneid,* book VI, vv. 550–1199.

50 Bart D. Ehrman, *Journeys to Heaven and Hell: Tours of the Afterlife in the Early Christian Tradition* (New Haven, CT: Yale University Press, 2022); Catherine Ella Laufer, *Hell's Destruction: An Exploration of Christ's Descent to the Dead* (New York: Routledge, 2016).

51 Jared Wicks, S.J., "Christ's Saving Descent to the Dead: Early Witnesses from Ignatius of Antioch to Origen," *Pro Ecclesia* 17, no. 3 (2008): 298.

52 See Christopher Beiting, "The Nature and Structure of Limbo in the Works of Albertus Magnus," *New Blackfriars* 85, no. 999 (2004): 498–509.

53 Christopher Beiting, "The Idea of Limbo in Thomas Aquinas," *The Thomist* 62, no. 2 (1998): 228.

54 Dante Alighieri, *Inferno* IV.28–30, trans. Robert and Jean Hollander (New York: Anchor, 2000), 69.

55 David H. Price, *In the Beginning Was the Image: Art and the Reformation Bible* (New York: Oxford University Press, 2020).

56 John Haldane and Patrick Lee, "Aquinas on Human Ensoulment, Abortion and the Value of Life," *Philosophy* 78, no. 2 (2003): 257.

57 Robert Pasnau, *Thomas Aquinas on Human Nature: A Philosophical Study of* Summa Theologiae *1a 75–89* (Cambridge: Cambridge University Press, 2002), esp. 74–75, 159–60, 163–64.

58 Pasnau, *Thomas Aquinas on Human Nature*, 154.

59 Jason T. Eberl, "Aquinas's Account of Human Embryogenesis and Recent Interpretations," *Journal of Medicine and Philosophy* 30, no. 4 (2005): 383.

60 Patrick Toner, "Critical Study of Fabrizio Amerini's *Aquinas on the Beginning and End of Human Life*," in *Oxford Studies in Medieval Philosophy*, ed. Robert Pasnau, vol. 2 (Oxford: Oxford University Press, 2014), 220, in italics in the original.

61 "The vegetative soul, which is present first, when the embryo lives the life of a plant, is corrupted, and a more perfect soul follows, which is at once nutritive and sensory, and then the embryo lives the life of an animal. With its corruption, the rational soul follows, infused from without." Aquinas, quoted in Robert Pasnau, "Souls and the Beginning of Life (A Reply to Haldane and Lee)," *Philosophy* 78, no. 306 (2003): 528.

62 Pasnau indicates that Aquinas defers to Aristotle's view on the timing of ensoulment but does not firmly commit to it. See Pasnau, *Thomas Aquinas on Human Nature*, 419n13.

63 Aquinas concluded that early abortion was "less than homicide." Aquinas, quoted in Pasnau, *Thomas Aquinas on Human Nature*,

418n7. See Fabrizio Amerini, *Aquinas on the Beginning and End of Human Life*, trans. M. Henninger, S.J. (Cambridge, MA: Harvard University Press, 2013), 230n4.

64 John Haldane and Patrick Lee, "Aquinas on Human Ensoulment, Abortion and the Value of Life," *Philosophy* 78, no. 2 (2003): 274n26.

65 Toner, "Critical Study of Fabrizio Amerini's *Aquinas*," 223.

66 Haldane and Lee, "Aquinas on Human Ensoulment," 271, italics added.

67 Haldane and Lee, "Aquinas on Human Ensoulment," 277.

68 Pasnau, "Souls and the Beginning of Life," 526. "Cells and/or cell parts cannot be considered 'organs' from Aquinas' perspective." Fabrizio Amerini, "Aquinas on the Beginning and End of Human Life: A Rejoinder to Patrick Toner," in *Oxford Studies in Medieval Philosophy*, ed. Robert Pasnau, vol. 3 (Oxford: Oxford University Press, 2015), 191.

69 Aquinas, quoted in Pasnau, *Thomas Aquinas on Human Nature*, 111.

70 See Hugo Lagercrantz, "The Emergence of Consciousness: Science and Ethics," *Seminars in Fetal and Neonatal Medicine* 19, no. 5 (2014): 300–305.

71 Pasnau, *Thomas Aquinas on Human Nature*, 392. See Terrence Ehrman, C.S.C., "Disability and Resurrection Identity," *New Blackfriars* 96, no. 1066 (2015): 734n48.

72 Benjamin Breckinridge Warfield, *The Development of the Doctrine of Infant Salvation* (New York: Christian Literature, 1891), 43–44, 49; https://tinyurl.com/2p83f2fs.

73 Myk Habets, "'Suffer the Little Children to Come to Me, for Theirs Is the Kingdom of Heaven': Infant Salvation and the Destiny of the Severely Mentally Disabled," in *Evangelical Calvinism: Essays Resourcing the Continuing Reformation of the Church*, ed. Myk Habets and Bobby Grow (Eugene, OR: Wipf and Stock, 2012), 303n54.

74 See Susan C. Karant-Nunn, "'Suffer the Little Children to Come unto Me, and Forbid Them Not': The Social Location of Baptism in Early Modern Germany," in *Continuity and Change: The Harvest of Late Medieval and Reformation History: Studies in Honor of Heiko A. Oberman on His Seventieth Birthday*, ed. Andrew C. Gow and Robert J. Bast (Leiden: Brill, 2000), 364.

75 Price, *In the Beginning Was the Image*, 230.
76 See Jonathan D. Trigg, *Baptism in the Theology of Martin Luther* (Leiden: Brill, 1994), 103–4.
77 Luke 1:39–45. For typical prolife uses of this story see William Ross Blackburn, "Abortion and the Voice of Scripture," *Human Life Review* 31, no. 2 (2005): 74; John Piper, "The Baby in My Womb Leaped for Joy," *Desiring God* (blog), January 25, 2009, https://tinyurl.com/ypsa4xn5.
78 Mark Ellingsen, *Martin Luther's Legacy: Reforming Reformation Theology for the 21st Century* (New York: Palgrave Macmillan, 2017), 192.
79 Karant-Nunn, "Suffer the Little Children," 370.
80 Kirsi Stjerna, *Women and the Reformation* (Malden, MA: Blackwell, 2011), 58. Katharina gave birth to six children between 1526 and 1534.
81 Kristen E. Kvam finds it "striking" that Luther did not definitively repudiate the Catholic notion of infants locked in limbo. "Introduction" to Martin Luther, "Consolation for Women Whose Pregnancies Have Not Gone Well, 1542," in *The Annotated Luther*, vol. 4, *Pastoral Writings*, ed. Mary Jane Haemig, Hans J. Hillerbrand, Kirsi I. Stjerna, and Timothy J. Wengert (Minneapolis: Fortress, 2016), 423.
82 Kristen Kvam, "Comfort," in *Hope Deferred: Heart-Healing Reflections on Reproductive Loss*, ed. Nadine Pence Frantz and Mary T. Stimming (Cleveland: Pilgrim 2010), 80.
83 Notger Slenczka, "Luther's Anthropology," in *The Oxford Handbook of Martin Luther's Theology*, ed. Robert Kolb, Irene Dingel, and Ľubomír Batka (Oxford: Oxford University Press, 2014), 244.
84 Luther, "Consolation for Women Whose Pregnancies Have Not Gone Well, 1542," 424.
85 Luther colorfully recounted that "we are to sleep until [Christ] comes and knocks on the grave and says, 'Dr. Martin, get up.'" Luther quoted in Jeffrey G. Silcock, "A Lutheran Approach to Eschatology," *Lutheran Quarterly* 31, no. 4 (2017): 391n32. See also Jane E. Strohl, "Luther's Eschatology," in *The Oxford Handbook of Martin Luther's Theology*, ed. Robert Kolb, Irene Dingel, and Ľubomír Batka (Oxford: Oxford University Press, 2014); David P. Scaer, "Luther's

Concept of the Resurrection in His Commentary on 1 Corinthians 15," *Concordia Theological Quarterly* 47 (1983): 222.

86 God "adopts our babies for his own before they are born. . . . Few realize how much injury the dogma that baptism is necessary to salvation . . . has entailed." John Calvin, *Institutes of the Christian Religion* (1536), IV.15.20, trans. Ford Lewis Battles, ed. John T. McNeill (Philadelphia: Westminster, 1960), 1321.

87 Karen E. Spierling, *Infant Baptism in Reformation Geneva: The Shaping of a Community, 1536–1564* (New York: Routledge, 2016), 34.

88 Spierling, *Infant Baptism in Reformation Geneva*, 33. Exorcisms were still part of Luther's version of the baptismal ceremony (32).

89 See Spierling, *Infant Baptism in Reformation Geneva*, 72–76. Along with theological reasons for suppressing emergency baptisms, authorities in Geneva and other Reformed cities disapproved of midwives conducting baptisms. See Will Coster, *Baptism and Spiritual Kinship in Early Modern England* (New York: Routledge, 2017), 52–53.

90 Calvin defends these fetal deaths in the biblical story of the destruction of Sodom, saying that "God would never have suffered any infants to be destroyed, except those which He had already reprobated." John Calvin, *Commentaries on the Four Last Books of Moses*, vol. 2, trans Charles William Bingham (Edinburgh: Calvin Translation Society, 1853), 87, https://tinyurl.com/mrxymjnw.

91 See John Witte Jr., and Robert M. Kingdon, *Sex, Marriage, and Family in John Calvin's Geneva*, vol. 1, *Courtship, Engagement, and Marriage* (Grand Rapids: Eerdmans, 2005), 99–100.

92 Witte Jr. and Kingdon, *Sex, Marriage, and Family*, 100n24.

93 Idelette was an Anabaptist, but she and Calvin apparently agreed on infant baptism. See Witte and Kingdon, *Sex, Marriage, and Family*, 358n22.

94 Warfield wrote that "it is probable, from the superabundance of the gift of grace . . . that death in infancy is a sign of election." Warfield, *The Development of the Doctrine of Infant Salvation*, 37–38.

95 See David Albert Jones, *The Soul of the Embryo: An Inquiry into the Status of the Human Embryo in the Christian Tradition* (London: Continuum, 2004), 146.

96  Calvin, quoted in Margaret R. Miles, "Theology, Anthropology, and the Human Body in Calvin's *Institutes of the Christian Religion*," *Harvard Theological Review* 74, no. 3 (1981): 313.

97  Calvin asserted that "souls when divested from their bodies" would "still retain their essence, and have capacity of blessed glory." Calvin, *Institutes of the Christian Religion*, III.25.6 (997).

98  At the resurrection, God "does not call forth new matter from the four elements to fashion men, but [calls forth] dead men from their graves." Calvin, *Institutes of the Christian Religion*, III.25.7 (999).

99  John Calvin, *Commentaries on the Four Last Books of Moses*, vol. 3, trans. Charles William Bingham (Edinburgh: Calvin Translation Society, 1853), 42; https://tinyurl.com/2vxhmmbv.

100 Abortion or attempted abortion was not rigorously prosecuted and apparently mostly overlooked by the Genevan Consistory (religious council) and the Small Council (legal court). See Witte and Kingdon, *Sex, Marriage, and Family*, 74–76.

101 Warfield was aware of the challenging issue of the salvation of "children dying in the womb," and he referenced Luther's miscarriage consolation letter. Warfield, *The Development of the Doctrine of Infant Salvation*, 17, 25.

102 Jean-François Lyotard, *The Postmodern Condition: A Report on Knowledge* (Minneapolis: University of Minnesota Press, 1984).

103 Foucault, "Two Lectures," 81. Foucault calls the methodology for this discernment "genealogy," characterized as "the attempt to emancipate historical knowledges . . . to render them . . . capable of opposition and of struggle against the coercion of a theoretical, unitary, formal and scientific discourse" (85).

104 See Genesis 4:10.

105 Anne Stensvold, *A History of Pregnancy in Christianity: From Original Sin to Contemporary Abortion Debates* (New York: Routledge, 2015), 71–73.

106 "Infancy Gospel of James," trans. Shelly Matthews, 17:10–18:1, https://tinyurl.com/2sjbuter.

107 The birth helpers in the story perform a postpartum vaginal exam. "Infancy Gospel of James," 20:1–3.

108 *Didascalia* quoted in Charlotte Elisheva Fonrobert, *Menstrual Purity: Rabbinic and Christian Reconstructions of Biblical Gender* (Stanford, CA: Stanford University Press, 2002), 175.

109 A yearly gathering of women to lament the death of the daughter of Jephthah is mentioned in Judges 11:39–40.

110 Tertullian, *Treatise on the Soul*, XXV.

111 In a typical seventeenth-century Lutheran prayer, a pious pregnant woman is encouraged to address God with these words: "It has pleased you to burden me and the entire feminine sex, because of our sins, with having to bear children with pain and suffering in order to populate the world." Judith Popovich Aikin, "Gendered Theologies of Childbirth in Early Modern Germany and The Devotional Handbook for Pregnant Women by Aemilie Juliane, Countess of Schwarzburg-Rudolstadt (1683)," *Journal of Women's History* 15, no. 2 (2003): 42.

112 Aikin, "Gendered Theologies of Childbirth," 49.

113 *Solls aber ja nicht seyn/muß ich meines Kindes Grab werden* (Aikin, "Gendered Theologies of Childbirth," 67n47).

114 "The Acts of Perpetua and Felicitas," VI.1, https://tinyurl.com/yt5yetdb.

115 Illiterate, she left a book of her experiences, which is thought to be the first woman's spiritual autobiography. *The Book of Margery Kempe*, trans. and ed. Lynn Staley (New York: Norton, 2001). For a discussion of Margery being "like a virgin," see Sarah Salih's chapter, "White Clothes," in *Versions of Virginity in Late Medieval England* (Woodbridge, Suffolk, UK: Boydell & Brewer, 2001), 217–23.

116 Mary Dunn, *The Cruelest of All Mothers: Marie de l'Incarnation, Motherhood, and Christian Tradition* (New York: Fordham University Press, 2015), 48.

117 Maeve Callan, *Sacred Sisters: Gender, Sanctity, and Power in Medieval Ireland* (Amsterdam: Amsterdam University Press, 2019), 100–101. Callan notes the uniqueness not only of the saintly pregnancy termination but that the tradition recorded the woman giving thanks to God for it (101).

118 Callan, *Sacred Sisters*, 101–2.

## 3. Finding Resurrection in Buried Grain

1 "Concepts of soul are ubiquitous throughout history and across human societies." Jonathan J. Loose, "Materialism Most Miserable: The Prospects for Dualist and Physicalist Accounts of Resurrection," in *The Blackwell Companion to Substance Dualism*, ed. Jonathan J. Loose, Angus J. L. Menuge, and J. P. Moreland (Hoboken, NJ: Wiley, 2018), 474, 472.

2 Marvin M. Ellison and Kelly Brown Douglas, eds., *Sexuality and the Sacred: Sources for Theological Reflection*, 2nd ed. (Louisville: Westminster John Knox, 2010); Richard Bourne and Imogen Adkins, *A New Introduction to Theology: Embodiment, Experience and Encounter* (London: T&T Clark, 2020).

3 Sallie McFague, *Metaphorical Theology: Models of God in Religious Language* (Philadelphia: Fortress, 1982), 23, 38.

4 McFague, *Metaphorical Theology*, 23.

5 McFague, *Metaphorical Theology*, 108.

6 Caroline Walker Bynum, *The Resurrection of the Body in Western Christianity, 200–1336* (New York: Columbia University Press, 1995), 3.

7 Bynum, *Resurrection of the Body*, 8.

8 Bynum, *Resurrection of the Body*, 57.

9 Bynum, *Resurrection of the Body*, 61.

10 Bynum, *Resurrection of the Body*, 70.

11 Bynum, *Resurrection of the Body*, 96.

12 Irenaeus, quoted in Bynum, *Resurrection of the Body*, 39.

13 Aphrahat, quoted in Bynum, *Resurrection of the Body*, 73. Tertullian makes a similar point that only wheat comes from wheat or barley from barley. Outi Lehtipuu, *Debates over the Resurrection of the Dead: Constructing Early Christian Identity* (Oxford: Oxford University Press, 2015), 138.

14 Bynum, *Resurrection of the Body*, 66.

15 Guerric of Igny, quoted in Bynum, *Resurrection of the Body*, 169. Another Cistercian bishop analogized the final resurrection as sown seed "dying in the winter's cold but . . . revived by the kindly moisture of spring." Otto of Freising, quoted in Bynum, *Resurrection of the Body*, 185.

16 Peter the Venerable, quoted in Bynum, *Resurrection of the Body*, 179.
17 A strike against resurrection metaphorized as flowering may have been the widespread use of "flowers" as a euphemism for a woman's menses, which would have triggered a blood taboo reaction among church leaders and believers. Monica H. Green, ed., *The Trotula: An English Translation of the Medieval Compendium of Women's Medicine* (Philadelphia: University of Pennsylvania Press, 2013), 21. By the seventeenth century, "'flowers' was the most common alternative name for menstruation." Sara Read, *Menstruation and the Female Body in Early Modern England* (New York: Palgrave Macmillan, 2013), 24.
18 Bynum, *Resurrection of the Body*, 113.
19 The papal proclamation *Benedictus Deus* (1336) was seen "as a victory for the position that emphasizes soul" (Bynum, *Resurrection of the Body*, 10). Manuele Gragnolati, *Experiencing the Afterlife: Soul and Body in Dante and Medieval Culture* (Notre Dame, IN: University of Notre Dame Press, 2005), 67–74.
20 John W. Cooper, *Body, Soul, and Life Everlasting: Biblical Anthropology and the Monism-Dualism Debate* (Grand Rapids: Eerdmans, 2000), xv. Other Christian philosophers look approvingly to Cooper's work on this issue. Dean W. Zimmerman, "Should a Christian Be a Mind-Body Dualist?" in *Contemporary Debates in Philosophy of Religion*, ed. Michael L. Peterson and Raymond J. Van Arragon (Malden, MA: Blackwell, 2004), 316n3; Stephen T. Davis, *Risen Indeed: Making Sense of the Resurrection* (Grand Rapids: Eerdmans, 1993), xi; J. P. Moreland and Scott B. Rae, *Body & Soul: Human Nature & the Crisis in Ethics* (Downers Grove, IL: InterVarsity, 2001), 23; Alvin Plantinga, "Materialism and Christian Belief," in *Persons: Human and Divine*, ed. Peter van Inwagen and Dean Zimmerman (New York: Oxford University Press, 2007), 118.
21 Evangelical philosophers who are critics of this hardline position have tried to soften the insistence that Christians must believe in the soul, arguing that "contemporary Christians are free to adopt either physicalism or dualism." Nancey Murphy, *Bodies and Souls, or Spirited Bodies?* (Cambridge: Cambridge University Press, 2006), 37.

22  McFague, *Metaphorical Theology*, 5.

23  Cooper, *Body, Soul, and Life Everlasting*, 39–40. "Old Testament" is the term Cooper uses.

24  Cooper, *Body, Soul, and Life Everlasting*, 64. I quote the version of the Bible Cooper uses. The NRSVue calls them "shades."

25  Cooper, *Body, Soul, and Life Everlasting*, 81.

26  See Cooper, *Body, Soul, and Life Everlasting*, 81–85, 89–90. Mark Finney does not read Josephus as anticipating the notion of bodily resurrection. See his *Resurrection, Hell and the Afterlife: Body and Soul in Antiquity, Judaism and Early Christianity* (New York: Routledge, 2016), 63–64.

27  "Do not be afraid of those who kill the body (*sōma*) but cannot kill the soul (*psychē*)" (Matt 10:28). Cooper, *Body, Soul, and Life Everlasting*, 117.

28  Cooper, *Body, Soul, and Life Everlasting*, 146. Cooper believes this interpretation is reaffirmed in Philippians 1:23: "I desire to depart and be with Christ" (151).

29  See Cooper, *Body, Soul, and Life Everlasting*, 115–16.

30  Cooper, *Body, Soul, and Life Everlasting*, 142. Cooper has no qualms about saying that Paul most likely espoused an "anthropological dualism" (164).

31  Stewart Goetz, "Substance Dualism," in *The Ashgate Research Companion to Theological Anthropology*, ed. Joshua R. Farris and Charles Taliaferro (New York: Routledge, 2016), 130.

32  Paul probably thought of "this 'nakedness' (γυμνός, *gymnos*) with abhorrence" rather than a state of blessedness. Joel B. Green, "Eschatology and the Nature of Humans: A Reconsideration of Pertinent Biblical Evidence," *Science and Christian Belief* 14, no. 1 (2002): 47.

33  Joseph A. Fitzmyer, S.J., *First Corinthians*, Anchor Yale Bible 32 (New Haven, CT: Yale University Press, 2008), 588.

34  Jerry Sumney, "Post-mortem Existence and Resurrection of the Body in Paul," *Horizons in Biblical Theology* 31, no. 1 (2009): 19.

35  N.T. Wright, "Mind, Spirit, Soul and Body: All for One and One for All; Reflections on Paul's Anthropology in His Complex Contexts," Society of Christian Philosophers: Regional Meeting, Fordham University, March 2011, https://tinyurl.com/ycyk8jp9.

36 Dale B. Martin, *The Corinthian Body* (New Haven, CT: Yale University Press, 1999), 15. Stoics tended to see the soul as corporeal; Platonists saw the soul comprised of levels, the highest being the ethereal, rational soul (see 115–16).

37 *Sarx* (flesh) versus *pneuma* (spirit), the mortal versus the immortal, the earthly versus the heavenly. See Martin, *Corinthian Body*, 127.

38 Martin, *Corinthian Body*, 126. For Cooper's views on the "*sōma pneumatikon*," see *Body, Soul, and Life Everlasting*, 152.

39 Martin, *Corinthian Body*, 128. To Paul's mind, the substance of the spiritual body will probably be of "a thinner, higher nature" (128). Martin's contextualized explanation of the spiritual body in 1 Corinthians 15 has been widely affirmed by other scholars. See Candida Moss, *Divine Bodies: Resurrecting Perfection in the New Testament and Early Christianity* (New Haven, CT: Yale University Press, 2019), 12; Sumney, "Post-mortem Existence and Resurrection," 14–15; Claudia Setzer, *Resurrection of the Body in Early Judaism and Early Christianity: Doctrine, Community, and Self-Definition* (Boston: Brill Academic, 2004), 63–66.

40 Luke 23:43, quoted in Cooper, *Body, Soul, and Life Everlasting*, 127. The NRSVue: "Truly I tell you, today you will be with me in paradise."

41 The verse is theologically perplexing because there is no other biblical reference to Jesus's soul going to heaven before his resurrection. Candida R. Moss, *The Other Christs: Imitating Jesus in Ancient Christian Ideologies of Martyrdom* (New York: Oxford University Press, 2010), 123.

42 Joel B. Green, *Body, Soul, and Human Life: The Nature of Humanity in the Bible* (Grand Rapids: Baker, 2008), 163–65.

43 Thomas Farrar, "'Today in Paradise?' Ambiguous Adverb Attachment and the Meaning of Luke 23:43," *Neotestamentica* 51, no. 2 (2017): 186. I will give an emergent materialist reading of this verse in ch. 4.

44 Lazarus (John 11); the widow's son (Luke 7:11–17); Jairus's daughter (Luke 8:52–56); the dead who exit their tombs at the moment of Jesus's death (Matt 27:50–53); Tabitha (Acts 9:36–43); and Eutychus (Acts 20:7–12).

45 Martin, *Corinthian Body*, 130.

46 C. Stephen Evans and Brandon L. Rickabaugh, "What Does It Mean to Be a Bodily Soul?," *Philosophia Christi* 17, no. 2 (2015): 315. Substance dualism is a view "held by the overwhelming number of humankind now and throughout history." J. P. Moreland, "Substance Dualism and the Diachronic/Synchronic Unity of Consciousness," in *Christian Physicalism?: Philosophical Theological Criticisms*, ed. R. Keith Loftin and Joshua R. Farris (Lanham, MD: Lexington, 2018), 43.

47 R. Keith Loftin and Joshua R. Farris, "Christian Physicalism: An Introduction," in Loftin and Farris, *Christian Physicalism?*, xiv.

48 See Sophie Cartwright, "Soul and Body in Early Christianity: An Old and New Conundrum," in *A History of Mind and Body in Late Antiquity*, ed. Anna Marmodoro and Sophie Cartwright (Cambridge: Cambridge University Press, 2018), 176.

49 Moss, *The Other Christs*, 119.

50 Eliezer Gonzalez, "Anthropologies of Continuity: The Body and Soul in Tertullian, Perpetua, and Early Christianity," *Journal of Early Christian Studies* 21, no. 4 (2013): 485.

51 Finney, *Resurrection, Hell and the Afterlife*, 150.

52 Marie-Hélène Congourdeau, "Debating the Soul in Late Antiquity," in *Reproduction: Antiquity to the Present Day*, ed. Nick Hopwood, Rebecca Flemming, and Lauren Kassell (Cambridge: Cambridge University Press, 2018), 115. See also Peter W. Martens, "Embodiment, Heresy, and the Hellenization of Christianity: The Descent of the Soul in Plato and Origen," *Harvard Theological Review* 108, no. 4 (2015): 594.

53 Origen quoted in Paul L. Gavrilyuk, "The Incorporeality of the Soul in Patristic Thought," in Loftin and Farris, *Christian Physicalism?*, 13.

54 See Congourdeau, "Debating the Soul in Late Antiquity," 118.

55 Augustine quoted in Stewart Goetz and Charles Taliaferro, *A Brief History of the Soul* (Chichester, UK: John Wiley, 2011), 33.

56 Goetz and Taliaferro, *Brief History of the Soul*, 20

57 Augustine quoted in Bynum, *Resurrection of the Body*, 104.

58 Bynum, *Resurrection of the Body*, 100.

59 Susan Wessel, "The Reception of Greek Science in Gregory of Nyssa's *De hominis opificio*," *Vigiliae Christianae* 63, no. 1 (2009): 26.

60 Wessel, "Reception of Greek Science," 36.

61 Gregory of Nyssa, quoted in Catharine P. Roth, "Platonic and Pauline Elements in the Ascent of the Soul in Gregory of Nyssa's Dialogue on the Soul and Resurrection," *Vigiliae Christianae* 46, no. 1 (1992): 22–23.

62 Benjamin P. Blosser, "The Ensoulment of the Body in Early Christian Thought," in Marmodoro and Cartwright, *History of Mind and Body in Late Antiquity*, 211. N. T. Wright argues that the church fathers firmly rejected transmigration. *The Resurrection of the Son of God* (Minneapolis: Fortress, 2003), 77–79.

63 Moss, *The Other Christs*, 120–21.

64 Moss, *The Other Christs*, 118.

65 Bynum, *Resurrection of the Body*, 56.

66 Peter Brown, *The Body and Society: Men, Women, and Sexual Renunciation in Early Christianity*, 20th anniv. ed. with new introduction (New York: Columbia University Press, 2008), lx.

67 Teresa M. Shaw, *The Burden of the Flesh: Fasting and Sexuality in Early Christianity* (Minneapolis: Fortress, 1998), 78.

68 Quoting Gregory of Nyssa, in Bynum, *Resurrection of the Body*, 85.

69 Shaw, *The Burden of the Flesh*, ch. 6.

70 "The Anathemas against Origen," ¶ X, in the "Fifth Ecumenical Council: Second Council of Constantinople" (553), *Nicene and Post-Nicene Fathers*, Series II: *Seven Ecumenical Councils*, vol. 14, ed. Philip Schaff and Henry Wace, https://tinyurl.com/364fyd6u.

71 Brian Schmisek, *Resurrection of the Flesh or Resurrection from the Dead: Implications for Theology* (Collegeville, MN: Liturgical, 2013), 35.

72 I am not implying that substance dualism throughout history or today incites misogyny. It is noteworthy, however, that in two major anthologies on the subject, no female scholars contributed essays defending this ontology: Loose, Menuge, and Moreland, *The Blackwell Companion to Substance Dualism;* Loftin and Farris, *Christian Physicalism?*

73 The notion of a paradigm shift is borrowed from Thomas S. Kuhn's classic, *The Structure of Scientific Revolutions* (Chicago: University of Chicago Press, 1970).

74 Goetz and Taliaferro, *Brief History of the Soul*, 22.

75  Aquinas, quoted in Eleonore Stump, "Resurrection, Reassembly, and Reconstitution: Aquinas on the Soul," in *Die Menschliche Seele: Brauchen Wir den Dualismus?*, ed. Bruno Niederbacher and Edmund Runggaldier (Frankfurt: ontos verlag, 2006), 166.

76  Notger Slenczka, "Luther's Anthropology," in *The Oxford Handbook of Martin Luther's Theology*, ed. Robert Kolb, Irene Dingel, and L'ubomir Batka (Oxford: Oxford University Press, 2014), 214–17.

77  On Calvin's exposure to the thought of Scholastic and other theologians, see Anthony N. S. Lane, *John Calvin: Student of Church Fathers* (Edinburgh: T & T Clark, 1999), ch. 2.

78  John Calvin *Institutes of the Christian Religion* (1536), trans. Ford Lewis Battles, ed. John T. McNeill (Philadelphia: Westminster, 1960), 192 (I.15.6). Calvin believed that the soul's incorporeality was a biblical teaching (see 184–88; I.15.2).

79  Substance dualists "accept a metaphysic of soul and body that is deceptively similar to Plato's: one *is* an immaterial soul." Peter van Inwagen, "I Look for the Resurrection of the Dead and the Life of the World to Come," in Loose, Menuge, and Moreland, *Blackwell Companion to Substance Dualism*, 491.

80  Evans and Rickabaugh, "What Does It Mean to Be a Bodily Soul?," 315.

81  Alvin Plantinga, "Materialism and Christian Belief," in van Inwagen and Zimmerman, *Persons: Human and Divine*, 100.

82  Jonathan J. Loose, "Materialism Most Miserable: The Prospects for Dualist and Physicalist Accounts of Resurrection," in Loose, Menuge, and Moreland, *Blackwell Companion to Substance Dualism*, 471–72.

83  It is sometimes called "integrative dualism." Charles Taliaferro, "Substance Dualism: A Defense," in Loose, Menuge, and Moreland, *Blackwell Companion to Substance Dualism*, 44–45.

84  Brandon Rickabaugh, "Dismantling Bodily Resurrection Arguments against Mind-Body Dualism," in Loftin and Farris, *Christian Physicalism?*, 306.

85  Moreland and Rae, *Body & Soul*, 21, italics added.

86  Brandon L. Rickabaugh, "Responding to N.T. Wright's Rejection of the Soul," *Heythrop Journal* 59, no. 2 (2018): 209, italics added.

87 Goetz, "Substance Dualism," 135.

88 Pew Research Center, "Few Americans Blame God or Say Faith Has Been Shaken amid Pandemic, Other Tragedies" (Nov. 23, 2021), https://tinyurl.com/mshbxvt5.

89 Rickabaugh, "Responding to N.T. Wright's Rejection of the Soul," 212.

90 Moreland and Rae, *Body & Soul*, 200.

91 It is questionable that Thomistic substance dualism succeeds as an ontology, since a soul cannot be both a separable subsistent entity and a form, as Aquinas defined it. How the soul in substance dualism differs from the soul in hylomorphism is explained well in Robert Pasnau, *Thomas Aquinas on Human Nature: A Philosophical Study of* Summa Theologiae, *1a 75–89* (Cambridge: Cambridge University Press, 2002), 65–72.

92 Moreland and Rae, *Body & Soul*, 201.

93 Gary R. Habermas and J. P. Moreland, *Beyond Death: Exploring the Evidence for Immortality* (Eugene, OR: Wipf and Stock, 2004), 227. The intermediate state will be a mentally active time of "intensified fellowship with Christ" and possibly the ability to "communicate" telepathically with other souls (231, 232).

94 Rickabaugh sees the risk in positing a soul fully conscious of and enjoying God. He waffles between saying "the soul may still be able to function in some regular ways" but will not able to "function in its normal and intended way" ("Responding to N.T. Wright's Rejection of the Soul," 212).

95 Rickabaugh, "Responding to N.T. Wright's Rejection of the Soul," 212.

96 Moreland and Rae, *Body & Soul*, 21

97 Moreland and Rae, *Body & Soul*, 211. Any hylomorphic approach to the resurrection (including Aquinas's) faces this problem. I will say more about Aquinas on the resurrection in ch. 4.

98 Jonathan J. Loose, "Christian Materialism and Christian Ethics: Moral Debt and an Ethic of Life," in Loftin and Farris, *Christian Physicalism?*, 363, 362.

99 There is a "heaven for aborted fetuses." Habermas and Moreland, *Beyond Death*, 372.

100 Some philosophers require not just belief in a soul but a traducian soul. Moreland and Rae argue that an embryo's or a fetus's

right to life derives from it having the soul it received at conception, itself generated by the "soulish potentialities" in the sperm and egg (*Body & Soul*, 221). On John Cooper's traducianism, see "The Current Body-Soul Debate: A Case for Dualistic Holism," *Southern Baptist Journal of Theology* 13, no. 2 (2009): 49n27.

101  Timothy O'Connor and Jonathan D. Jacobs, "Emergent Individuals and the Resurrection," *European Journal for Philosophy of Religion* 2, no. 2 (2010): 86, 77.

102  See Nancey Murphy, "Nonreductive Physicalism," in *In Search of the Soul: Perspectives on the Mind-Body Problem*, ed. Joel B. Green and Stuart L. Palmer (Downers Grove, IL: InterVarsity, 2005), 115–38.

103  R. Keith Loftin and Joshua R. Farris, "Christian Physicalism: An Introduction," in Loftin and Farris, *Christian Physicalism?*, xiii.

104  Trenton Merricks, "How to Live Forever without Saving Your Soul: Physicalism and Immortality," in *Soul, Body, and Survival: Essays on the Metaphysics of Human Persons*, ed. Kevin Corcoran (Ithaca, NY: Cornell University Press, 2001), 183.

105  Merricks, "How to Live Forever," 184.

106  Corcoran, *Rethinking Human Nature*, 127.

107  O'Connor and Jacobs, "Emergent Individuals and the Resurrection," 84.

108  Peter van Inwagen, "The Possibility of Resurrection," *International Journal for Philosophy of Religion* (1978): 119.

109  See Kevin Corcoran, "Physical Persons and Postmortem Survival without Temporal Gaps," in Corcoran, *Soul, Body, and Survival*, 201–17.

110  Adam Wood, "Mind the Gap? The Principle of Non-repeatability and Aquinas's Account of the Resurrection," in *Oxford Studies in Medieval Philosophy*, vol. 3, ed. Robert Pasnau (Oxford: Oxford University Press, 2015), 99–127.

111  See John Hick, *Death and Eternal Life* (Louisville: Westminster John Knox, 1994), 279–84. Hick's notion of a resurrected replica is linked to his proposal for serial cycles of personal existence "in other worlds . . . other than that in which we are now" (456).

112  Van Inwagen, "The Possibility of Resurrection," 121.

113 Dean W. Zimmerman, "The Compatibility of Materialism and Survival: The 'Falling Elevator' Model," *Faith and Philosophy* 16, no. 2 (1999): 196. Zimmerman is actually a substance dualist, but he generously offers his best take on what a successful materialist argument might look like.

114 Corcoran, *Rethinking Human Nature*, 132.

115 Individual postmortem survival is possible only if the "resurrection jump works for the organism as a whole." Dean Zimmerman, "Bodily Resurrection: The Falling Elevator Model Revisited," in *Personal Identity and Resurrection*, ed. Georg Gasser (Burlington, VT: Ashgate, 2010), 44.

116 Hick speaks of the afterlife replica of a "Mr X" (Hick, *Death and Eternal Life*, 290); van Inwagen imagines reanimating the corpse of "Socrates" (van Inwagen, "I Look for the Resurrection," 493); Zimmerman debates the best way to think of the resurrection of "Jones" and "Smith" (Zimmerman, "Bodily Resurrection," 41–43).

117 There is also the issue of disabled bodies in a materialist approach to the resurrection. I will discuss this issue in ch. 5.

118 It is difficult to determine whether materialist philosophers' lack of comment on this issue is influenced by their position on fetal personhood. Only a few have even commented on it. Hick sees fetal personhood only "as a potentiality" and implies that laws allowing for early abortions are morally permissible (Hick, *Death and Eternal Life*, 45). Peter van Inwagen disputes the pro-life claim that you and I "were once zygotes," and he identifies fetal neurocortical development as decisive for "the beginning of a life," *Material Beings* (Ithaca, NY: Cornell University Press, 1990), 152, 154.

119 Merricks, "How to Live Forever," 184.

120 Zimmerman, "Bodily Resurrection," 36–37.

121 Dean Zimmerman, "Personal Identity and the Survival of Death," in *The Oxford Handbook of Philosophy of Death*, ed. Ben Bradley, Fred Feldman, and Jens Johansson (New York: Oxford University Press, 2013), 142. Budding would allow for the "arrangement of atoms that appear at a distance [to be] directly immanent-causally connected to my body at the time of my death" (142).

122 The hymn was written by early twentieth-century Anglican minister J. M. C. Crum at some point after the childbirth death of his wife of two years. See C. Michael Hawn, "History of Hymns: 'Now the Green Blade Riseth,'" Discipleship Ministries, United Methodist Church (Apr. 22, 2014), https://tinyurl.com/4fsfhjac.

123 Wright, "Mind, Spirit, Soul, and Body."

124 Paul Ricoeur, "Biblical Hermeneutics," *Semeia* 4 (1975): 75.

125 Ricoeur, "Biblical Hermeneutics," 78.

## 4. Emerging into Resurrected Life

1 John E. Thiel, "For What May We Hope? Thoughts on the Eschatological Imagination," *Theological Studies* 67, no. 3 (2006): 527.

2 T. S. Eliot, "Little Gidding," https://tinyurl.com/3s27nruw.

3 "Is Emergence Fundamental?" Closer to Truth, https://tinyurl.com/3s27nruw.

4 William Hasker, "The Case for Emergent Dualism," in *The Blackwell Companion to Substance Dualism*, ed. Jonathan J. Loose, Angus J. L. Menuge, and J. P. Moreland (Hoboken, NJ: Wiley, 2018), 65.

5 Hasker, "Case for Emergent Dualism," 65.

6 Timothy O'Connor and Jonathan D. Jacobs, "Emergent Individuals and the Resurrection," *European Journal for Philosophy of Religion* 2, no. 2 (2010): 84. Technically speaking, "the simples that compose us . . . have latent dispositions such that, when *organically* arranged in the right sorts of ways—in the first instance, into cells, then into more complex structures such as functioning nervous systems—they collectively cause and sustain emergent mental phenomena."

7 It makes sense to conclude that a fetus would also "be capable of the same sort of development" without having to be "infused with an immaterial soul" (William Hasker, "A Critique of Thomistic Dualism," in Loose, Menuge, and Moreland, *Blackwell Companion to Substance Dualism*, 126).

8 William Hasker, "The Emergence of Persons," in *The Blackwell Companion to Science and Christianity*, ed. James B. Stump and Alan G. Padgett (Walden, MA: Blackwell, 2012), 483.

9 O'Connor and Jacobs, "Emergent Individuals and the Resurrection," 76. "The emergent things we are are none other than living organisms."

10 Emergent materialism differs from emergent dualism. The latter argues that human bodily development produces "an *emergent immaterial entity*" (call it mind, soul, consciousness), which survives the death of the body in an interim state (Hasker, "Case for Emergent Dualism," 67, italics in original). By positing the bodiless survival of the mind/soul/consciousness, emergent dualism reiterates a traditional soul-based view of the resurrection.

11 Timothy O'Connor and Jonathan D. Jacobs, "Emergent Individuals," *Philosophical Quarterly* 53, no. 213 (2003): 551.

12 O'Connor and Jacobs, "Emergent Individuals," 546. O'Connor and Jacobs suggest the basis for a perduring self is a kind of primitive "*thisness*"—something between a substance, property, and process. The idea is obscure, as other philosophers have noted. See James T. Turner Jr., *On the Resurrection of the Dead: A New Metaphysics of Afterlife for Christian Thought* (New York: Routledge, 2018), 83–96; William Hasker, "Is Materialism Equivalent to Dualism?" in *After Physicalism*, ed. Paul Göcke Benedikt (Notre Dame, IN: University of Notre Dame Press, 2012), 194–95.

13 O'Connor and Jacobs, "Emergent Individuals," 551.

14 See ch. 3, "Materialist Resurrection without a Soul."

15 O'Connor and Jacobs, "Emergent Individuals and the Resurrection," 79. The "dead body in the grave is not just a replica of something that once was a living organism, but is instead the remains of such an organism," lacking only the *thisness* that went with the "glorified individual far away from *terra firma*" (79).

16 See ch. 3, "Materialist Resurrection without a Soul."

17 James L. Bernat, "The Whole-Brain Concept of Death Remains Optimum Public Policy," *Journal of Law, Medicine & Ethics* 34, no. 1 (2006): 37, 38.

18 Alexander E. Pozhitkov and Peter A. Noble, "Gene Expression in the Twilight of Death," *Bioessays* 39, no. 9 (2017): 1700066.

19 Eliot, "Little Gidding."

20 As discussed in ch. 3, Dean Zimmerman suggests a materialist approach to bodily resurrection where God endows each "atom

within the corpse" with its own "miraculous 'budding' power." "Personal Identity and the Survival of Death," in *The Oxford Handbook of Philosophy of Death*, ed. Ben Bradley, Fred Feldman, and Jens Johansson (New York: Oxford University Press, 2013), 142.

21  Budding materialist resurrection would have to address other concerns as well. Hershenov thinks the idea of materialist resurrection might work, but only if "part replacement does not happen too quickly and the replacement parts are not too large." David B. Hershenov, "Van Inwagen, Zimmerman, and the Materialist Conception of Resurrection," *Religious Studies* 38, no. 4 (2002): 461. My model of budding emergence is guilty of adding great amounts of new organic matter but at least it happens very slowly, presumably over a very long stretch of time.

22  Hershenov, "Van Inwagen, Zimmerman," 459.

23  If many contenders for the deceased me suddenly appear in the afterlife, my identity would be the result of some external, arbitrary factor that determines the closest contender for the real me. See Dean Zimmerman, "Bodily Resurrection: The Falling Elevator Model Revisited," in *Personal Identity and Resurrection*, ed. Georg Gasser (Burlington, VT: Ashgate, 2016), 38–44.

24  I agree with Kevin Corcoran that the materialist who is a theist can appeal to God to solve the closest continuer problem. "Physical Persons and Postmortem Survival without Temporal Gaps," in *Soul, Body, and Survival: Essays on the Metaphysics of Human Persons*, ed. Kevin Corcoran (Ithaca, NY: Cornell University Press, 2001), 215.

25  There is no genetically "gappy" existence. See my discussion of this notion in ch. 3, "Materialist Resurrection without a Soul."

26  Peter van Inwagen, "I Look for the Resurrection of the Dead and the Life of the World to Come," in Loose, Menuge, and Moreland, *Blackwell Companion to Substance Dualism*, 496.

27  For more on the materialist principle of immanent causality, see ch. 3, "Materialist Resurrection without a Soul."

28  See Christina Van Dyke, "I See Dead People: Disembodied Souls and Aquinas's 'Two-Person' Problem," in *Oxford Studies in Medieval Philosophy*, ed. Robert Pasnau, vol. 2 (Oxford: Oxford University Press, 2014).

29 O'Connor and Jacobs judge that Aquinas leaves woefully unexplained how the rules of hylomorphism can be temporarily suspended. How is it "possible for a mere 'form' of something to persist absent any underlying stuff that it is the form *of*'? ("Emergent Individuals and the Resurrection," 86).

30 That Aquinas's hylomorphic ideas might translate well into an emergence model is not surprising. Brian Leftow sees hylomorphism as a type of protoemergentism. "Souls Dipped in Dust," in Corcoran, *Soul, Body, and Survival,* 128–29. According to Christopher Shields and Robert Pasnau, "Aquinas prefigures . . . emergentist approaches to life." *The Philosophy of Aquinas*, 2nd ed. (New York: Oxford University Press, 2016), 200.

31 In Greek myth, the souls in the underworld preparing for reincarnation must drink the waters of forgetting from the river Lethe.

32 These four categories are suggested in Nancey Murphy, "A Nonreductive Physicalist Response," in *In Search of the Soul: Four Views of the Mind-Body Problem*, ed. Joel B. Green and Stuart L. Palmer (Downers Grove, IL: InterVarsity, 2005), 185–88. See also David H. Kelsey, *Eccentric Existence: A Theological Anthropology*, vol. 1 (Louisville: Westminster John Knox, 2009), 556.

33 Constitutionalism, a type of materialism, defines a person as a human organism with a "first-person perspective." Lynne Rudder Baker, "Persons and the Metaphysics of Resurrection," *Religious Studies* 43 (2007): 335. Persons are constituted by their biological bodies but are not "identical with the physical organisms that constitute them." Kevin Corcoran, *Rethinking Human Nature: A Christian Materialist Alternative to the Soul* (Grand Rapids: Baker Academic, 2006), 69.

34 Resurrection is the event of one's first-person perspective property transferred by "God's free decree" into a new risen body. Baker, "Persons and the Metaphysics of Resurrection," 346. Baker's pithy formula: "Same person, different body, no soul." Lynne Rudder Baker, "Resurrecting Material Persons," in *The Palgrave Handbook of the Afterlife*, ed. Yujin Nagasawa and Benjamin Matheson (London: Palgrave Macmillan, 2017), 315.

35 Marya Schechtman, *The Constitution of Selves* (Ithaca, NY: Cornell University Press, 1996), 94, 97.

36 Hilde Lindemann Nelson, "What Child Is This?," *Hastings Center Report* 32, no. 6 (2002): 36.

37 Michael W. DeLashmutt, "Paul Ricoeur at the Foot of the Cross: Narrative Identity and the Resurrection of the Body," *Modern Theology* 25, no. 4 (2009): 590.

38 John Polkinghorne defines the self as a "dynamic, information-bearing pattern" that is "perfectly preserved in the divine memory." "Eschatological Credibility: Emergent and Teleological Processes," in *Resurrection: Theological and Scientific Assessments*, ed. Ted Peters, Robert John Russell, and Michael Welker (Grand Rapids: Eerdmans, 2002), 51, 52.

39 See Stanley B. Klein and Shaun Nichols, "Memory and the Sense of Personal Identity," *Mind* 121, no. 483 (2012): 677–702.

40 Song of Songs 7:5.

41 Augustine, *City of God*, 22.13, in *The Nicene and Post-Nicene Fathers*, vol. 2, trans. Marcus Dodd, ed. Philip Schaff and Henry Wace (Grand Rapids: Eerdmans, 1972), 494, https://tinyurl.com/4dbcj2ws.

42 Hasker (emergent dualism) is skeptical of embryonic or fetal resurrection, finding it unacceptable to conclude that "the greater part of the citizenry of the eternal kingdom is made up of . . . [creatures] who never drew a breath on the earth." William Hasker, "Abortion and the Definition of a Person," *The Human Life Review* 5, no. 2 (1979): 31. Baker (constitutionalism) concludes that a first-person perspective develops later in gestation ("Christian Materialism in a Scientific Age," *International Journal for Philosophy of Religion* 70, no. 1 [2011]: 49n11). Before that point, there is no person to be resurrected—nor is there a person killed by abortion. Lynne Rudder Baker, "When Does a Person Begin?," *Social Philosophy and Policy* 22, no. 2 (2005): 45. Peter van Inwagen (materialism) discounts fetal personhood prior to brain development (*Material Beings* [Ithaca, NY: Cornell University Press, 1990], 152, 154).

43 Marija Gimbutas, *The Living Goddesses* (Berkeley: University of California Press, 2001).

44 See Diana W. Bianchi, "Fetal Cells in the Mother: From Genetic Diagnosis to Diseases Associated with Fetal Cell Microchimerism," *European Journal of Obstetrics & Gynecology and*

*Reproductive Biology* 92, no. 1 (2000): 103–8; Suzanne Peterson et al., "Fetal Cellular Microchimerism in Miscarriage and Pregnancy Termination," *Chimerism*, 4, no. 3 (2013): 136–38.

45 Claire T. Roberts, "Premature Lambs Grown in a Bag," *Nature* 546 (June 2017): 45–46.

46 My argument here is not an apologetic attempt to convert scientists to believe in Christian resurrection. For the theologian working with the notion of God as Creator, however, all scientific discoveries are fair game to use in explicating doctrine.

47 Lindemann Nelson recounts her family's experience of caring for her anencephalic sister, Carla, who lived only eighteen months ("What Child Is This?").

48 Schechtman, *The Constitution of Selves*, 94. In an agency-based notion of narrative identity an anencephalic infant or person with dementia lives on the margins of personhood (146–48). Schechtman has amended this view in later writings, arguing that imputed narrative identity renders a fetus a person about whom moral questions may be discussed. Marya Schechtman, *Staying Alive: Personal Identity, Practical Concerns, and the Unity of a Life* (New York: Oxford University Press, 2014), 105–6. I question relying solely on the notion of imputed personhood. One can and should ask moral questions about uterine beings even if one thinks the category of person does not apply.

49 Loftin and Farris, "Christian Physicalism," xiv.

50 See ch. 3, "Saving the Soul and Losing Orthodoxy."

51 Richard Price and Michael Gaddis, *The Acts of the Council of Chalcedon, 400–700* (Liverpool: Liverpool University Press, 2005).

52 *Grammar* is a Wittgensteinian term Lindbeck uses to display how the normativity of doctrinal formulations can be seen in terms of rules for Christian life, analogous to how languages are spoken using accepted linguistic rules. George A. Lindbeck, *The Nature of Doctrine: Religion and Theology in a Postliberal Age* (Philadelphia: Westminster John Knox, 1984), 106–7.

53 See my discussion of how to use Lindbeck's theory to adjudicate among differing theological positions. *Feminist Theology and the Challenge of Difference* (New York: Oxford University Press, 2007), 116–23.

54 Evans and Rickabaugh, "What Does It Mean to Be a Bodily Soul?," 316.

55 Heidelberg Catechism (1563), Faith Alive Christian Resources (2011), part II, question 57; available at: https://tinyurl.com/3rvke9k3.

56 Adapted from Heidelberg Catechism, questions 57 and 58.

57 The answers to 57 and 58 are prefaced by the question, "How does [the teaching] comfort you?"

58 I see emergent resurrection as entailing some kind of universal shalom. I base this perspective on philosophical arguments that blessedness is not possible if a separate realm of eternal hellish suffering exists. See Eric Reitan, "Eternal Damnation and Blessed Ignorance: Is the Damnation of Some Incompatible with the Salvation of Any?," *Religious Studies* 38 (2002): 429–50.

59 In this way, a materialist emergence model for personal postmortem survival is compatible with feminist and ecotheologies that critique anthropocentrism and demand a broader focus on the redemption of this planet, spoken of as "deep resurrection." Elizabeth A. Johnson, "Jesus and the Cosmos: Soundings in Deep Christology," in *Incarnation: On the Scope and Depth of Christology*, ed. Niels Henrik Gregersen (Minneapolis: Fortress, 2015), 133–56.

60 I am not implying a millennialist age on earth that various Christians groups associate with Christ's return.

61 Kelsey, *Eccentric Existence*, 554.

62 Robert W. Jenson, *Systematic Theology*, vol. 2, *The Works of God* (New York: Oxford University Press, 1999), 19, 222, 351.

63 Athanasian Creed.

64 On the conjunction of apophaticism and rule theory, see Margaret D. Kamitsuka, *Abortion and the Christian Tradition: A Pro-choice Theological Ethic* (Louisville: Westminster John Knox, 2019), 88–90.

65 Mark Harris, "Will Resurrection Be a Law of Nature? Science as Divine Action at the End of the World," in *Chance or Providence: Religious Perspectives on Divine Action* (Newcastle upon Tyne, UK: Cambridge Scholars, 2014), 41.

66 Jesus invites being touched (John 20:27); he avoids being touched (John 20:17); he walks along a road (Luke 24: 15, 28); he eats (Luke 24:42–43).

67 Luke 24:31, 51; Acts 1:9–10.

68 "It is even conceivable that the gospels were written as a kind of polemic against Paul's thinking." Alan F. Segal, "Paul's Thinking about Resurrection in Its Jewish Context," *New Testament Studies* 44, no. 3 (1998): 419.

69 Luke 23:46.

70 "Truly I tell you, today you will be with me in Paradise." For my discussion of the placement of the adverbial "today," see ch. 3, "Finding the Soul in the New Testament."

71 Lazarus (John 11: 1–44). See also the widow's son (Luke 7:11–17), and Jairus's daughter (Luke 8:49–56).

72 Richard B. Hays, *First Corinthians* (Louisville: Westminster John Knox, 2011), 270. The gospels also have Jesus using "a grain of wheat" metaphor (John 12:24).

73 Sallie McFague, *Metaphorical Theology: Models of God in Religious Language* (Minneapolis: Fortress, 1982), 44.

74 McFague, *Metaphorical Theology*, 23.

75 Guerric of Igny, quoted in Caroline Walker Bynum, *The Resurrection of the Body in Western Christianity, 200–1336* (New York: Columbia University Press, 1995), 169.

## 5. Envisioning Disabled Bodies in Heaven and Reproductive Agency on Earth

1 The type of selective abortion to be discussed in this chapter is the termination of a pregnancy when a disabling genetic condition, malformation, or other anomaly is detected prenatally. I will not discuss sex-related selective abortion or genetic testing of embryos in IVF.

2 Disability theorists have advocated for various preferred terms. *Disability* is widely used, but some theorists critique that term as a cultural label about "broken 'parts.'" Brian Brock, *Wondrously Wounded: Theology, Disability, and the Body of Christ* (Waco, TX: Baylor University Press 2019), 195. Other prodisability advocates use medicalized terms, such as *affected fetus*. Adrienne Asch, "Why I Haven't Changed My Mind about Prenatal Diagnosis: Reflections and Refinements," in *Prenatal Testing and Disability Rights*, ed. Erik Parens and Adrienne Asch (Washington, DC:

Georgetown University Press, 2000), 240. I acknowledge these complexities and will vary my word usage accordingly.

3 Pope John Paul II, quoted in Hans S. Reinders, *Receiving the Gift of Friendship: Profound Disability, Theological Anthropology, and Ethics* (Grand Rapids: Eerdmans, 2008), 120, 32. Some disability scholars argue positively for a new attitude toward "conserving disability" as an ethical and epistemic resource. Rosemarie Garland-Thomson, "The Case for Conserving Disability," *Journal of Bioethical Inquiry* 9, no. 3 (2012): 345–49.

4 Christopher Kaczor, *The Ethics of Abortion: Women's Rights, Human Life, and the Question of Justice*, 3rd ed. (New York: Routledge, 2023), 200. Likewise, Reinders believes any pregnancy termination constitutes "an act of homicide." Hans S. Reinders, *The Future of the Disabled in Liberal Society* (Notre Dame, IN: University of Notre Dame Press, 2000), 23.

5 Adrienne Asch and David Wasserman, "Where Is the Sin in Synecdoche? Prenatal Testing and the Parent-Child Relationship," in *Quality of Life and Human Difference: Genetic Testing, Health Care, and Disability*, ed. David Wasserman, Robert Wachbroit, and Jerome Bickenbach (Cambridge: Cambridge University Press, 2005), 203. Asch and Wasserman consider selective abortion might be morally permissible in only three instances: "severe, comprehensive cognitive impairments; very early death; and virulently oppressive social environments" (205); however, even these reasons strike them as weak.

6 Amos Yong, *Theology and Down Syndrome: Reimagining Disability in Late Modernity* (Waco, TX: Baylor University Press, 2007), 65.

7 Yong acknowledges the problem of "spontaneous abortions" due to genetic abnormalities but does not comment on the eternal destiny of these uterine beings (*Theology and Down Syndrome*, 180).

8 This chapter is an attempt to take seriously the challenge for feminist theologians to reflect on how women and disabled persons are marginalized as "that which culture holds abject" in different but possibly related ways. Sharon V. Betcher, "Becoming Flesh of My Flesh: Feminist and Disability Theologies on the Edge of Posthumanist Discourse," *Journal of Feminist Studies in Religion* 26, no. 2 (2010): 115.

9 Terrence Ehrman, "Disability and Resurrection Identity," *New Blackfriars* 96, no. 1066 (2015): 735, 738.

10 Ehrman, "Disability and Resurrection Identity," 734.

11 Ehrman, "Disability and Resurrection Identity," 732.

12 Ehrman, "Disability and Resurrection Identity," 738.

13 James Barton Gould, "The Hope of Heavenly Healing of Disability, Part 1: Theological Issues," *Journal of Disability & Religion* 20, no. 4 (2016): 321.

14 James Barton Gould, "The Hope of Heavenly Healing of Disability, Part 2: Philosophical Issues," *Journal of Disability & Religion* 21, no. 1 (2017): 101. R.T. Mullins agrees that theology should attend seriously to those disabled persons who hope for "God's future curing of their bodies." "Some Difficulties for Amos Yong's Disability Theology of the Resurrection," *Ars Disputandi* 11, no. 1 (2011): 30.

15 Mullins, "Some Difficulties," 31.

16 Gould, "The Hope of Heavenly Healing of Disability, Part 1," 330.

17 Yong, *Theology and Down Syndrome*, 269.

18 Yong, *Theology and Down Syndrome*, 259.

19 This motto is attributed to Stanley Hauerwas in Amos Yong, "Disability and the Love of Wisdom: De-forming, Re-forming, and Per-forming Philosophy of Religion," *Ars Disputandi* 9, no. 1 (2009): 61; Yong, *Theology and Down Syndrome*, 270.

20 See Nancy L. Eiesland, "Liberation, Inclusion, and Justice: A Faith Response to Persons with Disabilities," *Impact* 14, no. 3 (2001/02).

21 Timpe tries to thread the needle with a taxonomy of disabilities. He suggests that beatitude-interfering disabilities might be healed, but other disabilities (e.g., blindness) would be retained in the resurrected body. Kevin Timpe, "Defiant Afterlife: Disability and Uniting Ourselves to God," in *Voices from the Edge: Centring Marginalized Perspectives in Analytic Theology*, ed. Michelle Panchuk and Mike Rea (Oxford: Oxford University Press, 2020), 223–27.

22 Amos Yong, "Disability Theology of the Resurrection: Persisting Questions and Additional Considerations—a Response to Ryan Mullins," *Ars Disputandi* 12, no. 1 (2012): 9. See Brock, *Wondrously Wounded*, 184–85, 192.

23  Brock references his son Adam, who has severe intellectual disabilities. *Wondrously Wounded*, 192.

24  Lisa D. Powell, "Disability and Resurrection: Eschatological Bodies, Identity, and Continuity," *Journal of the Society of Christian Ethics* 41, no. 1 (2021): 90, 103. See also Devan Joy Stahl, "A Christian Ontology of Genetic Disease and Disorder," *Journal of Disability & Religion* 19, no. 2 (2015): 119–45.

25  Yong, *Theology and Down Syndrome*, 188. Yong endorses a kind of emergent dualism. "Mental (cognitional) properties . . . are dependent on but not fully explicable by physical (brain) properties" (170), and "souls are emergent from and constituted by human bodies and brains without being reducible to the sum of these biological parts" (188).

26  Yong, *Theology and Down Syndrome*, 190.

27  Yong, *Theology and Down Syndrome*, 282. Timpe argues that not all people with cognitive disabilities need to be completely healed in heaven as long as the "degree of cognitive disability [does not] fall below the relevant limit such that . . . their union with God is impaired" ("Defiant Afterlife," 226–27).

28  A materialist emergence view of the resurrection does not specify whether disabilities acquired in one's life from disease, ageing, and so on, would remain in the afterlife. Yong does not see these types of disabilities as "identity-constitutive" in the way that congenital disabilities are (Yong, "Disability and the Love of Wisdom," 68).

29  Even retention models imply the need for some slow process of healing change in heaven, appealing to Gregory of Nyssa's notion of *epectasis* (Yong, *Theology and Down Syndrome*, 274). Gould also appeals to this concept ("The Hope of Heavenly Healing of Disability, Part 2," 111–12).

30  Powell, "Disability and Resurrection."

31  See Kathryn Joyce, *Quiverfull: Inside the Christian Patriarchy Movement* (Boston: Beacon, 2009); Emily Hunter McGowin, *Quivering Families: The Quiverfull Movement and Evangelical Theology of the Family* (Minneapolis: Fortress, 2018).

32  See ch. 1, "Reproduction in Bondage," in Dorothy Roberts, *Killing the Black Body: Race, Reproduction, and the Meaning of Liberty* (New York: Vintage, 1999), 22–55.

33 Lisa Sowle Cahill, "Abortion and Argument by Analogy," *Horizons* 9, no. 2 (1982): 284.

34 Kaczor, *The Ethics of Abortion*, 185.

35 Kaczor, *The Ethics of Abortion*, 187.

36 On rising mortality rates in pregnancy, see Priya Agrawal, "Maternal Mortality and Morbidity in the United States of America," *Bulletin of the World Health Organization* 93 (2015): 135. https://tinyurl.com/fd2f79ds.

37 Candida R. Moss and Joel S. Baden, *Reconceiving Infertility: Biblical Perspectives on Procreation and Childlessness* (Princeton, NJ: Princeton University Press, 2015).

38 Delores S. Williams, *Sisters in the Wilderness: The Challenge of Womanist God-Talk* (Maryknoll, NY: Orbis, 1993).

39 For example, Jacob and Esau (Gen 25:23); the prophet Jeremiah (Jer 1:5); John the Baptist (Luke 1:13–17); Jesus (Luke 1:31–33).

40 Thomas Aquinas warned against drawing universalizing conclusions. See *Summa Theologica*, trans. Fathers of the Eastern Dominican Province (New York: Benzinger, 1947), III Q. 27, a. 6, respondeo; https://tinyurl.com/mr23364m.

41 See Frances Gray, "Original Habitation: Pregnant Flesh as Absolute Hospitality," in *Coming to Life: Philosophies of Pregnancy, Childbirth, and Mothering*, ed. Sarah LaChance Adams and Caroline R. Lundquist (New York: Fordham University Press, 2013), 71–87.

42 Margaret Olivia Little, "Abortion, Intimacy, and the Duty to Gestate," *Ethical Theory and Moral Practice* 2, no. 3 (1999): 299.

43 Patricia Beattie Jung, "Abortion and Organ Donation: Christian Reflections on Bodily Life Support," *Journal of Religious Ethics* 16, no. 2 (1988): 281.

44 Justin M. Anderson, *Virtue and Grace in the Theology of Thomas Aquinas* (Cambridge: Cambridge University Press, 2020), 293–94.

45 These are the words of Gandalf in J. R. R. Tolkien's *The Lord of the Rings*, quoted in Craig Boyd, "Prudence and Human Providence: Love and Wisdom," in *Divine and Human Providence: Philosophical, Psychological and Theological Approaches*, ed. Ignacio Silva and Simon Maria Kopf (New York: Routledge, 2020), 16–17.

46  Yong, "Disability and the Love of Wisdom," 58.

47  Charles M. Wood, *The Question of Providence* (Louisville: Westminster John Knox, 2008), xi.

48  Heidelberg Catechism, Christian Reformed Church (2011), https://tinyurl.com/3azbweth.

49  James A. Metzger, "Reclaiming 'a Dark and Malefic Sacred' for a Theology of Disability," *Journal of Religion, Disability & Health* 15, no. 3 (2011): 300. Metzger notes that many disability theologians accept a limited but benevolent deity.

50  A third cliff is possible: an atheism that finds it "almost inconceivable that this deity would have absolutely *no* ability to intervene or alter the underlying structures of the world just a little to ameliorate the enormity of pointless suffering," which is the reality for many disabling conditions and diseases (Metzger, "Reclaiming 'a Dark and Malefic Sacred,'" 303).

51  "We shall overcome because the arc of the moral universe is long but it bends toward justice." Dr. Martin Luther King Jr., "Remaining Awake through a Great Revolution," speech given at the National Cathedral, Washington, DC (March 31, 1968), https://tinyurl.com/57peu85d.

52  Emmanuel Levinas, "Ethics as First Philosophy," in *The Levinas Reader*, ed. Seán Hand (Oxford: Blackwell, 1989), 83.

53  Deborah Beth Creamer, *Disability and Christian Theology: Embodied Limits and Constructive Possibilities* (New York: Oxford University Press, 2009), 93.

54  Darla Schumm draws on feminist care ethics and Buddhist thought in "Reimaging Disability," *Journal of Feminist Studies in Religion* 26, no. 2 (2010): 132–37.

55  Paul Ricoeur, *The Course of Recognition* (Cambridge, MA: Harvard University Press, 2005), 257.

56  Brock, *Wondrously Wounded*, 26. All italics in quotes from this book are in the original.

57  Brock speaks personally of his family's experience of being pressured by medical specialists into having their newborn son's disability diagnosed and, hence, named as an abnormality, when they just wanted to celebrate his entry into their family. See *Wondrously Wounded*, 65–71. Reinders also recounts a story of a woman being pressured by doctors to run diagnostic

tests for disability (Reinders, *Disability, Providence, and Ethics*, 178).

58  Brock, *Wondrously Wounded*, 67.

59  Brock, *Wondrously Wounded*, 16, 74.

60  A urine pregnancy test detects human chorionic gonadotropin (HCG), a hormone that indicates a pregnancy.

61  "If things are deprived of all good, they cease altogether to be; and this means that as long as things are, they are good. Therefore, whatever is, is good." Augustine, *Confessions*, VII.12, trans. R. S. Pine-Coffin (Harmondsworth, Middlesex, UK: Penguin, 1962), 148.

62  Ian McFarland, "Evil, Wonder, and Chance: A Reflection on Categories in *Wondrously Wounded*," *Syndicate*, Oct. 14, 2020, https://tinyurl.com/bdf7d8z9.

63  David Fergusson, *The Providence of God: A Polyphonic Approach* (Cambridge: Cambridge University Press, 2018), 335.

64  Martin Luther, "Consolation for Women Whose Pregnancies Have Not Gone Well, 1542," in *The Annotated Luther*, vol. 4, *Pastoral Writings*, ed. Mary Jane Haemig, Hans J. Hillerbrand, Kirsi I. Stjerna, and Timothy J. Wengert (Minneapolis: Fortress, 2016), 423.

65  Brock, *Wondrously Wounded*, 239.

66  A similar idea is beautifully presented in Eva F. Kittay's essay about her disabled daughter, "Not My Way, Sesha. Your Way. Slowly," in *Love's Labor: Essays on Women, Equality, and Dependency* (New York: Routledge, 1999): 147–61.

67  David H. Kelsey, *Eccentric Existence: A Theological Anthropology*, vol. 1 (Louisville: Westminster John Knox, 2009), 212. McFarland argues similarly that "except where God is confessed to be speaking or acting directly (e.g., miracles, sacraments, Scripture, the incarnation), the relationship between creaturely happenings and divine will seem to me just too obscure to be able to make such judgments." McFarland, "Evil, Wonder, and Chance."

68  Reinders, *Disability, Providence, and Ethics*, 17–18.

69  Reinders, *Disability, Providence, and Ethics*, 160.

70  Prolife websites abound with stories of mothers who, for religious reasons, reject the pressure to have prenatal testing. See Katherine Mayne Wheeler, "Why It Is Imperative to Reject

Prenatal Screening for Down Syndrome," Human Defense Initiative (June 10, 2018), https://tinyurl.com/44sys5nv.

71 Prodisability advocates protest disability bias in genetic counseling; however, this bias may happen less than what these advocates claim. Brian G. Skotko, "Prenatally Diagnosed Down Syndrome: Mothers Who Continued Their Pregnancies Evaluate Their Health Care Providers," *American Journal of Obstetrics and Gynecology* 192, no. 3 (2005): 670, 674. See also Susan Markens, "'Is This Something You Want?': Genetic Counselors' Accounts of Their Role in Prenatal Decision Making," *Sociological Forum* 28, no. 3 (2013): 431–51.

72 Natalie Stoljar, "Feminist Perspectives on Autonomy," *The Stanford Encyclopedia of Philosophy* (2018), https://tinyurl.com/7n54pjdt.

73 For several classic arguments on these positions see Judith Jarvis Thomson, "A Defense of Abortion," *Philosophy & Public Affairs* 1, no. 1 (1971): 47–66; Eileen McDonagh, "Adding Consent to Choice in the Abortion Debate," *Society* 42, no. 5 (2005): 18–26; Mary Anne Warren, "On the Moral and Legal Status of Abortion," *The Monist* 57, no. 4 (1973): 43–61.

74 Carolyn McLeod, *Self-Trust and Reproductive Autonomy* (Cambridge, MA: MIT Press, 2002), 1, 6.

75 McLeod, *Self-Trust and Reproductive Autonomy*, 104.

76 McLeod, *Self-Trust and Reproductive Autonomy*, 113.

77 Rebecca Todd Peters, *Trust Women: A Progressive Christian Argument for Reproductive Justice* (Boston: Beacon, 2018), 72.

78 Dorothy E. Roberts, *Killing the Black Body: Race, Reproduction, and the Meaning of Liberty* (New York: Vintage, 1997), 11; Claudia Malacrida, "Mothering and Disability: Implications for Theory and Practice," in *Routledge Handbook of Disability Studies*, ed. Nick Watson and Simo Vehmas, 2nd ed. (New York: Routledge, 2020), 398–409.

79 There are apparently waiting lists for adopting babies with a disability. Heidi L. Lindh et al., "Characteristics and Perspectives of Families Waiting to Adopt a Child with Down Syndrome," *Genetics in Medicine* 9, no. 4 (2007): 235–40. However, few women consider adoption in abortion decision-making. Gretchen Sisson et al., "Adoption Decision Making among Women Seeking Abortion," *Women's Health Issues* 27, no. 2

(2017): 136–44. Rates are low for adopting older disabled children in the foster care system. "Older Youth with Disabilities in Foster Care," Center for the Advanced Studies in Child Welfare, University of Minnesota School of Social Work (2013), https://tinyurl.com/yms2emkj.

80 Fergusson, *The Providence of God*, 119.

81 Asch and Wasserman, "Where Is the Sin in Synecdoche," 181.

82 Asch and Wasserman, "Where Is the Sin in Synecdoche," 189.

83 Creamer may not have envisioned her concept of a theology of limits applying to reproductive decision-making, but it rings true to me.

84 See Sarah Zhang, "The Last Children of Down Syndrome," *Atlantic*, Dec. 2020, https://tinyurl.com/4he5afsd; Carolin Ahlvik-Harju, "The Invisible Made Visible? The Ethical Significance of Befriending People with Disabilities," *Studia Theologica-Nordic Journal of Theology* 68, no. 2 (2014): 122–46.

85 American College of Obstetrics and Gynecology, "Cell-Free DNA Prenatal Screening Test" (2019), https://tinyurl.com/56wkhwdm.

86 A recent study on Down syndrome in multiple countries finds that termination rates remained the same or decreased with the use of NIPT. Melissa Hill et al., "Has Noninvasive Prenatal Testing Impacted Termination of Pregnancy and Live Birth Rates of Infants with Down Syndrome?," *Prenatal Diagnosis* 37, no. 13 (2017): 1281–90.

87 Carolin Ahlvik-Harju, "Disturbing Bodies—Reimagining Comforting Narratives of Embodiment through Feminist Disability Studies," *Scandinavian Journal of Disability Research* 18, no. 3 (2016): 231.

88 For a critique of expressivism see James Lindemann Nelson, "Prenatal Diagnosis, Personal Identity and Disability," *Kennedy Institute of Ethics Journal* 10, no. 3 (2000): 218.

89 C. Ben Mitchell, "The Vulnerable—Abortion and Disability," in *The Oxford Handbook of Evangelical Theology*, ed. Gerald R. McDermott (New York: Oxford University Press, 2010), 492.

90 Jay J. Bringman, "Invasive Prenatal Genetic Testing: A Catholic Healthcare Provider's Perspective," *Linacre Quarterly* 81, no. 4 (2014): 307.

91 Brock, *Wondrously Wounded*, 197.

92  Brock, *Wondrously Wounded*, 90.

93  Reinders entertains the idea of laws where women are required to "take a leave of absence . . . to consider their decision" (Reinders, *Future of the Disabled in Liberal Society*, 95); Denise Cooper-Clarke, "Grounding Our Discussion of Abortion," in *Grounded in the Body, in Time and Place, in Scripture: Papers by Australian Women Scholars in the Evangelical Tradition*, ed. Jill Firth and Denise Cooper-Clarke (Eugene, OR: Wipf and Stock, 2021), 215.

94  Hille Haker, "Recognition and Responsibility," *Religions* 12 (2021): 467, https://tinyurl.com/yc2mt6f7.

95  Paul Stark, "Is Abortion Justified after an Adverse Prenatal Diagnosis?" *Minnesota Citizens Concerned for Life* (May 9, 2018), https://tinyurl.com/yekja6y8. The filicide rhetoric, it should be noted, does little to foster beneficence because the underlying concern is not the moral principle, "How can I love my neighbor as myself?" but, rather, "How can I avoid a murder charge?" Daniel Callahan, "The Roman Catholic Position," in *Abortion: A Reader*, ed. Lloyd Steffen (Eugene, OR: Wipf and Stock, 1996), 90.

96  See Brian G. Skotko, Susan P. Levine, and Richard Goldstein, "Having a Son or Daughter with Down Syndrome: Perspectives from Mothers and Fathers," *American Journal of Medical Genetics*, part A 155, no. 10 (2011): 2335–47. The parents in this study were mostly white, religious, married, well educated, and caring for a Down syndrome child under the age of ten. See Jennifer Guon et al., "Our Children Are Not a Diagnosis: The Experience of Parents Who Continue Their Pregnancy after a Prenatal Diagnosis of Trisomy 13 or 18," *American Journal of Medical Genetics Part A* 164, no. 2 (2014): 308–18. Participants were recruited from trisomy support groups, 85 percent self-identified as religious, and 61 percent felt pressured to abort, though none of the participants did.

97  Asch and Wasserman, "Where Is the Sin in Synecdoche," 183. "No one ought to shame, blame, or in any way coerce a woman into taking these responsibilities." Eva Feder Kittay, *Learning from My Daughter: The Value and Care of Disabled Minds* (New York: Oxford University Press, 2019), 133.

98 See Ellen Painter Dollar, *No Easy Choice: A Story of Disability, Parenthood, and Faith in an Age of Advanced Reproduction* (Louisville: Westminster John Knox, 2011).

99 In one study, slightly over 65 percent wished to avoid a future pregnancy where they might face a decision regarding disability. Susan E. Kelly, "Choosing Not to Choose: Reproductive Responses of Parents of Children with Genetic Conditions or Impairments," *Sociology of Health & Illness* 31, no. 1 (2009): 82.

100 Kelly, "Choosing Not to Choose," 90.

101 M. Antonia Biggs, Heather Gould, and Diana Greene Foster, "Understanding Why Women Seek Abortions in the US," *BMC Women's Health* 13, no. 1 (2013): 1–13. Rebecca Todd Peters, "Listening to Women: Examining the Moral Wisdom of Women Who End Pregnancies," *Journal of Religious Ethics* 49, no. 2 (2021): 290–313.

102 Brock, *Wondrously Wounded*, 93.

103 Linda Ellison, "Abortion and the Politics of God: Patient Narratives and Public Rhetoric in the American Abortion Debate" (ThD diss., Harvard Divinity School, 2008), 91.

104 Skotko, "Prenatally Diagnosed Down Syndrome," 674. This factor had a higher ranking than religious teachings.

105 Dollar, *No Easy Choice*, 143.

106 Yong, *Theology and Down Syndrome*, 12.

107 Yong, *Theology and Down Syndrome*, 13–14.

108 Catriona Mackenzie, "Abortion and Embodiment," *Australasian Journal of Philosophy*, 70, no. 2 (1992): 152.

109 Brock, *Wondrously Wounded*, 97.

110 Sharon V. Betcher, *Spirit and the Politics of Disablement* (Minneapolis: Fortress, 2007), 46.

111 Betcher, *Spirit and the Politics of Disablement*, 47.

112 Williams, *Sisters in the Wilderness*; Rita Nakashima Brock, "Losing Your Innocence but Not Your Hope," in *Reconstructing the Christ Symbol: Essays in Feminist Christology*, ed. Maryanne Stevens (Mahwah, NJ: Paulist, 1993), 30–53.

113 1 Cor 13:12 KJV.

## Conclusion

1  Delores S. Williams, *Sisters in the Wilderness: The Challenge of Womanist God-Talk* (Maryknoll, NY: Orbis, 1993), 165

2  Mary Catherine Sommers, "Living Together: Burdensome Pregnancy and the Hospitable Self," in *Abortion: A New Generation of Catholic Responses*, ed. Stephen J. Heaney (Braintree, MA: Pope John Center, 1992), 259.

3  Priya Agrawal, "Maternal Mortality and Morbidity in the United States of America," *Bulletin of the World Health Organization* 93 (2015): 135.

4  Emily E. Petersen et al., "Racial/Ethnic Disparities in Pregnancy-Related Deaths—United States, 2007–2016," *Morbidity and Mortality Weekly Report* 68, no. 35 (2019): 762.

5  Elisabeth Clare Larsen et al., "New Insights into Mechanisms behind Miscarriage," *BMC Medicine* 11, no. 1 (2013): 1–2.

6  William R. Rice, "The High Abortion Cost of Human Reproduction," *bioRxiv* (2018): 17.

7  Serene Jones, *Trauma and Grace: Theology in a Ruptured World* (Louisville: Westminster John Knox, 2009), 147–49.

8  *Demonarchy* is a term coined by Delores Williams referring to black women's oppressions of race and sex at the hands of white people. "The Color of Feminism: On Speaking the Black Woman's Tongue," in *Feminist Theological Ethics*, ed. Lois K. Daly (Louisville: Westminster John Knox, 1994), 49–50.

9  The allusion is to Maya Angelou's poem, "Still I Rise."

10  The allusion is to the Dylan Thomas poem "Do not go gentle into that good night."

11  Jaroslav Pelikan, *The Christian Tradition: A History of the Development of Doctrine*, 5 vols. (Chicago: University of Chicago Press, 1971–89).

12  George A. Lindbeck, *The Nature of Doctrine: Religion and Theology in a Postliberal Age* (Philadelphia: Westminster John Knox, 1984).

13  Serene Jones and Paul Lakeland, eds., *Constructive Theology: A Contemporary Approach to Classical Themes* (Minneapolis: Fortress, 2005).

14  Virgil, *The Aeneid*, bk. VI. 702, trans. H. R. Fairclough, https://tinyurl.com/4v7az4cx.

15 Dante Alighieri, *Purgatorio* II. 79–80, trans. Allen Mandelbaum, https://tinyurl.com/3hnjvx74.

16 The allusion is to Democratic strategist James Carville's edgy yet on-point commentary (now a meme) on a principal issue in the 1992 elections.

17 The allusion is to Sallie McFague, *The Body of God: An Ecological Theology* (Minneapolis: Fortress, 1993).

18 T. S. Eliot, "Little Gidding," https://tinyurl.com/3hnjvx74.

19 Julian of Norwich, quoted in Liz Herbert McAvoy, *Authority and the Female Body in the Writings of Julian of Norwich and Margery Kempe* (Suffolk, UK: Boydell & Brewer, 2004), 83.

20 See the discussion of twilight death and microchimerism in ch. 4, "Embryonic and Fetal Demise."

21 Augustine, *City of God*, 22.13, *The Nicene and Post-Nicene Fathers*, vol. 2, trans. Marcus Dodd, ed. Philip Schaff and Henry Wace (Grand Rapids: Eerdmans, 1972), 494, https://tinyurl.com/3hnjvx74.

22 Caroline Walker Bynum, *The Resurrection of the Body in Western Christianity, 200–1336* (New York: Columbia University Press, 1995), 77.

# BIBLIOGRAPHY

"The Acts of Perpetua and Felicitas." Early Christian Writings. https://tinyurl.com/yt5yetdb.

Agrawal, Priya. "Maternal Mortality and Morbidity in the United States of America." *Bulletin of the World Health Organization* 93 (2015): 135. https://tinyurl.com/fd2f79ds.

Ahlvik-Harju, Carolin. "Disturbing Bodies—Reimagining Comforting Narratives of Embodiment through Feminist Disability Studies." *Scandinavian Journal of Disability Research* 18, no. 3 (2016): 222–33.

———. "The Invisible Made Visible? The Ethical Significance of Befriending People with Disabilities." *Studia Theologica-Nordic Journal of Theology* 68, no. 2 (2014): 122–46.

Aikin, Judith Popovich. "Gendered Theologies of Childbirth in Early Modern Germany and the Devotional Handbook for Pregnant Women by Aemilie Juliane, Countess of Schwarzburg-Rudolstadt (1683)." *Journal of Women's History* 15, no. 2 (2003): 40–67.

Alighieri, Dante. *Inferno.* Translated by Robert and Jean Hollander. New York: Anchor, 2000.

———. *Purgatorio.* Translated by Allen Mandelbaum. Digital Dante. https://tinyurl.com/3hnjvx74.

American College of Obstetrics and Gynecology. "Cell-Free DNA Prenatal Screening Test." 2019. https://tinyurl.com/56wkhwdm.

Amerini, Fabrizio. *Aquinas on the Beginning and End of Human Life.* Translated by M. Henninger, S.J. Cambridge, MA: Harvard University Press, 2013.

———. "Aquinas on the Beginning and End of Human Life: A Rejoinder to Patrick Toner." In *Oxford Studies in Medieval Philosophy,* edited by Robert Pasnau, vol. 3, 189–95. Oxford: Oxford University Press, 2015.

Anderson, Justin M. *Virtue and Grace in the Theology of Thomas Aquinas.* Cambridge: Cambridge University Press, 2020.

Aquinas, Thomas. *Summa Theologica*. Translated by Fathers of the Eastern Dominican Province. New York: Benzinger, 1947.

Asch, Adrienne. "Why I Haven't Changed My Mind about Prenatal Diagnosis: Reflections and Refinements." In *Prenatal Testing and Disability Rights*, edited by Erik Parens and Adrienne Asch, 234–60. Washington, DC: Georgetown University Press, 2000.

Asch, Adrienne, and David Wasserman. "Where Is the Sin in Synecdoche? Prenatal Testing and the Parent-Child Relationship." In *Quality of Life and Human Difference: Genetic Testing, Health Care, and Disability*, edited by David Wasserman, Robert Wachbroit, and Jerome Bickenbach, 172–16. Cambridge: Cambridge University Press, 2005.

Augustine. "City of God." In *The Nicene and Post-Nicene Fathers*, edited by Philip Schaff and Henry Wace, vol. 2. Grand Rapids: Eerdmans, 1972. https://tinyurl.com/5areazke.

———. *Confessions*. Translated by R. S. Pine-Coffin. Harmondsworth, Middlesex, UK: Penguin, 1962.

———. *Confessions and Enchiridion*. Translated by Albert C. Outler. Philadelphia: Westminster, 1955. https://tinyurl.com/efcc86yk.

Baker, Lynne Rudder. "Christian Materialism in a Scientific Age." *International Journal for Philosophy of Religion* 70, no. 1 (2011): 47–59.

———. "Persons and the Metaphysics of Resurrection." *Religious Studies* 43 (2007): 333–48.

———. "Resurrecting Material Persons." In *The Palgrave Handbook of the Afterlife*, edited by Yujin Nagasawa and Benjamin Matheson, 315–30. London: Palgrave Macmillan, 2017.

———. "When Does a Person Begin?" *Social Philosophy and Policy* 22, no. 2 (2005): 25–48.

Balfour, I. L. S. "The Fate of the Soul in Induced Abortion in the Writings of Tertullian." *Studia Patristica* 16, no. 2 (1985): 127–31.

Bardos, Jonah, et al. "A National Survey on Public Perceptions of Miscarriage." *Obstetrics and Gynecology* 125, no. 6 (2015): 1313–20.

Barilan, Y. Michael. "Abortion in Jewish Religious Law: Neighborly Love, Imago Dei, and a Hypothesis on the Medieval Blood Libel." *Review of Rabbinic Judaism* 8, nos. 1–2 (2005): 1–34.

Barkai, Ron. "A Medieval Hebrew Treatise on Obstetrics." *Medical History* 33, no. 1 (1989): 96–119.

Baun, Jane. "The Fate of Babies Dying before Baptism in Byzantium." *Studies in Church History* 31 (1994): 115–25.

Baxter, Darcy, and Colleagues. "Regeneration & Loss: Honoring Our Reproductive Lives." Side with Love. https://tinyurl.com/ysez55ja.

Beam, Sara. "Turning a Blind Eye: Infanticide and Missing Babies in Seventeenth-Century Geneva." *Law and History Review* 39, no. 2 (2021): 1–22.

Beattie, Tina. *God's Mother, Eve's Advocate.* New York: Continuum, 2002.

Beckwith, Francis J. "Taking Abortion Seriously: A Philosophical Critique of the New Anti-abortion Rhetorical Shift." *Ethics & Medicine* 17, no. 3 (2001): 155–66.

Bednarski, Steven, and Andrée Courtemanche. "'Sadly and with a Bitter Heart': What the Caesarean Section Meant in the Middle Ages." *Florilegium* 28, no. 1 (2011): 33–69.

Beiting, Christopher. "The Idea of Limbo in Thomas Aquinas." *The Thomist* 62, no. 2 (1998): 217–44.

———. "The Nature and Structure of Limbo in the Works of Albertus Magnus." *New Blackfriars* 85, no. 999 (2004): 492–509.

Bellinger, Charles K. *Othering: The Original Sin of Humanity.* Eugene, OR: Cascade, 2020.

Bernat, James L. "The Whole-Brain Concept of Death Remains Optimum Public Policy." *Journal of Law, Medicine & Ethics* 34, no. 1 (2006): 35–43.

Betcher, Sharon V. "Becoming Flesh of My Flesh: Feminist and Disability Theologies on the Edge of Posthumanist Discourse." *Journal of Feminist Studies in Religion* 26, no. 2 (2010): 107–18.

———. *Spirit and the Politics of Disablement.* Minneapolis: Fortress, 2007.

Bianchi, Diana W. "Fetal Cells in the Mother: From Genetic Diagnosis to Diseases Associated with Fetal Cell Microchimerism." *European Journal of Obstetrics & Gynecology and Reproductive Biology* 92, no. 1 (2000): 103–8.

Biggs, M. Antonia, Heather Gould, and Diana Greene Foster. "Understanding Why Women Seek Abortions in the US." *BMC Women's Health* 13, no. 1 (2013): 1–13.

Blackburn, William Ross. "Abortion and the Voice of Scripture." *The Human Life Review* 31, no. 2 (2005): 67–85.

Blosser, Benjamin P. "The Ensoulment of the Body in Early Christian Thought." In *A History of Mind and Body in Late Antiquity*, edited by Anna Marmodoro and Sophie Cartwright, 207–23. Cambridge: Cambridge University Press, 2018.

Bommaraju, Aalap, Megan L. Kavanaugh, Melody Y. Hou, and Danielle Bessett. "Situating Stigma in Stratified Reproduction: Abortion Stigma and Miscarriage Stigma as Barriers to Reproductive Healthcare." *Sexual & Reproductive Healthcare* 10 (2016): 62–69.

Bonopartis, Theresa. "The Souls of Aborted Babies and the 'Hope' of Heaven." Reclaiming Our Children. Blog. November 2, 2018. https://tinyurl.com/44pj7sk7.

Boswell, Parley Ann. *Pregnancy in Literature and Film*. Jefferson, NC: McFarland, 2014.

Bourne, Richard, and Imogen Adkins. *A New Introduction to Theology: Embodiment, Experience and Encounter*. London: T&T Clark, 2020.

Boyd, Craig A. "Prudence and Human Providence: Love and Wisdom." In *Divine and Human Providence: Philosophical, Psychological and Theological Approaches*, edited by Ignacio Silva and Simon Maria Kopf, 14–30. New York: Routledge, 2020.

Brier, Norman. "Anxiety after Miscarriage: A Review of the Empirical Literature and Implications for Clinical Practice." *Birth* 31, no. 2 (2004): 138–42.

Bringman, Jay J. "Invasive Prenatal Genetic Testing: A Catholic Healthcare Provider's Perspective." *The Linacre Quarterly* 81, no. 4 (2014): 302–13.

Brock, Brian. *Wondrously Wounded: Theology, Disability, and the Body of Christ*. Waco, TX: Baylor University Press, 2019.

Brock, Rita Nakashima. "Losing Your Innocence but Not Your Hope." In *Reconstructing the Christ Symbol: Essays in Feminist Christology*, edited by Maryanne Stevens, 30–53. Mahwah, NJ: Paulist, 1993.

Brown, Peter. *The Body and Society: Men, Women, and Sexual Renunciation in Early Christianity*, 20th anniv. ed. with new introduction. New York: Columbia University Press, 2008.

Butler, Judith. *Bodies That Matter: On the Discursive Limits of Sex*. New York: Routledge, 1993.

———. *Frames of War: When Is Life Grievable?* New York: Verso, 2016.

————. *Gender Trouble: Feminism and the Subversion of Identity.* 10th anniv. ed. New York: Routledge, 2002.

Bynum, Caroline Walker. *The Resurrection of the Body in Western Christianity, 200–1336.* New York: Columbia University Press, 1995.

Cahill, Ann J. "Miscarriage and Intercorporeality." *Journal of Social Philosophy* 46, no. 1 (2015): 44–58.

Cahill, Lisa Sowle. "Abortion and Argument by Analogy." *Horizons* 9, no. 2 (1982): 271–78.

Callahan, Daniel. "The Roman Catholic Position." In *Abortion: A Reader*, edited by Lloyd Steffen, 82–93. Eugene, OR: Wipf and Stock, 1996.

Callan, Maeve. *Sacred Sisters: Gender, Sanctity, and Power in Medieval Ireland.* Amsterdam: Amsterdam University Press, 2019.

Calvin, John. *The Four Last Books of Moses.* Translated by Charles William Bingham. Edinburgh: Calvin Translation Society, 1853.

————. *Institutes of the Christian Religion, 1536.* Translated by Ford Lewis Battles, edited by John T. McNeill. Philadelphia: Westminster, 1960.

Cannon, Katie G. *Black Womanist Ethic.* Atlanta: Scholars, 1988.

Cartwright, Sophie. "Soul and Body in Early Christianity: An Old and New Conundrum." In *A History of Mind and Body in Late Antiquity*, edited by Anna Marmodoro and Sophie Cartwright, 173–90. Cambridge: Cambridge University Press, 2018.

Cave, Holly. "The Miscarriage Taboo." *Atlantic*, March 2, 2016. https://tinyurl.com/29m6kb2u.

Center for Reproductive Rights. "The World's Abortion Laws." Feb. 23, 2021. https://tinyurl.com/32w76wce.

Cockrill, Kate, Ushma D. Upadhyay, Janet Turan, and Diana Greene Foster. "The Stigma of Having an Abortion: Development of a Scale and Characteristics of Women Experiencing Abortion Stigma." *Perspectives on Sexual and Reproductive Health* 45, no. 2 (2013): 79–88.

*Code of Canon Law.* The Vatican. 1983. https://tinyurl.com/mr22srnn.

Coleman, Monica A. "Sacrifice, Surrogacy and Salvation: Womanist Reflections on Motherhood and Work." *Black Theology* 12, no. 3 (2014): 200–212.

Congourdeau, Marie-Hélène. "Debating the Soul in Late Antiquity." In *Reproduction: Antiquity to the Present Day*, edited by Nick

Hopwood, Rebecca Flemming, and Lauren Kassell, 109–21. Cambridge: Cambridge University Press, 2018.

Cooper, John W. *Body, Soul, and Life Everlasting: Biblical Anthropology and the Monism-Dualism Debate.* Grand Rapids: Eerdmans, 2000.

———. "The Current Body-Soul Debate: A Case for Dualistic Holism." *Southern Baptist Journal of Theology* 13, no. 2 (2009): 32–50.

Cooper-Clarke, Denise. "Grounding Our Discussion of Abortion." In *Grounded in the Body, in Time and Place, in Scripture: Papers by Australian Women Scholars in the Evangelical Tradition,* edited by Jill Firth and Denise Cooper-Clarke, 203–18. Eugene, OR: Wipf and Stock, 2021.

Corcoran, Kevin. "Physical Persons and Postmortem Survival without Temporal Gaps." In *Soul, Body, and Survival: Essays on the Metaphysics of Human Persons,* edited by Kevin Corcoran, 201–17. Ithaca, NY: Cornell University Press, 2001.

———. *Rethinking Human Nature: A Christian Materialist Alternative to the Soul.* Grand Rapids: Baker Academic, 2006.

Coster, Will. *Baptism and Spiritual Kinship in Early Modern England.* New York: Routledge, 2017.

Cowchock, F. Susan, et al. "Spiritual Needs of Couples Facing Pregnancy Termination Because of Fetal Anomalies." *Journal of Pastoral Care & Counseling* 65, no. 2 (2011): 1–10.

Creamer, Deborah Beth. *Disability and Christian Theology: Embodied Limits and Constructive Possibilities.* New York: Oxford University Press, 2009.

Crow, Madison, Colleen Zori, and Davide Zori. "Doctrinal and Physical Marginality in Christian Death: The Burial of Unbaptized Infants in Medieval Italy." *Religions* 11, no. 12 (2020): 678. https://tinyurl.com/ys9ympj7.

Cuffel, Alexandra. *Gendering Disgust in Medieval Religious Polemic.* Notre Dame, IN: University of Notre Dame Press, 2007.

Daly, Mary. *Gyn/Ecology: The Metaethics of Radical Feminism.* Boston: Beacon, 2016.

Davis, Stephen T. *Risen Indeed: Making Sense of the Resurrection.* Grand Rapids: Eerdmans, 1993.

De Anda, Neomi. "Miscarriage Matters, Stillbirth's Significance, and the Tree of Many Breasts." In *Parenting as Spiritual Practice and*

*Source for Theology*, edited by Claire Bischoff, Elizabeth O'Donnell Gandolfo, and Annie Hardison-Moody, 173–85. Cham, Switzerland: Palgrave Macmillan, 2017.

DeLashmutt, Michael W. 2009. "Paul Ricoeur at the Foot of the Cross: Narrative Identity and the Resurrection of the Body." *Modern Theology* 25, no. 4 (2009): 589–616.

Dingle, Shannon. "I Was in the Pro-Life Movement. But Then, Widowed with 6 Kids, I Prepared for an Abortion." *USA Today.* Opinion. October 11, 2020. https://tinyurl.com/49rwyfza.

Dollar, Ellen Painter. *No Easy Choice: A Story of Disability, Parenthood, and Faith in an Age of Advanced Reproduction.* Louisville: Westminster John Knox, 2011.

Dugas, Carla, and Valori H. Slane. "Miscarriage." National Center for Biotechnology Information. June 29, 2021. https://tinyurl.com/44effnrc.

Dunn, Mary. *The Cruelest of All Mothers: Marie de l'Incarnation, Motherhood, and Christian Tradition.* New York: Fordham University Press, 2015.

Eaton, Heather. "An Earth-Centric Theological Framing for Planetary Solidarity." In *Planetary Solidarity: Global Women's Voices on Christian Doctrine and Climate Justice*, edited by Grace Ji-Sun Kim and Hilda P. Koster, 19–46. Minneapolis: Fortress, 2017.

Eberl, Jason T. "Aquinas's Account of Human Embryogenesis and Recent Interpretations." *Journal of Medicine and Philosophy* 30, no. 4 (2005): 379–94.

Ehrman, Bart D. *Journeys to Heaven and Hell: Tours of the Afterlife in the Early Christian Tradition.* New Haven, CT: Yale University Press, 2022.

Ehrman, Terrence, C.S.C. "Disability and Resurrection Identity." *New Blackfriars* 96, no. 1066 (2015): 723–38.

Eiesland, Nancy L. "Liberation, Inclusion and Justice: A Faith Response to People with Disabilities." *Impact* 14, no. 3 (2001): 2–3, 35.

Eliot, T. S. "Little Gidding." https://tinyurl.com/3s27nruw.

Elledge, C. D. *Resurrection of the Dead in Early Judaism, 200 BCE–CE 200.* Oxford: Oxford University Press, 2014.

Ellingsen, Mark. *Martin Luther's Legacy: Reforming Reformation Theology for the 21st Century.* New York: Palgrave Macmillan, 2017.

Ellison, Linda. "Abortion and the Politics of God: Patient Narratives and Public Rhetoric in the American Abortion Debate." ThD diss., Harvard Divinity School, 2008.

Ellison, Marvin M., and Kelly Brown Douglas, eds. *Sexuality and the Sacred: Sources for Theological Reflection.* 2nd ed. Louisville: Westminster John Knox, 2010.

Evans, C. Stephen, and Brandon L. Rickabaugh. "What Does It Mean to Be a Bodily Soul?" *Philosophia Christi* 17, no. 2 (2015): 315–30.

Faro, Laurie. "Monuments for Stillborn Children and Disenfranchised Grief in the Netherlands: Recognition, Protest and Solace." *Mortality* 26, no. 3 (2020): 1–20.

Farrar, Thomas. "Today in Paradise? Ambiguous Adverb Attachment and the Meaning of Luke 23:43." *Neotestamentica* 51, no. 2 (2017): 185–207.

Ferguson, Everett. *Baptism in the Early Church: History, Theology, and Liturgy in the First Five Centuries.* Grand Rapids: Eerdmans, 2009.

Fergusson, David. *The Providence of God: A Polyphonic Approach.* Cambridge: Cambridge University Press, 2018.

"Fifth Ecumenical Council: Second Council of Constantinople" (553). In *Nicene and Post-Nicene Fathers,* series 2, *Seven Ecumenical Councils,* edited by Philip Schaff and Henry Wace, vol. 14. https://tinyurl.com/364fyd6u.

Finney, Mark. *Resurrection, Hell and the Afterlife: Body and Soul in Antiquity, Judaism and Early Christianity.* New York: Routledge, 2016.

Fitzmyer, Joseph A., S.J. *First Corinthians.* Anchor Yale Bible. New Haven, CT: Yale University Press, 2008.

Fonrobert, Charlotte Elisheva. *Menstrual Purity: Rabbinic and Christian Reconstructions of Biblical Gender.* Stanford, CA: Stanford University Press, 2002.

Foucault, Michel. *Power/Kowledge: Selected Interviews and Other Writings, 1972–1977.* Translated and edited by Colin Gordon et al. New York: Pantheon, 1972.

Frantz, Nadine Pence, and Mary T. Stimming, eds. *Hope Deferred: Heart-Healing Reflections on Reproductive Loss.* Cleveland: Pilgrim, 2010.

Freedman, Lori R., Uta Landy, and Jody Steinauer. "When There's a Heartbeat: Miscarriage Management in Catholic-Owned Hospitals." *American Journal of Public Health* 98, no. 10 (2008): 1774–78.

Frei, Hans. *The Identity of Jesus Christ: The Hermeneutical Bases of Dogmatic Theology.* Philadelphia: Fortress, 1975.

———. "The 'Literal Reading' of Biblical Narrative in the Christian Tradition: Does It Stretch or Will It Break?" In *The Bible and the Narrative Tradition*, edited by Frank McConnell, 36–77. New York: Oxford University Press, 1986.

Gamble, Elette, and Wilbur L. Holz. "A Rite for the Stillborn." *Word & World* 15, no. 3 (1995): 349–53.

Garland-Thomson, Rosemarie. "The Case for Conserving Disability." *Journal of Bioethical Inquiry* 9, no. 3 (2012): 339–55.

Gasser, Georg, ed. *Personal Identity and Resurrection*. Burlington, VT: Ashgate, 2010.

Gavrilyuk, Paul L. "The Incorporeality of the Soul in Patristic Thought." In *Christian Physicalism?: Philosophical Theological Criticisms*, edited by R. Keith Loftin and Joshua R. Farris, 1–26. Lanham, MD: Lexington, 2018.

Gilchrist, Roberta. *Medieval Life: Archaeology and the Life Course.* Woodbridge, Suffolk, UK: Boydell, 2012.

Gimbutas, Marija. *The Living Goddesses.* Berkeley: University of California Press, 2001.

Goetz, Stewart. "Substance Dualism." In *The Ashgate Research Companion to Theological Anthropology*, edited by Joshua R. Farris and Charles Taliaferro, 145–58. New York: Routledge, 2016.

Goetz, Stewart, and Charles Taliaferro. *A Brief History of the Soul.* Malden, MA: Wiley-Blackwell, 2011.

Gonzalez, Eliezer. "Anthropologies of Continuity: The Body and Soul in Tertullian, Perpetua, and Early Christianity." *Journal of Early Christian Studies* 21, no. 4 (2013): 479–502.

Gorman, Michael J. *Abortion and the Early Church: Christian, Jewish and Pagan Attitudes in the Greco-Roman World.* Eugene, OR: Wipf and Stock, 1998.

Gould, James Barton. "The Hope of Heavenly Healing of Disability Part 1: Theological Issues." *Journal of Disability & Religion* 20, no. 4 (2016): 317–34.

————. "The Hope of Heavenly Healing of Disability, Part 2: Philosophical Issues." *Journal of Disability & Religion* 21, no. 1 (2017): 98–116.

Gray, Frances. "Original Habitation: Pregnant Flesh as Absolute Hospitality." In *Coming to Life: Philosophies of Pregnancy, Childbirth, and Mothering*, edited by Sarah LaChance Adams and Caroline R. Lundquist, 71–87. New York: Fordham University Press, 2013.

Greasley, Kate. *Arguments about Abortion: Personhood, Morality, and Law*. Oxford: Oxford University Press, 2017.

Green, Joel B. *Body, Soul, and Human Life: The Nature of Humanity in the Bible*. Grand Rapids: Baker, 2008.

————. "Eschatology and the Nature of Humans: A Reconsideration of Pertinent Biblical Evidence." *Science and Christian Belief* 14, no. 1 (2002): 33–50.

Green, Monica H., ed. *The Trotula: An English Translation of the Medieval Compendium of Women's Medicine*. Philadelphia: University of Pennsylvania Press, 2013.

Guon, Jennifer, et al. "Our Children Are Not a Diagnosis: The Experience of Parents Who Continue Their Pregnancy after a Prenatal Diagnosis of Trisomy 13 or 18." *American Journal of Medical Genetics*, part A 164, no. 2 (2014): 308–18.

Guttmacher Institute. "Induced Abortion in the United States." 2019. https://tinyurl.com/4u9vtp8r.

Habermas, Gary R., and J. P. Moreland. *Beyond Death: Exploring the Evidence for Immortality*. Eugene, OR: Wipf and Stock, 2004.

Habets, Myk. "'Suffer the Little Children to Come to Me, for Theirs is the Kingdom of Heaven': Infant Salvation and the Destiny of the Severely Mentally Disabled." In *Evangelical Calvinism: Essays Resourcing the Continuing Reformation of the Church*, edited by Myk Habets and Bobby Grow, 287–328. Eugene, OR: Wipf and Stock, 2012.

Haker, Hille. "Recognition and Responsibility." *Religions* 12 (2021): 467. https://tinyurl.com/yc2mt6f7.

Haldane, John, and Patrick Lee. "Aquinas on Human Ensoulment, Abortion and the Value of Life." *Philosophy* 78, no. 304 (2003): 255–78.

Hallstein, Lynn O'Brien, Andrea O'Reilly, and Melinda Vandenbeld Giles, eds. *The Routledge Companion to Motherhood*. New York: Routledge, 2020.

Hanson, Clare. *A Cultural History of Pregnancy: Pregnancy, Medicine and Culture, 1750–2000*. Houndmills, Basingstoke, Hampshire, UK: Palgrave Macmillan, 2004.

Harris, Mark. "Will Resurrection Be a Law of Nature? Science as Divine Action at the End of the World." In *Chance or Providence: Religious Perspectives on Divine Action*, edited by Louise Hickman, 21–44. Newcastle upon Tyne, UK: Cambridge Scholars, 2014.

Harrison, Beverly Wildung. *Our Right to Choose: Toward a New Ethic of Abortion*. Boston: Beacon, 1983.

———. "The Power of Anger in the Work of Love: Christian Ethics for Women and Other Strangers." In *Making the Connections: Essays in Feminist Social Ethics*, edited by Carol S. Robb, 3–21. Boston: Beacon, 1985.

Harrison, Brian, O.S. "Aborted Infants as Martyrs: Are There Wider Implications?" In *Abortion and Martyrdom. The Papers of the Solesmes Consultation and an Appeal to the Catholic Church*, edited by Aidan Nichols, O.P., 103–19. Leominster, Herefordshire, UK: Gracewing, 2003.

Hasker, William. "Abortion and the Definition of a Person." *Human Life Review* 5, no. 2 (1979).

———. "The Case for Emergent Dualism." In *The Blackwell Companion to Substance Dualism*, edited by Jonathan J. Loose, Angus J. L. Menuge, and J. P. Moreland, 61–72. Hoboken, NJ: Wiley Blackwell, 2018.

———. "A Critique of Thomistic Dualism." In *The Blackwell Companion to Substance Dualism*, edited by Jonathan J. Loose, Angus J. L. Menuge, and J. P. Moreland, 123–31. Hoboken, NJ: Wiley Blackwell, 2018.

———. "The Emergence of Persons." In *The Blackwell Companion to Science and Christianity*, edited by James B. Stump and Alan G. Padgett, 480–90. Walden, MA: Blackwell, 2012.

———. "Is Materialism Equivalent to Dualism?" In *After Physicalism*, edited by Paul Göcke Benedikt, 180–99. Notre Dame, IN: University of Notre Dame Press, 2012.

Hawn, C. Michael. "History of Hymns: 'Now the Green Blade Riseth.'" Discipleship Ministries, United Methodist Church. Apr. 22, 2014. https://tinyurl.com/4fsfhjac.

Hayford, Jack W. *I'll Hold You in Heaven: Healing and Hope for the Parent Who Has Lost a Child through Miscarriage, Stillbirth, Abortion or Early Infant Death.* Ventura, CA: Gospel Light, 2003.

Hays, Richard B. *First Corinthians.* Louisville: Westminster John Knox, 2011.

Heidelberg Catechism (1563). Faith Alive Christian Resources. 2011. https://tinyurl.com/3rvke9k3.

Hershenov, David B. "Van Inwagen, Zimmerman, and the Materialist Conception of Resurrection." *Religious Studies* 38, no. 4 (2002): 451–69.

Heyward, Carter. *Touching Our Strength: The Erotic as Power and the Love of God.* San Francisco: Harper & Row, 1989.

Hick, John. *Death and Eternal Life.* Louisville: Westminster John Knox, 1994.

Hill, Melissa, et al. "Has Noninvasive Prenatal Testing Impacted Termination of Pregnancy and Live Birth Rates of Infants with Down Syndrome?." *Prenatal Diagnosis* 37, no. 13 (2017): 1281–90.

"Infancy Gospel of James." Translated by Shelly Matthews. https://tinyurl.com/2sjbuter.

International Theological Commission. *The Hope of Salvation for Infants Who Die without Being Baptized.* The Vatican. 2007. https://tinyurl.com/67e59dkh.

"Is Emergence Fundamental?" Closer to Truth. Created by Robert Lawrence Kuhn. https://tinyurl.com/4dbcj2ws.

Isasi-Díaz, Ada María. "Mujerista Narratives: Creating a New Heaven and a New Earth." In *Liberating Eschatology: Essays in Honor of Letty M. Russell,* edited by Margaret A. Farley and Serene Jones, 227–43. Louisville: Westminster John Knox, 1999.

Isherwood, Lisa, and Elizabeth Stuart. *Introducing Body Theology.* Sheffield, UK: Sheffield Academic, 1998.

Jantzen, Grace. *Becoming Divine: Toward a Feminist Philosophy of Religion.* Bloomington: Indiana University Press, 1999.

Jeal, Roy R., and Linda A. West. "Rolling Away the Stone: Post-abortion Women in the Christian Community." *Journal of Pastoral Care & Counseling* 57, no. 1 (2003): 53–64.

Jenson, Robert W. *Systematic Theology.* Vol. 2: *The Works of God.* New York: Oxford University Press, 1999.

Johnson, Elizabeth A. "Jesus and the Cosmos: Soundings in Deep Christology." In *Incarnation: On the Scope and Depth of Christology,* edited by Niels Henrik Gregersen, 133–56. Minneapolis: Fortress, 2015.

Johnson, Nicole. "Invisible Grief? Theological Reflections on Miscarriage." *Other Journal,* March 17, 2014. https://tinyurl.com/ycxeth72.

Jones, David Albert. *The Soul of the Embryo: An Inquiry into the Status of the Human Embryo in the Christian Tradition.* London: Continuum, 2004.

———. "An Unholy Mess: Why 'the Sanctity of Life Principle' Should Be Jettisoned." *The New Bioethics* 22, no. 3 (2016): 185–201.

Jones, Serene. *Trauma and Grace: Theology in a Ruptured World.* Louisville: Westminster John Knox, 2009.

Jones, Serene, and Paul Lakeland, eds. *Constructive Theology: A Contemporary Approach to Classical Themes.* Minneapolis: Fortress, 2005.

Joyce, Kathryn. *Quiverfull: Inside the Christian Patriarchy Movement.* Boston: Beacon, 2009.

Jung, Patricia Beattie. "Abortion and Organ Donation: Christian Reflections on Bodily Life Support." *Journal of Religious Ethics* 16, no. 2 (1988): 273–305.

———. *Sex on Earth as It Is in Heaven: A Christian Eschatology of Desire.* Albany: SUNY Press, 2016.

Kaczor, Christopher. *The Ethics of Abortion: Women's Rights, Human Life, and the Question of Justice.* 3rd ed. New York: Routledge, 2023.

Kamitsuka, Margaret D. *Abortion and the Christian Tradition: A Prochoice Theological Ethic.* Louisville: Westminster John Knox, 2019.

———. *Feminist Theology and the Challenge of Difference.* New York: Oxford University Press, 2007.

———. "Prolife Christian Romance Novels: A Sign That the Abortion-as-Murder Center Is Not Holding?." *Christianity & Literature* 69, no. 1 (2020): 36–52.

———. "Sex in Heaven? Eschatological Eros and the Resurrection of the Body." In *The Embrace of Eros: Bodies, Desires, and Sexuality in Christianity*, edited by Margaret D. Kamitsuka, 261–75. Minneapolis: Fortress, 2010.

Karant-Nunn, Susan C. "'Suffer the Little Children to Come unto Me, and Forbid Them Not': The Social Location of Baptism in Early Modern Germany." In *Continuity and Change: The Harvest of Late Medieval and Reformation History: Studies in Honor of Heiko A. Oberman on His Seventieth Birthday*, edited by Andrew C. Gow and Robert J. Bast, 359–78. Leiden: Brill, 2000.

Keane, Helen. "Foetal Personhood and Representations of the Absent Child in Pregnancy Loss Memorialization." *Feminist Theory* 10, no. 2 (2009): 153–71.

Kelly, Ewan R. *Marking Short Lives: Constructing and Sharing Rituals Following Pregnancy Loss*. Oxford: Peter Lang, 2007.

Kelly, Kimberly. "The Spread of 'Post Abortion Syndrome' as Social Diagnosis." *Social Science & Medicine* 102 (2014): 18–25.

Kelly, Susan E. "Choosing Not to Choose: Reproductive Responses of Parents of Children with Genetic Conditions or Impairments." *Sociology of Health & Illness* 31, no. 1 (2009): 81–97.

Kelsey, David H. *Eccentric Existence: A Theological Anthropology*. 2 vols. Louisville: Westminster John Knox, 2009.

Kennedy, Liam. "Afterlives: Testimonies of Irish Catholic Mothers on Infant Death and the Fate of the Unbaptized." *Journal of Family History* 46, no. 2 (2021): 236–55.

King, Jr., Martin Luther. "Remaining Awake through a Great Revolution." Speech given at the National Cathedral. Washington, DC. March 31, 1968. https://tinyurl.com/57peu85d.

Kittay, Eva Feder. *Learning from My Daughter: The Value and Care of Disabled Minds*. New York: Oxford University Press, 2019.

———. *Love's Labor: Essays on Women, Equality, and Dependency*. New York: Routledge, 1999.

Kitzler, Petr. "Tertullian and Ancient Embryology in De Carne Christi 4, 1 and 19, 3–4." *Zeitschrift für Antikes Christentum/Journal of Ancient Christianity* 18, no. 2 (2014): 204–9.

Klein, Stanley B., and Shaun Nichols. "Memory and the Sense of Personal Identity." *Mind* 121, no. 483 (2012): 677–702.

Kuhn, Thomas S. *The Structure of Scientific Revolutions*. Chicago: University of Chicago Press, 1970.

Kvam, Kristen. "Comfort." In *Hope Deferred: Heart-Healing Reflections on Reproductive Loss*, edited by Nadine Pence Franz and Mary T. Stimming, 71–84. Cleveland: Pilgrim, 2010.

———. "Introduction" to Martin Luther, "Consolation for Women Whose Pregnancies Have Not Gone Well, 1542." In *The Annotated Luther*. Vol. 4: *Pastoral Writings*, edited by Mary Jane Haemig, Hans J. Hillerbrand, Kirsi I. Stjerna, and Timothy J. Wengert, 419–21. Minneapolis: Fortress, 2016.

Kwasniewski, Peter. "King Herod and the Martyr-Children." In *Abortion and Martyrdom. The Papers of the Solesmes Consultation and an Appeal to the Catholic Church*, edited by Aidan Nichols, O.P., 32–50. Leominster, Herefordshire, UK: Gracewing, 2003.

Lagercrantz, Hugo. "The Emergence of Consciousness: Science and Ethics." *Seminars in Fetal and Neonatal Medicine* 19, no. 5 (2014): 300–305.

Larsen, Elisabeth Clare, et al. "New Insights into Mechanisms behind Miscarriage." *BMC Medicine* 11, no. 1 (2013): 1–10.

Laufer, Catherine Ella. *Hell's Destruction: An Exploration of Christ's Descent to the Dead.* New York: Routledge, 2016.

Layne, Linda L. "Troubling the Normal: 'Angel Babies' and the Canny/Uncanny Nexus." In *Understanding Reproductive Loss: Perspectives on Life, Death and Fertility*, edited by Sarah Earle, Carol Komaromy, and Linda Layne, 129–41. Farnham, UK: Ashgate, 2012.

Leever, Martin, et al. "'Baptizing' Deceased Infants? Is There a Catholic Ritual That Chaplains Can Perform to Relieve Grieving Parents?" *Health Progress* 85, no. 6 (2004): 44–49.

Leftow, Brian. "Souls Dipped in Dust." In *Soul, Body, and Survival: Essays on the Metaphysics of Human Persons*, edited by Kevin Corcoran, 120–38. Ithaca, NY: Cornell University Press, 2001.

Lehtipuu, Outi. *Debates over the Resurrection of the Dead: Constructing Early Christian Identity.* Oxford: Oxford Early Christian Studies, 2015.

Levinas, Emmanuel. "Ethics as First Philosophy." In *The Levinas Reader*, edited by Seán Hand, 75–87. Oxford: Blackwell, 1989.

Lindbeck, George A. *The Nature of Doctrine: Religion and Theology in a Postliberal Age.* Philadelphia: Westminster John Knox, 1984.

Lindemann Nelson, Hilde. "What Child Is This?" *Hastings Center Report* 32, no. 6 (2002): 29–38.

Lindemann Nelson, James. "Prenatal Diagnosis, Personal Identity and Disability." *Kennedy Institute of Ethics Journal* 10, no. 3 (2000): 213–28.

Lindh, Heidi L., et al. "Characteristics and Perspectives of Families Waiting to Adopt a Child with Down Syndrome." *Genetics in Medicine* 9, no. 4 (2007): 235–40.

Little, Margaret Olivia. "Abortion, Intimacy, and the Duty to Gestate." *Ethical Theory and Moral Practice* 2, no. 3 (1999): 295–312.

Loftin, R. Keith, and Joshua R. Farris. "Christian Physicalism: An Introduction." In *Christian Physicalism?: Philosophical Theological Criticisms*, edited by R. Keith Loftin and Joshua R. Farris, xiii–xxiii. Lanham, MD: Lexington, 2018.

Loose, Jonathan J. "Christian Materialism and Christian Ethics: Moral Debt and an Ethic of Life." In *Christian Physicalism?: Philosophical Theological Criticisms*, edited by R. Keith Loftin and Joshua R. Farris, 351–70. Lanham, MD: Lexington, 2018.

———. "Materialism Most Miserable: The Prospects for Dualist and Physicalist Accounts of Resurrection." In *The Blackwell Companion to Substance Dualism*, edited by Jonathan J. Loose, Angus J. L. Menuge, and J. P. Moreland, 469–87. Hoboken, NJ: Wiley, 2018.

Lowe, Jaime, and Stephanie Sinclair. "What a High-Risk Pregnancy Looks Like after Dobbs." *New York Times*. Sept. 13, 2022.

Lum, Kathryn Gin. *Damned Nation: Hell in America from the Revolution to Reconstruction*. New York: Oxford University Press, 2014.

Lupton, Deborah. *The Social Worlds of the Unborn*. Houndmills, Basingstoke, Hampshire, UK; New York: Palgrave Macmillan, 2013.

Luther, Martin. "Consolation for Women Whose Pregnancies Have Not Gone Well, 1542." Introduction by Kristen E. Kvam. In *The Annotated Luther*. Vol. 4: *Pastoral Writings*, edited by Mary Jane Haemig, Hans J. Hillerbrand, Kirsi I. Stjerna, and Timothy J. Wengert, 419–28. Minneapolis: Fortress, 2016.

Lyotard, Jean-François. *The Postmodern Condition: A Report on Knowledge*. Minneapolis: University of Minnesota Press, 1984.

MacArthur, John F. *Safe in the Arms of God: Truth from Heaven about the Death of a Child*. Nashville: Thomas Nelson, 2003.

Mackenzie, Catriona. "Abortion and Embodiment." *Australasian Journal of Philosophy* 70, no. 2 (1992): 136–55.

Malacrida, Claudia. "Mothering and Disability: Implications for Theory and Practice." In *Routledge Handbook of Disability Studies*, edited by Nick Watson and Simo Vehmas, 398–409. 2nd ed. New York: Routledge, 2013.

Markens, Susan. "'Is This Something You Want?': Genetic Counselors' Accounts of Their Role in Prenatal Decision Making." *Sociological Forum* 28, no. 3 (2013): 431–51.

Martin, Dale B. *The Corinthian Body*. New Haven, CT: Yale University Press, 1999.

Martin, Joan M. "A Sacred Hope and Social Goal: Womanist Eschatology." In *Liberating Eschatology: Essays in Honor of Letty M. Russell*, edited by Margaret A. Farley and Serene Jones, 209–26. Louisville: Westminster John Knox, 1999.

McAvoy, Liz Herbert. *Authority and the Female Body in the Writings of Julian of Norwich and Margery Kempe*. Suffolk, UK: Boydell & Brewer, 2004.

McDonagh, Eileen. "Adding Consent to Choice in the Abortion Debate." *Society* 42, no. 5 (2005): 18–26.

McFague, Sallie. *The Body of God: An Ecological Theology*. Minneapolis: Fortress, 1993.

———. *Metaphorical Theology: Models of God in Religious Language*. Philadelphia: Fortress, 1982.

McFarland, Ian. "Evil, Wonder, and Chance: A Reflection on Categories in *Wondrously Wounded*," *Syndicate*. Oct. 14, 2020. https://tinyurl.com/bdf7d8z9.

McGowin, Emily Hunter. *Quivering Families: The Quiverfull Movement and Evangelical Theology of the Family*. Minneapolis: Fortress, 2018.

McLeod, Carolyn. *Self-Trust and Reproductive Autonomy*. Cambridge, MA: MIT Press, 2002.

McMahan, Jeff. *The Ethics of Killing: Problems at the Margins of Life*. New York: Oxford University Press, 2002.

"Memorial Service." Rachel's Vineyard. https://tinyurl.com/2jsty45r.

Merricks, Trenton. "The Resurrection of the Body." In *The Oxford Handbook of Philosophical Theology*, edited by Thomas P. Flint and Michael C. Rea, 476–90. New York: Oxford University Press, 2009.

———. "How to Live Forever without Saving Your Soul: Physicalism and Immortality." In *Soul, Body, and Survival: Essays on the Metaphysics of Human Persons*, edited by Kevin Corcoran, 183–201. Ithaca, NY: Cornell University Press, 2001.

Metzger, James A. "Reclaiming 'a Dark and Malefic Sacred' for a Theology of Disability." *Journal of Religion, Disability & Health* 15, no. 3 (2011): 296–313.

Miles, Margaret R. "Theology, Anthropology, and the Human Body in Calvin's 'Institutes of the Christian Religion.'" *Harvard Theological Review* 74, no. 3 (1981): 303–23.

Mistry, Zubin. 2015. *Abortion in the Early Middle Ages, c. 500–900*. Woodbridge, Suffolk, UK: York Medieval.

Mitchell, C. Ben. "The Vulnerable—Abortion and Disability." In *The Oxford Handbook of Evangelical Theology*, edited by Gerald R. McDermott, 481–96. Oxford: Oxford University Press, 2010.

Moe, Thomas. *Pastoral Care in Pregnancy Loss: A Ministry Long Needed*. New York: Routledge, 2014.

Moreland, J. P. "Substance Dualism and the Diachronic/Synchronic Unity of Consciousness." In *Christian Physicalism?: Philosophical Theological Criticisms*, edited by R. Keith Loftin and Joshua R. Farris, 43–74. Lanham, MD: Lexington, 2017.

Moreland, J. P., and Scott B. Rae. *Body & Soul: Human Nature & the Crisis in Ethics*. Downers Grove, IL: InterVarsity, 2001.

Morgan, Lynn M., and Meredith W. Michaels, eds. *Fetal Subjects, Feminist Positions*. Philadelphia: University of Pennsylvania Press, 1999.

Morris, Stephen. "Words in the Face of Unspeakable Tragedy: Eastern Christian Preaching at the Funeral of a Child." *Greek Orthodox Theological Review* 51, nos. 1–4 (2006): 71–89.

Moss, Candida R. *Divine Bodies: Resurrecting Perfection in the New Testament and Early Christianity*. New Haven, CT: Yale University Press, 2019.

———. *The Other Christs: Imitating Jesus in Ancient Christian Ideologies of Martyrdom*. Oxford: Oxford University Press, 2010.

Moss, Candida R., and Joel S. Baden. *Reconceiving Infertility: Biblical Perspectives on Procreation and Childlessness*. Princeton, NJ: Princeton University Press, 2015.

Moultrie, Monique. "#BlackBabiesMatter: Analyzing Black Religious Media in Conservative and Progressive Evangelical Communities." *Religions* 8, no. 11 (2017): 255. https://tinyurl.com/ms3vvxwc.

Mullins, R. T. "Some Difficulties for Amos Yong's Disability Theology of the Resurrection." *Ars Disputandi* 11, no. 1 (2011): 24–32.

Murphy, Nancey. "Nonreductive Physicalism." In *In Search of the Soul: Perspectives on the Mind-Body*, edited by Joel B. Green and Stuart L. Palmer, 115–38. 2nd ed. Eugene, OR: Wipf and Stock, 2010.

———. "A Nonreductive Physicalist Response." In *In Search of the Soul: Four Views of the Mind-Body Problem*, edited by Joel B. Green and Stuart L. Palmer, 185–88. 2nd ed. Eugene, OR: Wipf and Stock, 2010.

———. *Bodies and Souls, or Spirited Bodies?* Cambridge: Cambridge University Press, 2006.

"National Day of Remembrance for Aborted Children." https://tinyurl.com/2xpd2y4u.

Neal, Lynn S. *Romancing God: Evangelical Women and Inspirational Fiction*. Chapel Hill: University of North Carolina Press, 2006.

Neu, Diann L. "Women's Empowerment through Feminist Rituals." In *Women's Spirituality, Women's Lives*, edited by Judith Ochshorn and Ellen Cole, 185–200. New York: Hawthorne, 1995.

Nichols, Aidan, O.P., ed. *Abortion and Martyrdom: The Papers of the Solesmes Consultation and an Appeal to the Catholic Church*. Leominster, Herefordshire, UK: Gracewing, 2002.

O'Connor, June. "Ritual Recognition of Abortion: Japanese Buddhist Practices and US Jewish and Christian Proposals." In *Embodiment, Morality, and Medicine*, edited by Lisa Sowle Cahill and Margaret Farley, 93–111. Dordrecht: Kluwer Academic, 1995.

O'Connor, Timothy, and Jonathan D. Jacobs. "Emergent Individuals." *The Philosophical Quarterly* 53, no. 213 (2003): 540–55.

———. "Emergent Individuals and the Resurrection." *European Journal for Philosophy of Religion* 2, no. 2 (2010): 69–88.

O'Donnell, Karen. *The Dark Womb: Re-Conceiving Theology through Reproductive Loss*. London: SCM Press, 2022.

———. "Theology and Reproductive Loss." *Modern Believing* 60, no. 2 (2019): 123–33.

Oduyoye, Mercy Amba. "A Coming to Myself: The Childless Woman in the West African Space." In *Liberating Eschatology: Essays in Honor of Letty M. Russell,* edited by Margaret A. Farley and Serene Jones, 105–20. Louisville: Westminster John Knox, 1999.

O'Keefe, John J. "The Persistence of Decay: Bodily Disintegration and Cyrillian Christology." In *In the Shadow of the Incarnation: Essays on Jesus Christ in the Early Church in Honor of Brian E. Daley, S.J.,* edited by Peter William Martens, 228–45. Notre Dame, IN: University of Notre Dame Press, 2008.

"Older Youth with Disabilities in Foster Care." Center for the Advanced Studies in Child Welfare, University of Minnesota School of Social Work. 2013. https://tinyurl.com/yms2emkj.

Parsons, Kate. "Feminist Reflections on Miscarriage, in Light of Abortion." *International Journal of Feminist Approaches to Bioethics* 3, no. 1 (2010): 1–22.

Pasnau, Robert. "Souls and the Beginning of Life (A Reply to Haldane and Lee)." *Philosophy* 78, no. 306 (2003): 521–31.

———. *Thomas Aquinas on Human Nature: A Philosophical Study of Summa Theologiae, 1a 75–89.* New York: Cambridge University Press, 2002.

Paterson, Shaw James. "How Might Parish Ministers (and Other Pastoral Caregivers) Better Support Women Who Have Experienced an Early Miscarriage?" Ph.D. diss. University of Glasgow, 2020.

Pelikan, Jaroslav. *The Christian Tradition: A History of the Development of Doctrine.* 5 vols. Chicago: University of Chicago Press, 1971–89.

Pennington, Emily. *Feminist Eschatology: Embodied Futures.* London: Routledge, 2016.

Peretti, Frank E. *Tilly.* Wheaton, IL: Crossway, 1988.

Peters, Rebecca Todd. "Listening to Women: Examining the Moral Wisdom of Women Who End Pregnancies." *Journal of Religious Ethics* 49, no. 2 (2021): 290–313.

———. *Trust Women: A Progressive Christian Argument for Reproductive Justice.* Boston: Beacon, 2018.

Peters, Ted, Robert John Russell, and Michael Welker, eds. *Resurrection: Theological and Scientific Assessments.* Grand Rapids: Eerdmans, 2002.

Petersen, Emily E., et al. "Racial/Ethnic Disparities in Pregnancy-Related Deaths—United States, 2007–2016." *Morbidity and Mortality Weekly Report* 68, no. 35 (2019): 762–65.

Peterson, Suzanne E., et al. "Fetal Cellular Microchimerism in Miscarriage and Pregnancy Termination." *Chimerism* 4, no. 4 (2013): 136–38.

Pew Research Center. "Belief in Heaven." 2015. https://tinyurl.com/bdcrc7y8.

———. "Few Americans Blame God or Say Faith Has Been Shaken amid Pandemic, Other Tragedies." Nov. 23, 2021. https://tinyurl.com/mshbxvt5.

Planned Parenthood. "How does the Abortion Pill Work?" https://tinyurl.com/ycxvdh3m.

———. "What Happens during an in-Clinic Abortion?" https://tinyurl.com/58r7zj43.

———. "What Is a Miscarriage?" https://tinyurl.com/3n7fcmf3.

Piper, John. "The Baby in My Womb Leaped for Joy." Desiring God. January 25, 2009. https://tinyurl.com/ypsa4xn5.

Plantinga, Alvin. "Materialism and Christian Belief." In *Persons: Human and Divine*, edited by Peter van Inwagen and Dean Zimmerman, 99–141. New York: Oxford University Press, 2007.

Polkinghorne, John. "Eschatological Credibility: Emergent and Teleological Processes." In *Resurrection: Theological and Scientific Assessments*, edited by Ted Peters, Robert John Russell, and Michael Welker, 43–55. Grand Rapids: Eerdmans, 2002.

Pope Benedict XII. "Benedictus Deus: On the Beatific Vision of God." 1336. The Vatican. https://tinyurl.com/2xx6c3jj.

Powell, Lisa D. "Disability and Resurrection: Eschatological Bodies, Identity, and Continuity." *Journal of the Society of Christian Ethics* 41, no. 1 (2021): 89–106.

Pozhitkov, Alexander E., and Peter A. Noble. "Gene Expression in the Twilight of Death." *Bioessays* 39, no. 9 (2017): 1700066.

Prayer League of the Holy Innocents and St. Stylianos. https://tinyurl.com/ewdk9n64.

Price, David H. *In the Beginning Was the Image: Art and the Reformation Bible*. New York: Oxford University Press, 2020.

Price, Richard, and Michael Gaddis. *The Acts of the Council of Chalcedon, 400–700*. Liverpool: Liverpool University Press, 2005.

Rambo, Shelly. *Resurrecting Wounds: Living in the Afterlife of Trauma*. Waco, TX: Baylor University Press, 2017.

Read, Sara. *Menstruation and the Female Body in Early Modern England.* Houndmills, Basingstoke, Hampshire, UK; New York: Palgrave Macmillan, 2013.

Reagan, Leslie J. "From Hazard to Blessing to Tragedy: Representations of Miscarriage in Twentieth-Century America." *Feminist Studies* 29, no. 2 (2003): 357–78.

———. *When Abortion Was a Crime: Women, Medicine, and Law in the United States, 1867–1973.* Berkeley: University of California Press, 1997.

Reardon, David C. "A Defense of the Neglected Rhetorical Strategy (NRS)." *Ethics and Medicine* 18, no. 2 (2002): 23–32.

Reinders, Hans S. *Disability, Providence, and Ethics: Bridging Gaps, Transforming Lives.* Waco, TX: Baylor University Press, 2014.

———. *The Future of the Disabled in Liberal Society.* Notre Dame, IN: University of Notre Dame Press, 2000.

———. *Receiving the Gift of Friendship: Profound Disability, Theological Anthropology, and Ethics.* Grand Rapids: Eerdmans, 2008.

Reitan, Eric. "Eternal Damnation and Blessed Ignorance: Is the Damnation of Some Incompatible with the Salvation of Any?" *Religious Studies* 38 (2002): 429–50.

Religious Coalition for Reproductive Choice. "Abortions Welcome." https://tinyurl.com/38jxj354.

Reynolds, Susan Bigelow. "From the Site of the Empty Tomb: Approaching the Hidden Grief of Prenatal Loss." *New Theology Review: An American Catholic Journal for Ministry* 28, no. 2 (2016): 47–59.

Rickabaugh, Brandon. "Dismantling Bodily Resurrection Arguments Against Mind-Body Dualism." In *Christian Physicalism?: Philosophical Theological Criticisms*, edited by R. Keith Loftin and Joshua R. Farris, 295–317. Lanham, MD: Lexington, 2018.

———. "Responding to N.T. Wright's Rejection of the Soul." *Heythrop Journal* 59, no. 2 (2018): 201–20.

Rice, William R. "The High Abortion Cost of Human Reproduction." *bioRxiv* (2018): 17.

Ricoeur, Paul. "Biblical Hermeneutics." *Semeia* 4 (1975): 29–148.

———. *The Course of Recognition.* Cambridge, MA: Harvard University Press, 2005.

Roberts, Claire T. "Premature Lambs Grown in a Bag." *Nature* 546 (2017): 45–46.

Roberts, Dorothy E. *Killing the Black Body: Race, Reproduction, and the Meaning of Liberty*. New York: Vintage, 1999.

Robinson, Gail Erlick, et al. "Is There an 'Abortion Trauma Syndrome'? Critiquing the Evidence." *Harvard Review of Psychiatry* 17, no. 4 (2009): 268–90.

Roth, Catharine P. "Platonic and Pauline Elements in the Ascent of the Soul in Gregory of Nyssa's Dialogue on the Soul and Resurrection." *Vigiliae Christianae* 46, no. 1 (1992): 20–30.

Ruether, Rosemary Radford. "Eschatology in Christian Feminist Theologies." In *The Oxford Handbook of Eschatology*, edited by Jerry L. Walls, 328–42. New York: Oxford University Press, 2007.

———. *New Woman, New Earth: Sexist Ideologies and Human Liberation*. New York: Seabury, 1995.

———. *Sexism and God-Talk: Toward a Feminist Theology*, with a new introduction. Boston: Beacon, 1993.

———. *Women-Church: Theology and Practice of Feminist Liturgical Communities*. San Francisco: Harper & Row, 1988.

Salih, Sarah. *Versions of Virginity in Late Medieval England*. Woodbridge, Suffolk, UK: Boydell & Brewer, 2001.

Samson, Judith. "The Scars of the Madonna: The Struggle over Abortion in the Example of an American Post-abortion Pilgrimage to Mary." *Journal of Ritual Studies* 28, no. 2 (2014): 37–49.

Scaer, David P. "Luther's Concept of the Resurrection in His Commentary on 1 Corinthians 15." *Concordia Theological Quarterly* 47, no. 3 (1983): 209–25.

Schechtman, Marya. *The Constitution of Selves*. Ithaca, NY: Cornell University Press, 1996.

———. *Staying Alive: Personal Identity, Practical Concerns, and the Unity of a Life*. New York: Oxford University Press, 2014.

Schiff, Daniel. 2002. *Abortion in Judaism*. Cambridge: Cambridge University Press.

Schmisek, Brian. *Resurrection of the Flesh or Resurrection from the Dead: Implications for Theology*. Collegeville, MN: Liturgical, 2013.

Schumacher, Michele M. "The Martyr Status of the Aborted Child: A Share in Christ's Witness to the Father of Mercies." In *Abortion and Martyrdom. The Papers of the Solesmes Consultation and an Appeal to the Catholic Church*, edited by Aidan Nichols, O.P., 63–78. Leominster, Herefordshire, UK: Gracewing, 2003.

Schumm, Darla Y. "Reimaging Disability." *Journal of Feminist Studies in Religion* 26, no. 2 (2010): 132–37.

Segal, Alan F. "Paul's Thinking about Resurrection in Its Jewish Context." *New Testament Studies* 44, no. 3 (1998): 400–419.

Serfes, Archimandrite Nektarios. "The Massacre of 14,000 Holy Innocent Infants, in Bethlehem and Its Borders." *Orthodox Christianity*. Jan. 29, 2001. https://tinyurl.com/f742x5c6.

Setzer, Claudia. *Resurrection of the Body in Early Judaism and Early Christianity: Doctrine, Community, and Self.* Boston: Brill Academic, 2004.

Shanzer, Danuta. "Voices and Bodies: The Afterlife of the Unborn." *Numen* 56, nos. 2–3 (2009): 326–65.

Shaw, Teresa M. *The Burden of the Flesh: Fasting and Sexuality in Early Christianity.* Minneapolis: Fortress, 1998.

Shields, Christopher, and Robert Pasnau. *The Philosophy of Aquinas.* 2nd ed. New York: Oxford University Press, 2016.

"Shout Your Abortion." https://tinyurl.com/sy48wk67.

Shrine of the Holy Innocents. Saugerties, NY. https://tinyurl.com/368xekm5.

Silcock, Jeffrey G. "A Lutheran Approach to Eschatology." *Lutheran Quarterly* 31, no. 4 (2017): 373–95.

Singh, Puneet, Kearsley Stewart, and Scott Moses. "Pastoral Care Following Pregnancy Loss: The Role of Ritual." *Journal of Pastoral Care & Counseling* 58, nos. 1–2 (2004): 41–53.

Sisson, Gretchen, et al. "Adoption Decision Making among Women Seeking Abortion." *Women's Health Issues* 27, no. 2 (2017): 136–44.

Skotko, Brian G. "Prenatally Diagnosed Down Syndrome: Mothers Who Continued Their Pregnancies Evaluate Their Health Care Providers." *American Journal of Obstetrics and Gynecology* 192, no. 3 (2005): 670–77.

Skotko, Brian G., Susan P. Levine, and Richard Goldstein. "Having a Son or Daughter with Down Syndrome: Perspectives from Mothers and Fathers." *American Journal of Medical Genetics, Part A* 155, no. 10 (2011): 2335–47.

Slenczka, Notger. "Luther's Anthropology." In *The Oxford Handbook of Martin Luther's Theology*, edited by Robert Kolb, Irene Dingel, and L'ubomir Batka, 212–32. Oxford: Oxford University Press, 2014.

Sommers, Mary Catherine. "Living Together: Burdensome Pregnancy and the Hospitable Self." In *Abortion: A New Generation of Catholic Responses*, edited by Stephen J. Heaney, 243–61. Braintree, MA: Pope John Center, 1992.

Spierling, Karen E. *Infant Baptism in Reformation Geneva: The Shaping of a Community, 1536–1564*. New York: Routledge, 2017.

Stahl, Devan Joy. "A Christian Ontology of Genetic Disease and Disorder." *Journal of Disability & Religion* 19, no. 2 (2015): 119–45.

Staley, Lynn, trans. and ed. *The Book of Margery Kempe*. New York: Norton, 2001.

Standing Commission on Liturgy and Music. "A Rite for Mourning the Loss of a Pregnancy." In *Enriching Our Worship 5: Liturgies and Prayer Related to Childbearing, Childbirth, and Loss. Supplemental Liturgical Materials*, 21–23. New York: Church Publishing, 2009.

———. "A Rite of Repentance and Reconciliation for an Abortion." In *Enriching Our Worship 5: Liturgies and Prayer Related to Childbearing, Childbirth, and Loss. Supplemental Liturgical Materials*, 27–30. New York: Church Publishing, 2009.

Stanton, Elizabeth Cady. "On Marriage and Divorce." 1871. https://tinyurl.com/y85hvbvu.

Stark, Paul. "Is Abortion Justified after an Adverse Prenatal Diagnosis?" *Minnesota Citizens Concerned for Life*. May 9, 2018. https://tinyurl.com/yekja6y8.

Stensvold, Anne. *A History of Pregnancy in Christianity: From Original Sin to Contemporary Abortion Debate*. New York: Routledge, 2015.

Stjerna, Kirsi. *Women and the Reformation*. Malden, MA: Blackwell, 2011.

Stoljar, Natalie. "Feminist Perspectives on Autonomy." *Stanford Encyclopedia of Philosophy*. 2018. https://tinyurl.com/7n54pjdt.

Strohl, Jane E. "Luther's Eschatology." In *The Oxford Handbook of Martin Luther's Theology*, edited by Robert Kolb, Irene Dingel, and L'ubomír Batka, 353–62. Oxford: Oxford University Press, 2014.

Stump, Eleonore. "Resurrection, Reassembly, and Reconstitution: Aquinas on the Soul." In *Die Menschliche Seele: Brauchen Wir den Dualismus?*, edited by Bruno Niederbacher and Edmund Runggaldier, 151–71. Frankfurt: ontos verlag, 2013.

Sullivan, Francis A. "The Development of Doctrine about Infants Who Die Unbaptized." *Theological Studies* 72, no. 1 (2011): 3–14.

Sumney, Jerry. "Post-mortem Existence and Resurrection of the Body in Paul." *Horizons in Biblical Theology* 31, no. 1 (2009): 12–26.

Taliaferro, Charles. "Substance Dualism: A Defense." In *The Blackwell Companion to Substance Dualism*, edited by Jonathan J. Loose, Angus J. L. Menuge, and J. P. Moreland, 44–45. Hoboken, NJ: Wiley Blackwell, 2018.

Tasioulas, Jacqueline. "'Heaven and Earth in Little Space': The Foetal Existence of Christ in Medieval Literature and Thought." *Medium Aevum* 76, no. 1 (2007): 24–48.

Tertullian. "A Treatise on the Soul." In *The Ante-Nicene Fathers*, translated by D. D. Holmes, edited by Alexander Roberts and James Donaldson, vol. 3. New York: Scribner's, 1899. https://tinyurl.com/mtp7y999.

Thiel, John E. "For What May We Hope? Thoughts on the Eschatological Imagination." *Theological Studies* 67, no. 3 (2006): 517–41.

Thompson, Janice Allison. "Making Room for the Other: Maternal Mourning and Eschatological Hope." *Modern Theology* 27, no. 3 (2011): 395–413.

Thomson, Judith Jarvis. "A Defense of Abortion." *Philosophy and Public Affairs* 1, no. 1 (1971): 47–66.

Timpe, Kevin. "Defiant Afterlife: Disability and Uniting Ourselves to God." In *Voices from the Edge: Centring Marginalized Perspectives in Analytic Theology*, edited by Michelle Panchuk and Mike Rea, 206–31. Oxford: Oxford University Press, 2020.

Toner, Patrick. "Critical Study of Fabrizio Amerini's *Aquinas on the Beginning and End of Human Life*." In *Oxford Studies in Medieval Philosophy*, edited by Robert Pasnau, vol. 2, 212–29. Oxford: Oxford University Press, 2014.

Townes, Emilie M. *In a Blaze of Glory: Womanist Spirituality as Social Witness*. Nashville: Abingdon, 1995.

Trigg, Jonathan D. *Baptism in the Theology of Martin Luther*. Leiden: Brill, 1994.

"Turnaway Study." Advancing New Standards in Reproductive Health. University of California, San Francisco. https://tinyurl.com/2p8nxdvd.

Turner, James T. *On the Resurrection of the Dead: A New Metaphysics of Afterlife for Christian Thought*. New York: Routledge, 2018.

United States Conference of Catholic Bishops. *Ethical and Religious Directives for Catholic Health Care Services*. 2018. https://tinyurl.com 4a5a3vfc.

Van der Lugt, Maaike. "Formed Fetuses and Healthy Children in Scholastic Theology, Medicine and Law." In *Reproduction: Antiquity to the Present Day*, edited by Nick Hopwood, Rebecca Flemming, and Lauren Kassell, 167–80. Cambridge: Cambridge University Press, 2018.

Van Dyke, Christina. "I See Dead People: Disembodied Souls and Aquinas's 'Two-Person' Problem." In *Oxford Studies in Medieval Philosophy*, edited by Robert Pasnau, vol. 2, 25–45. Oxford: Oxford University Press, 2014.

Van Inwagen, Peter. "I Look for the Resurrection of the Dead and the Life of the World to Come." In *The Blackwell Companion to Substance Dualism*, edited by Jonathan J. Loose, Angus J. L. Menuge, and J. P. Moreland, 488–500. Hoboken, NJ: Wiley Blackwell, 2018.

———. *Material Beings*. Ithaca, NY: Cornell University Press, 1995.

———. "The Possibility of Resurrection." *International Journal for Philosophy of Religion* 9, no. 2 (1978): 114–21.

Virgil. *The Aeneid*. Translated by H. R. Fairclough. https://tinyurl.com/54xmpead.

Virk, Jasveer, Jun Zhang, and Jørn Olsen. "Medical Abortion and the Risk of Subsequent Adverse Pregnancy Outcomes." *New England Journal of Medicine* 357, no. 7 (2007): 648–53.

Walls, Jerry L., ed. *The Oxford Handbook of Eschatology*. New York: Oxford University Press, 2007.

Walsh, Maureen L. "Emerging Trends in Pregnancy-Loss Memorialization in American Catholicism." *Horizons* 44, no. 2 (2017): 369–98.

Ward, Keith. "Bishop Berkeley's Castle: John Polkinghorne on the Soul." In *God and the Scientist: Exploring the Work of John Polkinghorne*, edited by Fraser Watts and Christopher C. Knight, 127–37. London: Ashgate/Routledge, 2012.

Warfield, Benjamin Breckinridge. *The Development of the Doctrine of Infant Salvation*. New York: Christian Literature, 1891.

Warren, Mary Anne. "On the Moral and Legal Status of Abortion." *The Monist* 57, no. 1 (1973): 43–61.

Warren, Tish Harrison. "What Pro-lifers Can Learn from the Planned Parenthood Apology." *Christianity Today*. April 19, 2021.

Wessel, Susan. "The Reception of Greek Science in Gregory of Nyssa's De Hominis Opificio." *Vigiliae Christianae* 63, no. 1 (2009): 24–46.

Wheeler, Katherine Mayne. "Why It Is Imperative to Reject Prenatal Screening for Down Syndrome." *Human Defense Initiative*. June 10, 2018. https://tinyurl.com/44sys5nv.

Whitney, Donna Krupkin. "Emotional Sequelae of Elective Abortion: The Role of Guilt and Shame." *Journal of Pastoral Care & Counseling* 71, no. 2 (2017): 98–105.

"Why a Body in a Resurrection?" *Closer to Truth*. Created by Robert Lawrence Kuhn. Season 14, Episode 1407. 2015. https://tinyurl.com/yc7dd7ru.

Wicks, Jared, S.J. "Christ's Saving Descent to the Dead: Early Witnesses from Ignatius of Antioch to Origen." *Pro Ecclesia* 17, no. 3 (208): 281–309.

Williams, Delores S. "The Color of Feminism: On Speaking the Black Woman's Tongue." In *Feminist Theological Ethics*, edited by Lois K. Daly, 49–50. Louisville: Westminster John Knox, 1994.

———. *Sisters in the Wilderness: The Challenge of Womanist God-Talk*. Maryknoll, NY: Orbis, 1993.

Williams, Gareth E. "Stillborn Funeral Liturgies in Theological Perspective." *Whitefield Briefing* 3, no. 4 (1998): 1–4.

Witte, John, Jr., and Robert M. Kingdon. *Sex, Marriage, and Family in John Calvin's Geneva*. Vol. 1: *Courtship, Engagement, and Marriage*. Grand Rapids: Eerdmans, 2005.

Wood, Adam. "Mind the Gap? The Principle of Non-repeatability and Aquinas's Account of the Resurrection." In *Oxford Studies in Medieval Philosophy*, edited by Robert Pasnau, vol. 3, 99–127. Oxford: Oxford University Press, 2015.

Wood, Charles M. *The Question of Providence*. Louisville: Westminster John Knox, 2008.

Wright, David F. *Infant Baptism in Historical Perspective. Collected Studies.* Milton Keynes, UK: Paternoster, 2007.

Wright, J. Lenore. "Relationality and Life: Phenomenological Reflections on Miscarriage." *International Journal of Feminist Approaches to Bioethics* 11, no. 2 (2018): 135–56.

Wright, N. T. "Mind, Spirit, Soul and Body: All for One and One for All: Reflections on Paul's Anthropology in His Complex Contexts." Society of Christian Philosophers: Regional Meeting, Fordham University. March, 2011. https://tinyurl.com/ycyk8jp9.

———. *The Resurrection of the Son of God.* Minneapolis: Fortress, 2003.

Yong, Amos. "Disability and the Love of Wisdom: De-forming, Re-forming, and Per-forming Philosophy of Religion." *Ars Disputandi* 9, no. 1 (2009): 54–71.

———. "Disability Theology of the Resurrection: Persisting Questions and Additional Considerations–A Response to Ryan Mullins." *Ars Disputandi* 12, no. 1 (2012): 4–10.

———. *Theology and Down Syndrome: Reimagining Disability in Late Modernity.* Waco, TX: Baylor University Press, 2007.

Zhang, Sarah. "The Last Children of Down Syndrome." *Atlantic.* December, 2020. https://tinyurl.com/4he5afsd.

Zimmerman, Dean W. "Bodily Resurrection: The Falling Elevator Model Revisited." In *Personal Identity and Resurrection*, edited by Georg Gasser, 49–66. Burlington, VT: Ashgate, 2010.

———. "The Compatibility of Materialism and Survival: The 'Falling Elevator' Model." *Faith and Philosophy* 16, no. 2 (1999): 194–212.

———. "Personal Identity and the Survival of Death." In *The Oxford Handbook of Philosophy of Death*, edited by Ben Bradley, Fred Feldman, Jens Johansson, 97–154. New York: Oxford University Press, 2013.

———. "Should a Christian Be a Mind-Body Dualist?" In *Contemporary Debates in Philosophy of Religion*, edited by Michael L. Peterson and Raymond J. Van Arragon, 315–40. Malden, MA: Blackwell, 2004.

# INDEX OF SUBJECTS AND NAMES

stigma regarding, 23–24
taboo regarding, 19
treatment for, 23
misogyny, 5, 30, 69, 119–20
motherhood, 53–54

narrative theories of the self,
87–90, 92–94
Neoplatonism, 58, 68, 94
noninvasive prenatal testing
techniques (NIPT), 119
"Now the Green Blade Riseth,"
77, 166n122

Origen, 66
original sin, 41, 47, 56, 147n24,
155n111
orthodoxy, 69–73, 77, 94,
95, 97

paradise. *See* heaven
parousia, 63, 86, 99
paternalism, 120, 123
patriarchy, 1, 2, 6, 8, 28, 38, 55,
114, 126
Paul (apostle)
and 1 Corinthians 15, 8,
57–58, 59–60, 61, 63–64,
83, 84, 85, 97, 98–100, 129
dualisms use by, 62–63
metaphor use by, 77, 80, 100,
129
soul writings of, 62–63, 64
Pelagius, 147n24
Peretti, Frank, 15
Perpetua, 53
personhood, 19, 36–38, 42–44,
52, 69, 72, 92–94, 128–29

pneumatology, 105, 121–22. *See
also* Holy Spirit
postabortion rituals, 17–18,
137n23
postabortion trauma syndrome,
13–15, 25, 138n29
postmortem existence, 3, 30, 64,
71, 72, 86, 93, 107, 165n115
prayer, 18, 34, 47, 81, 54, 121
pregnancy
beginnings of, 9
in the Bible, 110
counterstories regarding,
52–53
death within, 91–92, 125–26
decision-making within, 117
emergence theological
approach to, 116
fragility/precarity of, 34, 104,
110, 111, 123–26
genetic testing during, 103,
115–17, 119
identity through, 10
knowledge within, 103, 117
moral authority within, 123,
126
providence within, 113–14,
116
self-care within, 120, 131
self-doubt within, 117
self-trust within, 118
as *sui generis*, 90, 111
surviving, 52–53
taboos regarding, 9
unpredictability regarding,
22–23
virtue and, 109–12, 124
women of color and, 110, 126